PRODUCTIVITY IN THE FOOD INDUSTRY:

PROBLEMS AND POTENTIAL

Gordon F. Bloom

The MIT Press
Cambridge, Massachusetts, and London, England

Library of Congress Cataloging in Publication Data

Bloom, Gordon Falk, 1918-
    Productivity in the food industry.

    1. Food industry and trade--United States.
I. Title.
HD9005.B65   338.1'9'73   72-1963
ISBN 0-262-02088-2

CONTENTS

PUBLISHER'S NOTE

The aim of this format is to close the time gap between
the preparation of certain works and their publication in book
form. A large number of significant though specialized manu-
scripts make the transition to formal publication either after
a considerable delay or not at all. The time and expense of
detailed text editing and composition in print may act to prevent publication or so to delay it that currency of content is
affected.

The text of this book has been photographed directly from
the author's typescript. It is edited to a satisfactory level
of completeness and comprehensibility though not necessarily to
the standard of consistency of minor editorial detail present
in typeset books issued under our imprint.

The MIT Press

FOREWORD

Understanding the basis for industrial productivity remains a complex and elusive goal in the present stage of the whole development of our society. The study of productivity in the food industry by Gordon F. Bloom of M.I.T. is an excellent example of the kind of work that must be undertaken on an industry-by-industry basis if we are to make progress in the analysis of the systems type problems of productivity.

Dr. Bloom's study is especially timely for the beginning of the decade of the seventies. There is an increasing public and professional concern about the lags in productivity that have characterized American industry in the last half of the sixties. Concern for our declining competitive balance in trade with Europe and Japan and the overriding need to provide rising real incomes for the lowest economic half of the country have placed new emphasis on the issue of improving productivity.

Controls have a short-lived attraction in dealing with the problem. There is a growing recognition that to affect fundamentally the many unmet needs—both economic and noneconomic—of our times, a larger base of national product must be established. Yet we know relatively little about the whole process by which an industry improves its productivity. A mass of related factors—social, economic, political and environmental—affect the final output. The broad definitions, once so simple, lose some of their meaning in dealing with situations on either a macro or micro basis. We need more studies of basic specific

industries if concrete steps to achieve improvements are to be
taken by management, by employees, by unions at the work place,
by consumers in the market place, and by public officials.

For these reasons Dr. Bloom's study of the food industry
offers a useful ground for such work. It is the largest industry in the United States. It is a notable service industry,
and by 1980 the service industries will be employing twice as
many people as manufacturing industries. The general difficulty
in improving productivity in the service industries makes a
special review of this archetype highly appropriate. New concepts, new approaches, new experiments, new devices must be
considered if headway is to be made in such vital areas. Let
us see if the present study can be helpful and, more, if it
can encourage new work both at M.I.T. and elsewhere on these
complex issues.

Howard W. Johnson

Chairman of the Corporation
Massachusetts Institute of Technology

PREFACE

For much of the past decade—and before productivity became a matter of national concern—the writer, both as an executive in the food industry and later as an academician, has espoused the need for a systems approach and industry cooperation as essential components of a program to accelerate the rate of improvement in manhour output in industry. Some of these ideas were set forth in an article entitled, "Productivity: Weak Link in our Economy", which appeared in the January-February 1971 issue of the Harvard Business Review. This book further elaborates the concept of a systems approach to productivity problems and examines the many influences—legal, technological, economic and institutional—which impinge upon the distribution system and ultimately determine the rate of productivity improvement.

The field study which provides the factual basis for this volume was originally undertaken at the request of the Working Group on Management Organization and Capital, a subcommittee of the National Commission on Productivity. Field work began about February 1, 1971 and ended June 9, 1971. During this period the writer personally discussed productivity problems and trends in the food industry with retailers, wholesalers, manufacturers, labor leaders, officials of government agencies, logistics experts, staff personnel of trade associations and numerous other knowledgeable people in the industry. Out of this investigation evolved the views and conclusions which are set forth in this book. Such views and conclusions are the writer's own and

are not to be construed as representing the opinion of the
National Commission on Productivity.

Because of the time constraints which faced the author in
his field survey and in view of the size and complexity of the
food industry, the writer has been compelled to be selective in
his discussion of productivity problems and potentials in the
food industry. This book does not, therefore, purport to be
an exhaustive review of productivity trends in the food industry.
It does, however, highlight some of the key areas in which major
breakthroughs in productivity improvement can be achieved through
proper governmental support and industry cooperation.

Although the discussion is set against the background of
the food industry, it is the author's hope that the approach
adopted and the conclusions recommended will have general applicability to many industries in our economy. In an effort to make
the discussion pertinent to physical distribution in general, the
writer has deliberately focused attention upon those problems within the food industry which seem to have most relevance to industry
at large while omitting reference to others which are more pecul-
iarly food oriented. Thus, productivity development in perishable
food products, such as dairy and frozen foods, has been slighted
while heavy emphasis has been placed upon problems such as transportation and unitized handling of grocery products, which raise
issues of more general concern to the economy at large.

This study could not have been completed without the cooperation of executives at all levels of the food industry who

in discussions with the writer have been frank in their views
and generous with their time. Staff personnel of the National
Association of Food Chains, the Grocery Manufacturers of America,
the National American Wholesale Grocers Association, the Super
Market Institute and the National Association of Convenience
Stores were most helpful in providing basic source material for
the report.

I am also grateful to Professor Sanford Belden of Cornell
University for research into certain aspects of the assemblage
problem and to fellow economists at the Massachusetts Institute
of Technology, the University of Massachusetts and Cornell
University for helpful comments.

In the final analysis, however, the writer must take the
sole responsibility for the views expressed in this volume. As
the discussion will indicate, statistics about productivity are
sparse and even the concept of productivity itself is abstruse.
What emerges then in the following discussion is a broad view
of trends in the food industry filtered through the eyes of
an individual who for twenty years has been both an observer
of and a participant in the industry and who continues to have
a deep conviction that the industry can, through cooperation
and leadership, achieve an accelerated rate of improvement in
productivity.

CHAPTER I

THE PROBLEM AND ITS SETTING

The American economy faces a productivity crisis. The full
impact and nature of this crisis is today becoming apparent to
the policy makers of government, to business and union leaders,
and to the public at large. The problem arises from the fact
that the rate of increase in money wages, which over most of the
past decade had advanced at a rate only slightly in excess of
the rate of increase in manhour output, has now commenced to step
ahead of productivity by such large increments as to threaten
increases in unit labor costs and prices of from five to ten
per cent per annum.

At this writing, governmental restrictions imposed upon
wages and prices have slowed the upward movement of wage rates
but little has been done to accelerate the long run upward movement of manhour output. At such time as wages and prices are
decontrolled, the full measure of the disequilibrium between
wage adjustments and manhour output will again reassert itself,
but even under Phase II it seems apparent that wage increases
will substantially exceed the rate of productivity growth.

The Widening Wage-Productivity Gap

During the decade of the sixties, average hourly earnings
in the private nonfarm economy rose at an average annual rate
of 5.2 per cent, while productivity measured by manhour output
advanced by 2.8 per cent per annum. The result was that unit

labor costs rose by about 2.3 per cent annually.[1] Labor cost is
the single most important component of price. For example, in
the period from 1965 to 1969, its relative importance varied from
$62\frac{1}{2}$ to 65 per cent of price.[2] In 1969, labor costs per unit of
product rose seven per cent—the sharpest advance for employees
in the private nonfarm sector since 1951[3]—while the consumer
price index rose 5.4 per cent.[4] In 1970, unit labor costs rose
6.3 per cent and in 1971 3.4 per cent.[5]

It is obvious that an acceleration in the rate of increase
in unit labor costs can be transmitted into a spiraling price
inflation of increasingly serious dimensions. When unit labor
costs rise, profit margins are reduced unless businessmen raise
prices. Thus, there is a strong incentive to offset rising unit
labor costs with increased prices. This cannot always be done—
competitive circumstances or depressed industry or general economic conditions may delay the adjustment. Eventually, however,
the adjustment must be made if industry is to remain profitable.
As a consequence, there is a fairly close correlation over time
between changes in unit labor costs and changes in prices. Thus,
years of large increases in unit labor costs such as 1948, 1951,
1956, and 1969, were also years of large increases in prices.

---

[1] U.S. Department of Labor data.

[2] Economic Report of the President, February, 1970, p. 53.

[3] Ibid., p. 51.

[4] Ibid., p. 56.

[5] U.S. Department of Labor data.

The sharp breakout in unit labor costs which occurred in
1969 reflected the influence of two trends. On the one hand,
there has been a steady escalation in the rate of increase of
employee compensation since 1965. From 1960 to 1965, the annual
increment in hourly compensation of workers in the private nonfarm economy averaged about 4.3 per cent.[6] Median first year wage
adjustments negotiated in collective bargaining fluctuated in a
narrow range, between annual increases of 2.8 and 3.2 per cent.[7]
In recent years, however, there has been a sharp escalation in
the magnitude of the annual increment in employee wages under
union wage settlements. In 1970 median first year increases in
wages under major collective bargaining agreements amounted to
12.0 per cent, compared to 10.9 per cent in 1969 and 8.1 per cent
in 1968. In 1971, despite wage restraints, median first year
increases amounted to 13.9 per cent.[8]

On the other hand, manhour output, which had grown at a rate
of approximately 4 per cent per annum from 1961 to 1966, commenced
to decline in 1967 and in 1969 grew at a rate of less than one
per cent—the smallest increase in 13 years.[9] In 1970 the rate of
improvement in manhour output remained below one per cent.[10]

Growth in output per manhour varies significantly from year

---

[6]Report to the National Commission on Productivity by the
    Council of Economic Advisers, August 7, 1970, p. II-9.

[7]Ibid.

[8]U.S. Department of Labor data.

[9]Manpower Report of the President, March, 1970, p. 36.

[10]Productivity and the Economy, Washington, D.C.: U.S.Department
    of Labor, Bureau of Labor Statistics, Bulletin 1710, 1971,
    p. 16.

to year and in manufacturing bears a close relationship to
capacity utilization. Typically, high rates of productivity
gains are registered in early stages of cyclical recovery when
unused human and capital resources are put into use. Thus, in
the postwar period, productivity gains were greatest in the
recovery years of 1950 (8.2%), 1955 (4.4%), and 1962 (4.7%).[11]
In 1971, output per manhour of nonfarm workers rose 3.2 per
cent after advancing only 0.7 per cent during 1970.[12]

Most economists believe that manhour output will resume its
historical trend once business recovers from its recession lows,
yet even such a resumption of productivity advance—which may or
may not materialize—will be totally inadequate to deal with the
rate of wage increases which now seem to lie ahead. The Bureau
of Labor Statistics of the U.S. Department of Labor has estimated
that during the decade of the seventies, output per manhour in
the private sector of the economy will grow by about 3 per cent
per year, a slightly slower pace than that registered in the
1960's.[13] If this prediction should prove to be valid, the nation
is facing a serious challenge of continuing inflation for the
years ahead. For we are faced on the one hand with a potential
wage explosion of unknown dimensions and, on the other hand, by a
changing economic and social environment which may make for a slower
rather than a more rapid, rise in manhour output in the future.

---

[11]Manpower Report of the President, April, 1967, p. 32.

[12]U.S. Department of Labor data.

[13]The U.S. Economy in 1980, Washington, D.C.: U.S. Department of
    Labor, Bureau of Labor Statistics, Bulletin 1673, 1970, p.1.

Not only will a 3 per cent annual improvement in manhour
output fail to meet our domestic needs, but also it may put us
at a substantial disadvantage in the world competitive market.
In manufacturing—the only industrial sector for which international comparisons are available—the growth rate in the
United States in manhour output lagged substantially behind
other industrial countries between 1965 and 1970. For example,
average annual percentage changes in output per manhour during
this period were 14.2 per cent in Japan; 7.9 per cent in Sweden;
6.6 per cent in France; 5.3 per cent in Germany; 5.1 per cent
in Italy; 3.6 per cent in the United Kingdom; 3.5 per cent in
Canada; and only 2.1 per cent in the United States.[14] Although
hourly compensation in these other nations also advanced more
rapidly than in the United States, unit labor costs did not rise
as fast as in the United States due to superior productivity
performance. Because of its slower productivity growth, unit
labor costs rose more sharply in the United States than in any
country except Canada and Italy.[15]

The Wage Explosion

It is evident from the foregoing discussion that practically
every industrialized nation is today witnessing what Professor
Raymond Salnier has aptly called a "wage explosion". In one

---

[14]Productivity and the Economy, op. cit., p. 30.

[15]Ibid.

country after another, wages continue their upward spiral in
an economic environment characterized by widespread discontent
among union members, strike action in the face of pleas by
government officials, and rank and file discontent with the
action of union leaders.

In the United States, extreme wage settlements have received so much publicity in the news media that it is safe to
say a new magnitude of wage adjustments is now part of the
thinking of every wage earner in the nation. It is easy to
blame such wage inflation upon unreasonable demands of union
leaders, but this is a simplistic solution which overlooks a
fundamental change which has occurred in the labor movement.
The fact is that union leaders today cannot control their
membership. In union after union, challenges to the leadership in elections are becoming more common. It is estimated
that only about 12 per cent of settlements arrived at by union
officials are rejected by the union membership,[16] but the
threat of rejection and its political implications are very
much in the minds of union negotiators. The militancy and
independence of union members makes union officials wary of
settling "too cheap" and injects extremism into union demands.

Rank and file discontent springs from a number of sources.
In the first place, most workers—union and nonunion—feel
that they are not keeping up with inflation. Despite the
improvement which has occurred in manhour output since 1965,

---

[16] Data from Federal Mediation and Conciliation Service.

real spendable earnings of workers with three dependents were
actually slightly less in 1970 than in 1965.[17]   Furthermore,
employees are becoming increasingly critical of the conditions
of daily work. The production line technique which was acceptable to workers of the past generation is today a source of
continuing frustration to younger employees who want something
more out of life than the monotony of tightening bolts all day.

The Drive for Leisure

Since employees cannot find satisfaction in their work,
they are seeking more leisure time so that they can find satisfaction in activities off the job. This objective will be reflected in two highly inflationary trends during the decade of
the seventies: the shorter workweek and early retirement.

During the past ten years actual hours of work per week
registered relatively little change. The coming decade, however, may witness the acceptance of the four-day week by an
important segment of American business. The movement has been
given some impetus by the Federal Government which has in
effect legislated a four-day week for certain weeks of the
year by prescribing that five national holidays shall fall on
Monday, rather than on other days of the week. In the automobile industry, Chrysler Corporation and the United Automobile
Workers have agreed to study the feasibility of a four-day week.
In Canada, the Retail Clerks Union has negotiated a contract
for a four-day 39 hour week in supermarkets, and West Coast food

----

[17] U.S. Department of Labor data.

chain executives believe that similar demands will soon be
pressed upon American companies. Achievement of union goals of
a four-day week of 35 hours with no reduction in pay will obviously impose substantial costs upon industry.

Another costly problem the economy must face is the growing
demand for early retirement. It is not commonly recognized
how much of a burden is added to the costs of funding a pension
plan by reducing the age for retirement. According to one
authority, a company which lowers the minimum age from 65 to
60 faces a 40-50 per cent increase in pension costs.[18] Early
retirement can also deplete the supply of skilled workers and
require expensive training programs to fill the gap. For
example, Earl R. Bramblett, General Motors Vice President for
Personnel, estimates:

> There are 16,820 G.M. hourly employees with 30 or
> more years of service. Of these, almost one third are
> skilled tradesmen. Coming right behind this large
> group are 24,235 with between 25 and 29 years of ser-
> vice...Of these, one fourth are skilled tradesmen.
> Losing such a large number of highly skilled and
> experienced personnel could be a crippling blow./19/

Both UAW and General Motors officials have predicted that about
half of those eligible for early retirement will take it. The impact upon the skilled labor force—and upon plant productivity—
therefore can be substantial.

Major improvements in pension plans present a special kind
of threat to price stability. On the one hand, such improvements

---

[18]
   Nation's Business, February, 1971, p. 22.

[19] Ibid.

create a substantial increase in unit labor costs and therefore may be expected to result in upward price adjustments by
business firms.[20] On the other hand, since these increased
costs do not end up in the employee's weekly pay envelope,
the gap between the employee's take-home pay and the employer's
cost of employing that worker widens. The employee sees prices
rising without a concomitant increase in his pay and therefore
is likely to demand large catch-up wage adjustments to make
him "whole". Thus a decade in which emphasis is placed upon
fringe benefits of any sort is likely to be characterized by a
double layer of costs for employers—higher fringe costs and
higher wage rates.

The Outlook for Productivity Gains

With wage, hour, and fringe adjustments of the magnitude
presaged by underlying trends in the labor market, annual increments in productivity of approximately 3 per cent for the
balance of the decade will hardly suffice if the American
economy is to regain some degree of price stability and if
American industry is to remain competitive in world markets.
Although wage controls were probably necessary to halt the
escalation in expectations concerning the magnitude of future
wage and price changes, they are unlikely to provide any long-

---

[20] The increase in fringe benefit costs in recent years
has undoubtedly contributed to the cost-push inflation.
In 1970, according to a biennial survey conducted by
the U.S. Chamber of Commerce, "fringes" cost employers
an average of $2,052 a year per worker, up 27.9 per
cent—or 98.3 cents per hour—since 1968. See Business
Week, December 12, 1970, p. 90.

run solution to the problem of rising unit labor costs in the American economy. No democratic industrial nation has succeeded in maintaining effective wage and price controls during peace-time for any extended period of time. The United States is unlikely to prove an exception to that rule. The long run economic health of our economy depends not upon artificial re-straints on the labor market but rather upon development of an economic environment in which the rate of growth of productivity can be materially increased.

This is no easy task; for the rate of productivity growth represents the interaction of many varied influences. For one thing, it reflects the change in composition of total output which year by year shifts more heavily to the service sector of the economy where historically the rate of productivity im-provement has been lower than in manufacturing. During the decade of the 1970's, it is estimated that this shift will detract about .2 per cent from the average annual productivity growth—that is, if there were no shift between sectors of the economy from 1970 to 1980, the growth rate in manhour output would probably amount to 3.2 per cent, rather than the 3.0 per cent now predicted.[21] Thus, the American economy in effect starts the race for improved productivity with a handicap to be overcome. Must the shift to service-producing from goods-producing result in a decline in manhour output in our economy? The opportunities for productivity improvement in the service

---

[21] Estimates provided by U.S. Department of Labor, Bureau of Labor Statistics.

industries are enormous. What needs to be done to exploit
them? Perhaps we shall find that the policies and practices
which worked so well in manufacturing are not well adapted to
the fragmented process of distribution and that new kinds of
analytical approaches, implemented by legal and technological
changes, must be devised to deal with this new situation.

In addition to reflecting changes in composition of GNP,
productivity also is influenced by a number of strategic variables: workers' effort; technological change; skill and education
of workers; and management techniques. These various factors have
always been subject to a variety of influences but during the
decade ahead their respective movements are particularly difficult
to predict. Most statistical series are projected by methods
which rely in part upon past trends. But the decade ahead is not
just another period of ten years. It is a decade in which basic
human values and concerns are in a state of upheaval. The revolution in our thinking about the environment, about wealth and
leisure, and physical production, may have incalculable repercussions upon physical productivity as customarily measured.

The future is full of unanswered questions about the key
variables in the productivity equation.

Technological change: Will the risk of government regulation,
class suits, minority stockholder action, community boycotts
and resistance, consumerism and other factors of similar nature
create such uncertainty in the economic environment that investment decisions involving technological development will be

slowed? The decade of the seventies has been characterized by
one writer as the "Age of Uncertainty"[22]—and with good reason.
The executive faced with the decision as to whether or not to
build a new atomic generating plant—or many other types of new
plants or processes—is faced today with a host of problems
which cannot be conveniently converted into monetary or quantitative terms.

<u>Worker effort</u>: Is the old Puritan ethic with its emphasis upon
hard work, savings, and monetary gains giving way to an ethic
which places greater stress on other values? What will happen
when the hippie, the campus activist, the long-haired intellec-
tual and the disaffected ghetto black become part of our industrial society? Will they become assimilated to the establishment, as generations before them, or will they retain their
critical attitudes and demand reforms which may have a detri-
mental effect upon productivity measured in conventional terms?

If there is in fact a new "zeitgeist" emerging among our
workers, it would probably be most apparent among the younger
workers in the labor force. As it happens, younger workers
will be the major source of growth in the labor force during
the 1970's. Workers aged 25-34 will increase by more than
50 per cent whereas workers over the age of 45 will increase
by only 4 per cent.[23]

---

[22] Charles Silberman, "The U.S.Economy in an Age of Uncertainty",
    <u>Fortune</u>, January, 1971, pp. 72-143.

[23] <u>Ibid</u>., p. 143.

Although the conventional wisdom states that "people
don't want to work anymore", the facts belie the contention.
More than one-half of married men in the 25 to 44-year old
age group have working wives. Multiple job holders—so-called
moonlighters—number approximately 4 million and account for
about 5 per cent of the work force.[24]   About 40 per cent of
men work overtime. Of all household heads approached by
the Survey Research Center of the University of Michigan,
40 per cent of those under 35 expressed a preference for
more work, while only 7 per cent opted for less.[25]

Despite all the rhetoric about our materialistic civi-
lization, most young people continue to want more of the
material things of life. Seventy-three per cent of household heads under 35 years of age who were surveyed by the
Survey Research Center said that they had unsatisfied wants
compared to only 36 per cent of those 35 years of age or
more.[26]   The problem is not so much that "people don't want
to work" but rather that they find most work dull, monotonous
and lacking challenge. This deficiency will unquestionably
become more and more of a problem as our work force becomes
more highly educated and therefore more capable of performing

---

[24]"Trends in Labor and Leisure", Monthly Labor Review,
      February, 1971, p. 7.

[25]Fortune, March, 1971, p. 94.

[26]Ibid.

tasks requiring thought and individual initiative.[27]

Skill of workers: How do we train and employ the uneducated

and the hard-core unemployed and still achieve an accelerated

rate of improvement in manhour output in industry? The number

of blacks aged 14 to 24 in central cities is increasing at

twice the rate of the black population generally and more than

twice as fast as the comparable white age group.[28]   As these

black youths enter the labor market, they will require increased

supervision, training and care by industry. Our brief exper-

ience with training hard-core unemployed under the National

Alliance of Businessmen JOBS Program suggests that the accom-

plishment of the employment objective may require a major com-

promise with productivity objectives. Trainees who lack skills

and educational background are not only less productive at

work, but also they require skilled personnel to train them,

teach them the three R's, and to take care of their pressing

personal and financial problems. All this takes manpower and

therefore the overall result of a concerted effort to make

---

[27]
    The production problems encountered by General Motors
        Corporation at its Vega plant—the newest and most tech-
        nologically advanced in the industry—dramatize this po-
        tential conflict between the monotonous routine imposed
        by sophisticated technology and the demands of a youth-
        ful educated work force. The average age of the workers
        in the Vega plant is 24. Workers take about 40 seconds
        to complete a task. According to the New York Times,
        the struggle which has developed between management and
        labor with regard to the speed and quality of work "has
        raised a wider issue of how management can deal with the
        younger worker who is determined to have a say as to how
        a job is to be performed..." New York Times, Jan. 23,
        1972, Sec. 1, p. 1.

[28]
    Report of the National Commission on Civil Disorders,
        1968, p. 269.

productive employees out of these disadvantaged members of the
work force may in the process actually reduce productivity
measured in output per manhour.

Education of workers: The increasing educational attainment
of the work force has in the past been a positive factor contributing to the continuing improvement in the productivity of
American labor.   Between 1952 and 1968, the proportion of
workers in the labor force with 8 years of school or less was
cut in half.[29]   Edward F. Denison has estimated that for the
period 1929-1957 about 42 per cent of the growth in output per
person employed was attributable to increased education.[30]

The upgrading in educational attainment is expected to
continue in the future.   By 1980 about 4 out of 5 young adult
workers (25 to 34 years old) will be high school graduates or
better, and 1 in 5 will have completed 4 years of college or
more.   By contrast, in the 1968 work force 3 out of 4 workers
in this age group were high school graduates, and 1 in 6 were
college graduates.[31]

---

[29]Educational Attainment of Workers, March, 1968. Washington,
    D.C.: U.S. Department of Labor, Bureau of Labor Statistics,
    Special Labor Force Report No. 103, 1968, p. 15.

[30]Edward F. Denison, The Sources of Economic Growth in the
    U.S. and the Alternatives Before Us, New York: Committee
    for Economic Development, 1962, p. 73.

    Other investigators have made lower estimates of the
    contribution of education.   See, for example, David
    Schwartzman, "Education and the Quality of Labor, 1929-63",
    American Economic Review, June, 1968, pp. 508-514.

[31]The U.S. Economy in 1980, op. cit., p. 30.

During the decade of the seventies there will be a heavy
influx to the labor force of relatively well-educated younger
workers which will occur at the same time that many less educated older workers are leaving the labor force. The result
will be a major change in the educational background of the
labor force. What effect will this change have on job attitudes? The U.S. Department of Labor has cautioned:

> ...The job mix and the education mix are already out
> of balance. New kinds of jobs will be needed in order
> to provide employment for the growing numbers of high
> school graduates that will fully use their skills
> and education. /32/

But the job mix may not change rapidly enough with the
result that many educated workers will be compelled to take
dull and undemanding jobs or have no jobs at all. What effect
will this possibility have on productivity? There is some
evidence to suggest that beyond a certain point increasing
educational attainment may be associated with declining,
rather than increasing, productivity on the job. Recent studies
of both blue collar and white collar performance indicate that
frequently there is an inverse relationship between performance
and educational achievement.[33]

It is a fact of economic life that many jobs in American
industry are dull, repetitive, and unsatisfying to a person
with a high school or college education. Data reveal that
education is more often than not an important factor accounting

---

[32] "Educational Attainment of Workers, March 1969 and 1970",
    Monthly Labor Review, October, 1970, p. 15

[33] Ivar Berg, Education and Jobs: The Great Training Robbery.
    Praeger Publishers, New York, 1970, pp. 85-94.

for dissatisfaction among workers in many occupational cate-

gories.[34]   Such dissatisfaction may be reflected in lack of

interest, impaired workmanship, "quickie" strikes, or a high

rate of absenteeism. A major threat to improvement of pro-

ductivity in American industry is the continuing increase in

absenteeism. For the nonagricultural work force, absenteeism

was 77 per cent higher in 1969 than in 1961, whereas the work-

ing population was up only 22 per cent.[35]   Personnel managers

in any line of business are well aware of the fact that Fridays

and Mondays are popular days for being "sick"!

Management dedication and ability: The seventies will be the

first decade to test the new social concern of management

against the back-drop of productivity. An increasingly signi-

ficant share of the decision-makers in industry will be young

men, graduates of our business schools and colleges, who in

academic surroundings have proclaimed the need for business

to temper profit objectives with social concerns. What will

happen to their attitudes when they become executives or

members of middle management in American business? According

to Fortune, "Corporations face unprecedented demands from

junior executives who want to reform the world on company

time."[36]

---

[34]Ibid., p. 17.

[35]The Morgan Guaranty Survey, April, 1970, p. 10.

[36]Judson Gooding, "The Accelerated Generation Moves Into
    Management", Fortune, March, 1971, p. 101.

Already there appears to be some erosion in the dedication
of business leaders to profits as the principal objective of
business effort. A study conducted by Fortune Magazine in
September, 1969, of 500 of the largest companies in the United
States revealed that 17 per cent of the executives responding
believed that business should assume social responsibilities
even at the cost of reduced profits while 42 per cent felt that
business must first make a profit but then assume public
responsibilities that may not be profitable.[37]

The desirability of such social involvement by business is
now a matter of public debate. However, there would probably
be general agreement that such efforts will tend to divert resources into channels where "output" is less easily quantifiable
with the result that the growth in manhour output may be adversely affected.

These then are some of the perplexing questions that cloud
the future trend of productivity in our economy. It is unfortunate—but nevertheless true—that change and progress are
becoming bad words among the intelligentsia as well as among
the ordinary citizens of this country. The sudden recognition of
the magnitude of the problems created by pollution, over-popula-
tion, and other ills of an industrial society has so overwhelmed
many Americans that subconsciously they are inclined to seek a
Ghandi-like, back-to-nature philosophy as a solution to our problems rather than a redirection of our efforts and capabilities
in the technological sphere.

---

[37] "The View from the Pinnacle: What Business Thinks",
Fortune, September, 1969, p. 94.

In this environment and in the face of an attitude revolution which can menace our progress as a world industrial power, it is important that the role of productivity in our scheme of national priorities be clarified.

The Need for a National Productivity Policy

The central domestic issue of the coming decade will be the need to accelerate the rate of improvement in our productivity. We shall come to recognize this basic fact as a nation, not by reason of a deep insight into the workings of our economic system, nor because of a clearer vision of the future perils which may result from the continuation of present policies. The recognition of the dominant importance of productivity will be brought home to us by default. We shall suddenly come to realize that nothing else will work without it. All of our ambitious national goals—to eliminate unemployment and pollution and the malaise of our cities—all will be rendered unattainable unless we can improve our productivity and scale down the tempo of inflation.

Efforts to control inflation will continue to be tried on all fronts. We shall find that wage and price controls will produce more speculation than stability; that fiscal and monetary policy are largely ineffective in a cost-push spiral; and that the over-riding social, political and human needs of maintaining a viable level of employment make efforts to control inflation by such policies virtually impossible in a democratic society.

Finally we shall have to direct our attention to the underlying and crucial problem: our economy cannot remain economically healthy with a 3 per cent annual improvement in productivity
in an era of 10 per cent wage adjustments. In agriculture, manhour output has been increasing at a rate of about 6 per cent
per annum or more than double the rate for the nonfarm private
economy. Can we adopt policies which will bring the rate of
improvement in the nonfarm private economy closer to that of
agriculture? If we cannot control wages and we cannot control
prices in a peacetime economy, can we through appropriate
governmental policies accelerate the rate of improvement in
productivity?

Before seeking answers to these questions, the nation must
first decide whether or not it really wants increased productivity
It must be recognized that increased productivity does not automatically mean lower prices; in semi-monopolistic industries,
the results of stepped-up productivity may simply be an increase
in profits. In the long run, of course, in a competitive
economy, increased productivity will tend to be reflected in
higher real income to employees, but the wisdom of policies
stimulating productivity change may be subject to serious attack
in the short run when the gains in real income are not evident.

Furthermore, improvement in productivity, like reduction
in unemployment, or curtailment of pollution, involves a trade-
off. We cannot as a nation attain all of our objectives at one
and the same time. Pursuit of the goal of maximum improvement

in productivity may require tax policies which at least temporarily appear to fuel inflationary forces. Likewise, acceleration of productivity change may aggravate problems of structural
unemployment.

Finally, the objective of improved productivity must be
viewed in proper perspective. It is not a panacea; it will not
cure inflation. It is quite unlikely that we shall be able to
achieve such an increase in manhour output that it will fully
offset the annual increment in wage changes. On the other hand,
it is possible that we can achieve sufficient gains in productivity
improvement so that the resultant rate of inflation is compatible
with the achievement of our domestic goals and will not put us
at a competitive disadvantage with our foreign competition.

Productivity deserves to be given a high national priority
in our agenda of goals for the decade of the seventies. This
means that all of our policies and laws should be re-examined
with a view to determining what needs to be done to provide an
environment favorable to increase in productivity. As will be
seen from the discussion in later chapters, many of our laws,
enacted under economic circumstances quite different from those
which now exist, act as a positive barrier to improvement in
productivity.

Definition and Measurement of Productivity

Once we have made a decision of national commitment to
productivity, we come face to face with a surprising enigma.
Productivity is a much more elusive and intractable problem

than pollution, or unemployment, or other social problems
which have confronted us in recent years. Unlike pollution,
government cannot pass a law and look forward to an improvement
in productivity. Unlike unemployment, the expenditure of funds
will not necessarily help productivity and may in fact deter
it. The rate of growth in productivity may be affected by
appropriate government policy but it cannot be turned on and
off like a spigot. Productivity is difficult to define, complex
to measure, and obdurate to manipulation.

Conventional Indexes

Productivity is simply a ratio between output measured in
specific units and any input factor, also measured in specific
units. As a matter of historical convenience, statistics of
productivity have generally been stated in terms of output
relative to manhours of labor and the resultant figure has,
therefore, been referred to as the productivity of labor. Such
a presentation tends to create the impression that in some way
labor is responsible for the increased output and so is entitled
to a lion's share of the gains deriving from improved productivity. Actually, productivity could just as well be stated in
terms of any other factor of production, such as per dollar of
capital invested.

However, since it seems likely that in the immediate future
the price of labor will rise more rapidly than the price of
capital, it is useful to have a series which, on the one hand,
indicates the change in output per manhour and, on the other,

the change in the cost of employing labor to obtain the hour of
output. In utilizing an index relating labor input and output,
it is important to recognize that output changes reflect the
combined influence of numerous variables, including changes in
technology, capital investment, rate of plant utilization,
managerial efficiency and scale of operations, as well as skill,
quality, and effort of the labor force.

The most widely used statistics on productivity are those
published by the Bureau of Labor Statistics of the United States
Department of Labor. The Bureau makes available two series, one
measuring productivity in terms of output per hour paid and the
other in terms of output per hour worked. The hours-worked data
are derived from a monthly survey of households while the hours-
paid data are based primarily on a monthly BLS survey of establishment payroll records. Theoretically the difference between
the two measures of labor input is equal to paid vacation time
and other paid leave. Most economists agree that hours worked
is the more desirable measure of labor input for productivity
measurement, but because of lack of data most productivity series
are generally based upon hours paid.[38]

The BLS measures output in terms of the constant dollar
value of the goods and services produced in the private sector
of the economy. This means that an estimate must be made of the
value of final goods and services produced and this figure must

---

[38] *The Meaning and Measurement of Productivity*, Bulletin
No. 1714, U.S. Department of Labor, Bureau of Labor
Statistics, September, 1971, p. 12.

then be deflated by a price index so as to eliminate the effect
of changing prices.

Because of the complexity of our economy, the millions of
individual operating units, and the paucity of accurate statistical data, productivity calculations whether made by the
Department of Labor or other research organizations are from
beginning to end based upon estimates, imputations and intelligent guesswork. A basic weakness which affects all aggregative
figures—whether used to measure inflation or productivity—is
our inability to define a unit of quantity of product where
quality is very heterogeneous and variable.[39] Certainly there
are grave doubts about the validity of imputing significance to
such statistics when they are carried out to decimal points.
Nevertheless, when we are dealing with a long period of years,
the statistics available can serve to give us a reasonable idea
of the basic underlying trend in productivity.

Social Versus Private Productivity

The definition of productivity in terms of physical output
harkens back to a decade when we were more concerned with the quantity of product than the quality of life, when we looked at the
productivity of an individual firm without taking account of the fa
that its high productivity may have been purchased at the expense
of imposing additional costs on society. If, for example, we compa
the efficiency of burning low sulphur fuel and high sulphur fuel

---

[39]Report to the National Commission on Productivity,
op. cit., p. I-9.

as a source of energy for electricity, we shall undoubtedly
find that the latter is less costly from the utility's point
of view. But what about the costs imposed upon society by air
pollution—for painting, laundry, medical attention, and so
forth? These costs—and the labor required to remedy them—
do not enter into the BLS figures which reflect only the changes
in output in the private economy.

By a strange quirk of fate, productivity as a concept has
become most important to us as an objective of national policy
at the very time that its meaning and definition have become
increasingly abstruse. There is a distinct possibility that
productivity, as we have conventionally measured it, could
actually decline over a given period of years during the coming
decade, yet "social productivity" might well gain.

Where should our concern lie? It can be urged that the
definition should suit the problem, and that if we are interested in accelerating the rate of improvement in productivity
to fight inflation, then the customary quantitative definition
is still more pertinent.

But the problem is not that simple. Inflation is a malaise
which results from a whole system of production and exchange in
our economy. To understand it we must look not only at the output of industry but also at the services of government, federal,
state and municipal. Consider, for example, the problem posed
by the nonreturnable bottle. If the nonreturnable bottle were
banned, productivity of bottlers and store operators would be
reduced. It is extremely time-consuming in terms of labor input

to transport, store, sort, and return bottles for refilling. On
the other hand, if the nonreturnable bottle were banned and the
returnable bottle were put back into use with recycling, the
amount of solid waste handled by municipalities would be reduced.
As a result, fewer rubbish collectors might be required. As a
consequence, municipal budgets for trash removal could be cut
and the rise in real estate taxes might be abated. In order to
obtain an index of the net effect on the economy of banning the
nonreturnable bottle, the decline in labor productivity in the
private sector would have to be weighed against the improvement
in labor productivity in the public sector.

The point is that on a national basis, the conventional
definition of productivity may not suffice. If we look upon an
accelerated rate of improvement in manhour output as a device to
combat inflation, we may have to inquire as to the costs which
were imposed upon the rest of society by an improvement in the
private sector.

At the present time, we have no way of measuring "social
productivity" and therefore this report will continue to speak
in terms of the conventional definition. However, the publication by the federal government of the document entitled "Toward
a Social Report"[40] and the growing interest in social accounting by businessmen, government officials, and academicians, all
suggest the need for a re-examination of our historic approach
to the definition and measurement of productivity.

---

[40]U.S. Department of Health, Education, and Welfare,
    Washington, D.C., 1969.

Outline of the Analysis

The discussion which follows in this report starts with a
general analysis of the problems facing the food industry so
that the issue of productivity improvement can be viewed in
proper context. Subsequent chapters look at productivity at
key points in the distribution process: manufacturing, transportation, warehousing, and retailing. Chapters VIII, IX, and
X discuss the possible impact of governmental policy on the
rate of improvement in productivity.

This division of the subject matter into separate chapters
is strictly for convenience in discussion. The entire process
of distribution must be viewed as a single system. For example,
the automatic checkout will be considered in the chapter dealing
with retailing but its impact will be felt throughout the entire
system.

The emphasis in this report is on the physical distribution system. Physical distribution costs represent about 50 per
cent of the total costs of most products. The possibilities for
productivity improvement and cost reduction in this area are
enormous, not only because of the magnitude of the costs involved, but also because most rationalization and management
attention has until now been focused on goods-producing activities. Physical distribution has been aptly called a wasteland—
the last great area in which we can expect massive breakthroughs
in cost reduction.

The reason that waste and inefficiency have gone unchecked

in this area is not hard to find. The problem is that elimination of inefficiency in distribution requires coordination of
functions throughout the system, but the integral parts of the
system are characteristically controlled by separate business
entities which may have quite diverse objectives and attitudes.
Manufacturing processes have become highly rationalized because
they are usually under the control of one entity. Distribution
processes are fragmented and separated; they are therefore
difficult to systematize. As a result, as Peter Drucker has so
aptly put it, "The industrial engineers are all where the machines are and very rarely does any of them poke his head into
the shipping room."[41] The key question is whether or not means
can be devised to implement improvements in distribution which
overall systems analysis indicates will improve productivity.

The emphasis in this book upon the application of an overall systems approach to problems of productivity in the field
of distribution is not intended to minimize the importance of
work in the motivational and psychological field to stimulate
greater interest and effort on the part of employees. Likewise
it is recognized that new processes and inventions can contribute materially to the overall rate of productivity growth in
the economy. The recommendations made in Chapter X are per-
fectly consistent with national productivity policies which
seek to encourage job enrichment and employee participation,
on the one hand, and stepped-up research and technological
change, on the other.

---

[41] Remarks made at Spring Meeting, National Council of Physical
Distribution Management, April 1965, Chicago, Illinois.

However, it is the writer's opinion that while the untapped
reservoir of human effort represents an enormous potential for
improving productivity, the changing attitudes, backgrounds,
and outlook of American workers will make it difficult to achieve
any net progress from this source in the decade ahead. As far
as technological progress is concerned, governmental efforts
to stimulate and support research and development expenditures
are to be applauded and should contribute materially to improved
productivity, especially in high technology industries. However,
in the area of distribution, as our discussion will indicate,
the need is not so much for new technology as for application of
technology already known. The problem is one of systematization
and implementation, rather than of invention.

In any case, it is apparent that there is no single high
road to improved productivity. We must explore every avenue
with vigor and concern. Gains are measured in percentage points
but the cumulative effect over the decade in terms of Gross
National Product can be enormous. As the discussion in the
following chapters will indicate, acceleration of the rate of
productivity growth in the food industry—and in the economy
at large—will require a coordinated program involving changes
in a whole spectrum of factors—institutional, legal, economic,
fiscal, and governmental—which ultimately affect the rate of
productivity growth in our economy. It is the purpose of this
text to identify and explore some of the more significant issues
which must be resolved if such a program is to be undertaken in
our nation.

CHAPTER II

THE OUTLOOK FOR THE FOOD INDUSTRY

The focus of this study is the food industry in the United States. It was selected for investigation because it is the largest industry in the nation, because its breadth and variety of operations mirror many of the problems which characterize industry in general, and because food prices are a critical element in the anatomy of inflation.

Food represents the single largest expenditure in consumers' budgets. Although for the nation as a whole food expenditures represent less than 17 cents of each dollar of disposable after-tax personal income, for the poor in our society food costs may take from 30 to 50 per cent of disposable income. A rise in the price of food, therefore, has the greatest impact upon those who can least afford it. Furthermore, since consumers in general are keenly aware of changes in the cost of food, an inflation in food prices is likely to cause a demand for higher wages, higher social security payments, and other compensatory increases in pay even if other costs entering into the family budget, such as clothing and shelter, remain stable. The cost of food is also a significant component of the Bureau of Labor Statistics Consumer Price Index which has been incorporated in many collective bargaining agreements as the index of changes in

the cost of living. Increases in food prices can have a
substantial effect upon the CPI and therefore trigger wage
adjustments under labor contracts in a variety of industries.

In a time of inflation, therefore, the strategic position
of the food industry in our economy takes on added importance.
Knowledge of cost, price, and productivity relationships
within this industry is essential to an understanding of
the broader currents and trends in our economy and of the
factors which affect a major portion of the budgets of all
consumers.

Definition of the Industry

What is the food industry? There is no single definition
that fits all purposes. There is no food industry in the same
sense that there is an automobile industry. In the latter
case, a relatively homogeneous line of products moves from
manufacturer through a limited number of channels of distribution to final users. The flow of distribution of physical
product can be neatly charted and traced.

But food is well nigh ubiquitous. It is sold on the
wayside stand, in the vending machine, at the candy store, in
the supermarket, in the department store, in the restaurant
and at the ballpark—to name only a few of the infinite number
of channels. How can one study productivity in such a system?

The food store of common parlance is not a food store
at all. The typical retail supermarket, for example, sells
a melange of items ranging from stockings to detergents; from
steaks to charcoal; from toys to razor blades. When the
average housewife complains about how little of her budget
money she has left after shopping for "food", she probably
has spent a significant part of her funds on nonfood items
at the "food" store.

With such complexity and diversity facing the investigator,
a definition of the industry must be sought which makes the
purpose of the research meaningful, the statistical analysis
manageable, and the conclusions capable of implementation. If
the purpose of this study were to consider how nutrition can
be improved in the American diet, it would be appropriate to
limit our inquiry to edible foods. But where our concern rests
with productivity, it is impossible to discuss in any meaningful way the number of manhours required to handle edible
items alone, because they move as part of an overall product
mix and the incorporation of nonfoods in that mix has a direct
effect upon the productivity of the entire distributive process.

In the typical retail supermarket, for example, it is
meaningless to talk about the productivity of handling food
items, in the narrow sense. When a load of merchandise comes
in from the warehouse, it is typically a mixed load of food
and nonfood products. If manufacturers of nonfood items sold

in supermarkets were to decide not to participate in implementation of the universal code (which is discussed in subsequent
chapters), they would effectively block what is likely to be
the most important single breakthrough in productivity in the
food industry during the coming decade.

Moreover, statistics presently collected in this industry
typically make no distinction between food and nonfood items.
At the warehouse level, statistics are usually maintained in
terms of tons per manhour, while at the store level the
appropriate figures are stated in terms of sales per manhour.
In neither case is there any attempt to isolate the edible
component of the merchandise mix.

Because of the intimate interrelationship between food
and nonfood items in the distribution process, implementation
of policy recommendations with respect to productivity improvement in this industry must, of necessity, apply to the entire
merchandising mix. Whether we look at the problem of the backhaul or the impact of the antitrust laws, productivity analysis
in the food industry requires a broad view of the entire mix
of merchandise which moves from manufacturer to warehouse to
store and to consumer.

We are led, therefore, to a definition of the food industry
which takes the retail store as the unifying focus in the study.
"Food products" are defined as all products, whether edible or
not, which are sold primarily through so-called food stores—

supermarkets, discount food departments, superettes, and small stores. The "food industry" encompasses all manufacturers, wholesalers, jobbers, and retailers who process, handle, or sell such products in the distribution channel from processing plant to consumer via such retail outlets.

This definition is not without its problems, but it has the merit of according with popular understanding both by consumers and by participants at all levels within the industry. Consumers normally include within their food budgets expenditures for a variety of nonfood items. Retailers customarily talk about the entire merchandising mix when they talk about productivity in food stores. Manufacturers have formed an association which expressly recognizes the unity of the retail outlet. The Grocery Manufacturers of America consists of approximately 165 firms which sell their products primarily through grocery stores. Included in this membership are companies which sell detergents, health and beauty aids, paper products, and many other nonfood items.

The Limits of the Study

Although the definition of the food industry set forth above is very broad, it specifically excludes three major segments which have been omitted from this study because of time constraints and because each of these sectors involves productivity considerations which are essentially different from the primary flow of product from manufacturer to the retail outlets

of the type enumerated above. These three sectors are: agriculture, institutional food business, and miscellaneous outlets.

Agriculture

Agriculture has been omitted from this study for two basic
reasons. First, government estimates predict that the average
annual rate of increase in manhour output in agriculture in the
decade ahead will be about 5.7 per cent.[1] This is almost twice
the predicted increase in the nonfarm segment of the industry.
It is in the distribution of food that the real breakthrough in
productivity must be achieved and it is therefore to this problem
that we shall direct our attention.

Second, farming still represents in large measure a struggle
of man against nature. Agricultural problems, therefore, are different in kind from those that affect the rest of industry. Since
it is hoped that this study will have some general applicability
through the suggestion of programs and directions which might
stimulate productivity in industry at large, the nonfarm segment
of the industry serves as a better testing ground for such ideas.

Institutional Food Business

Institutional food sales are made through restaurants, hos-
pitals, schools, in-plant feeding and similar institutions. Although this is an important and growing segment of the food industry, its inclusion in this study would render more complex
the already difficult task of developing a meaningful concept of
productivity for the industry. For example, in the restaurant

---

[1] "The U.S. Economy in 1980", Bulletin 1673, U.S. Department
of Labor, Bureau of Labor Statistics, p. 5.

business, service rather than efficiency in the use of manpower is often a dominant management objective and consumer
criterion of value received. It would be pointless to attempt
a comparison of "productivity" between a roadside hamburger
stand and an exclusive French restaurant! Therefore, no attempt
has been made to explicitly include institutional food outlets
in the scope of this study. However, sales to such outlets
may be distributed through wholesale food warehouses which are
included in this study.

Miscellaneous Outlets

Food items are sold through a diversity of outlets—
gasoline stations, drug stores, department stores, and other nonfood oriented businesses. Food is carried as an impulse item and
traffic generator; it is not the primary business of such establishments. Therefore, improvement of productivity in such outlets is likely to be more related to the nature of the major
business conducted therein than to the attributes of the relatively few food items carried. In any case, the physical distribution techniques and problems with which we shall be concerned
would generally have little applicability to such stores.

In addition to such predominantly non-food oriented outlets,
there are thousands of small specialty food stores in our economy.
There is the meat market, the bakery, the fruit store and the
candy shop. Most of the stores which fall in this category charge
higher prices than supermarkets, are owner-operated, and stress
quality, service, delivery, and credit, rather than low cost.
Like the restaurant business referred to above, the concept of

productivity is of secondary importance in this kind of enter-

prise.

The Profile of the Industry

The food industry, as defined in the previous section, is

unquestionably the largest industry in the United States. Just

how large it is is difficult to say because there are no sta-

tistics which cover the whole array of industries, both food and

nonfood, which make up the total system as we have defined it.

At the retail level, conventional statistics attest to the

size of the food business in the broad sense. Sales of food

stores as defined in this study exceeded 88 billion dollars in

1970.[2] Supermarkets accounted for 75 per cent of this total,

superettes 13 per cent, and small stores 12 per cent.[3] Al-

though the total number of food stores in all of the above

categories diminished over the past decade from 260,000 in

1960 to 208,300 in 1970,[4] the number of supermarkets increased

from 33,300 in 1960[5] to 38,300 in 1970.[6] Employment statistics

---

[2] *38th Annual Report of the Grocery Industry*, *Progressive Grocer*,
April, 1971, p. 60. Total sales were actually $88,415,000,000,
but this figure includes sales of country general and
delicatessen stores.

[3] Ibid., p. 66. Supermarket is defined as a food store doing
$500,000 or more per year; a superette is a food store doing
from $150,000 to $500,000 per year; and a small store is
a store with sales under $150,000 per year. Ibid., p. 61.

[4] Ibid., p. 69.

[5] *Progressive Grocer*, April, 1965, p. 59.

[6] *38th Annual Report*, op. cit., p. 66. The increase in number
of supermarkets was actually greater than these statistics
indicate. Progressive Grocer defined a supermarket differ-
ently in 1960 than in 1970. In 1960, the minimum sales
requirement was only $375,000 per annum.

are difficult to compile for this industry because of the high
proportion of part-time workers. However, in 1969 average
employment in all retail food stores was an estimated 1,692,000.[7]

Wholesaling represents another important segment of
activity in the food industry. All large and most medium-sized
supermarket chains operate their own warehouses and have integrated the wholesale and retail function. Food wholesalers,
however, are still very important in the marketing of food
products. In 1963 there were 1,977 general line grocery
wholesale companies with combined sales of $11.7 billion.[8]
The number of companies was little changed in 1970—1,930—
but sales had mushroomed to $26.6 billion.[9] About 600,000
workers were employed in food wholesaling establishments in
1969.[10]

Statistics with respect to the manufacturing segment of
the food industry are more difficult to compile because of
the diversity of types of firms which are included in the
breadth of the definition adopted. However, some idea of the
size of the manufacturing and processing stage of the industry
can be gained by reviewing the statistics for processing and

[7] Statistical Abstract of the United States, 1970, p. 222.

[8] Economic Report on the Structure and Competitive Behavior
of Food Retailing, Staff Report of the Federal Trade
Commission, January, 1966, p. 37.

[9] 38th Annual Report, op. cit., p. 90.

10 Marketing America's Food, Economic Research Service, U. S.
Department of Agriculture, October, 1970, p. 1.

distribution of agricultural products. Food manufacturing and

processing far overshadow in total employment such basic in-

dustries as primary metals, motor vehicles and petroleum. To-

tal employment in food manufacturing reached 1.4 million in

1969.[11] This is almost 40 per cent greater than in primary

metals, more than twice that in the motor vehicles industry and

over ten times greater than in petroleum refining.[12] Likewise,

value added in the food manufacturing business is far in ex-

cess of that in any other industry. Therefore, even on the

basis of a narrow definition of the food industry limited to

the production of edibles, the industry is the largest single

segment of American industry. A fortiori, if we include the

host of other industries which market nonfood products primari-

ly through food stores, we are obviously dealing with a huge

sector of the overall economic activity in our nation.

Inflationary Trends Affecting the Food Industry

In Chapter I, attention was directed to various trends

which will affect the rate of improvement in productivity and

the rate of increase in money wages and prices in the economy

at large. All of these general considerations are, of course,

relevant to the food industry. The food industry, for example,

---

[11] Ibid., p. 1.

[12] The Structure of Food Manufacturing, National Commission
     on Food Marketing, Technical Study No. 8, June, 1966,
     pp. 1-2.

is suffering from its own wage explosion, which derives its
impetus from settlements made in other industries. However,
in addition to such generalized woes, the food industry is the
focal point for a number of trends which are gathering momentum
and which will unquestionably impart a strong upward bias to
costs and prices in the years ahead. The impact of higher
wages will therefore be felt in an environment already charged
with inflationary cost pressures.

A brief review of these trends is relevant to our inquiry
into productivity for two reasons. In the first place, the
level of cost pressure faced by an industry has a significant
bearing on the motivation of management to improve productivity,
but may also adversely affect the ability of the industry to
obtain the capital funds required for mechanization and automation. This is a particularly significant factor for the
retail sector of the food industry where earnings of food chains
as a percentage of net worth have steadily declined over most
of the past decade from 11.25 per cent in 1961 to 8.88 per cent
in 1970-71.[13] Retail food store operators are finding it increasingly difficult to pass along higher costs in the form
of increased prices to consumers. Continuation of the escalation in costs may, therefore, subject the industry to a serious
cost-price squeeze with an unfavorable effect upon profit
margins.

---

[13] Operating Results of Food Chains, 1970-71. New York State
College of Agriculture and Life Sciences, Ithaca, N.Y.,
1972, p. 17.

In the second place, it is important to have some idea of the magnitude of the cost pressures which an industry faces in order to form some conclusions as to what would be a satisfactory level of productivity advance. Obviously, the larger the anticipated annual increment in costs—both wage and nonwage—the more serious the threat to price stability and the more reason for public concern with respect to those factors which may retard the rate of improvement in productivity.

The Trend in Farm Prices

Despite the rapid pace of productivity improvement in agriculture, farm prices may nevertheless advance sharply in the decade ahead. The fact is that the food on the table of the American consumer has been subsidized for many years by the substandard working conditions of agricultural—and particularly migratory—workers. These conditions are about to change. It seems likely that the decade of the seventies will see both an extension of the minimum wage on a uniform basis to agricultural workers and a major growth in union power on the farm. Farm operators are particularly vulnerable to strike action which is called at harvesting time—a fact which workers will hardly lose sight of in their bargaining strategy. The result will be either strikes with a loss of crops and/or substantial increases in wages, fringe benefits, and improvement in working conditions. Many American housewives who participated in the grape boycott will be shocked to learn what the success of Chavez means when converted into price on a head of lettuce.

Consumerism

A second possible source of inflationary influence on the

food industry is the growing strength of consumerism. The main

thrust of this movement has been directed at the supermarket. The

objectives of consumerism advocates are commendable, but in the

context of this study it must be observed that such legislation

will in the years ahead add to the cost of food. These added

costs may result from the requirement of additional labor at the

store or office level, specialized equipment, additional central

office controls or computer time, and similar factors.

The result of these expenditures may be a better shopping

experience for the customer, but it will not increase physical

product. Unit pricing, for example, cannot be weighed, packaged,

or sold. It is an intangible which does not enter into the calcu-

lation of physical productivity statistics. Productivity indexes

currently in use do not measure the "quality" of shopping any

more than they measure the quality of life. Therefore, it seems

likely that consumerist legislation directed at the food industry

will reduce productivity as currently measured by requiring more

labor to deliver a given quantity of product and as a consequence

will produce an upward pressure on food prices.

Control of Pollution

Legislation restricting emissions into the atmosphere will

affect food processing plants, warehouses and stores along with

all other establishments. Of particular significance to the

retail food industry is the effect of pollution controls on the

cost of electricity. It is not commonly recognized that the super-

market is a prodigious consumer of electric power. The average bill

in a large market with sales of three million dollars per year may

amount to as much as $20,000. If electricity costs jump 50 per cent over the next few years—as present trends suggest they will—the effect could be to impose an additional cost on such a store of approximately $10,000.

Since the average supermarket earns less than two per cent on sales before taxes, the increase in this one category of operating expense would require an increase in sales of over 16 per cent to provide the store with an equivalent pre-tax profit. Such an increase is hardly attainable for an entire industry. Therefore it will not be surprising if the cost of obtaining cleaner air ends up in a higher price for soup, beans and all the items sold in supermarkets.

The Return of the Returnable Bottle

The concern for our environment may lead to legislation banning the use of the nonreturnable bottle. Such action, although possibly beneficial from the point of view of society at large, would impose major costs upon the food industry. For the retailer in particular, handling of the returnable bottle is time-consuming and requires considerable space for collection, sorting, and storing. Indicative of the magnitude of these costs is the statement of one chain operator interviewed by the writer whose stores are presently 90 per cent converted to the nonreturnable bottle. He estimated that the total conversion to returnable would decrease productivity at store level, as measured by sales per manhour, approximately 4 per cent and would increase store labor costs .26 per cent. These percentages applied to the retail food industry at large would means millions of dollars in additional costs.

The Problem of Pilferage

The problem of customer pilferage has assumed alarming

proportions in retail trade in recent years. According to FBI
statistics, shoplifting increased by more than 150 per cent during
the past decade.[14] In the supermarket industry, inventory shortages ten years ago averaged about .5 per cent of sales. Today in
most urban areas the figure has doubled. In some cities, food
stores have experienced shortages as high as 2 per cent of sales
and in ghetto locations even higher.

A continuation of this trend will not only affect food prices
but also will raise serious questions about the future of self-
service in high pilferage areas. The development of the self-
service concept depended upon the prevalence of a standard of
morality and respect for private property which may no longer
exist in certain areas and among certain elements of the population.
If as a reaction to the threat of excessive pilferage there should
be any retrenchment by the retail food industry from the principle
of self-service in the direction of departmentalization of merchandise under the surveillance of a clerk, the result would be
a marked diminution of labor productivity.

Such a possibility is not a remote conjecture. In some stores,
cartons of cigarettes have already been taken off display and are
now sold only from behind a counter by a clerk. Health and beauty
aids may follow. A special study made by one large food chain
indicated that losses in this department may run as high as
10 per cent. Data provided by the automatic checkout (discussed
in Chapter VII) with respect to movement of individual products
may give operators second thoughts about the wisdom of displaying
high gross profit items on open gondolas.

---

[14] Peter Helleman, "One in Ten Shoppers is a Shoplifter",
New York Times Magazine, March 15, 1970, p. 35

The Outlook for the Food Industry

The Wage Explosion in the Food Industry

Of all the inflationary trends affecting the food industry, the most serious threat to cost stability is posed by the escalation which seems to be occurring in the rate of increase in wage rates in food manufacturing, wholesaling and retailing. [Although the imposition of wage and price controls has temporarily slowed the rate of advance in wage rates, the gains scored by unions prior to the wage freeze and the demands now being discussed over the bargaining table suggest that the food industry is on the threshold of a wage explosion which will rival that which occurred in the construction industry during the latter part of the past decade.

As can be seen from Table I, hourly earnings in all stages of the food industry have advanced steadily over the years with increases in the past decade averaging about 5 per cent per annum. However, beginning in 1970 wage increases sharply increased in magnitude. Food processors reported increases in hourly rates of 7-9 per cent. At the warehouse level, increases in rates per hour of 12 per cent were reported by a number of firms.

Nowhere was the acceleration of wage increases more apparent than in the retail sector of the food industry. A key contract was the Retail Clerks settlement in Chicago which provided increases in basic wages of 35 to 44 per cent over a 24-month period, and the Meatcutters settlement which provided increases of 31 to 39 per cent over a 24-month period. These percentages do not reflect the effect of improvement in fringe benefits which were also substantial and which added to the overall cost of the total wage package.

TABLE I

AVERAGE HOURLY EARNINGS
IN FOOD PROCESSING, WHOLESALING
AND RETAILING, 1940-1969

YEAR	FOOD PROCESSING	FOOD WHOLESALING	FOOD RETAILING	WEIGHTED AVERAGE
1940	$ .67	$ .74	$ .55	$ .61
1941	.65	.79	.58	.65
1942	.77	.86	.65	.72
1943	.80	.93	.70	.78
1944	.85	.98	.73	.83
1945	.88	1.03	.79	.87
1946	.99	1.15	.92	.99
1947	1.06	1.10	.95	1.03
1948	1.15	1.12	1.02	1.12
1949	1.21	1.22	1.07	1.17
1950	1.26	1.28	1.10	1.22
1951	1.35	1.37	1.19	1.30
1952	1.44	1.45	1.24	1.38
1953	1.53	1.53	1.30	1.46
1954	1.59	1.58	1.35	1.51
1955	1.66	1.65	1.41	1.58
1956	1.76	1.74	1.47	1.67
1957	1.85	1.82	1.54	1.75
1958	1.94	1.89	1.59	1.82
1959	2.02	1.97	1.60	1.88
1960	2.10	2.03	1.68	1.96
1961	2.17	2.09	1.76	2.03
1962	2.24	2.16	1.83	2.10
1963	2.31	2.25	1.89	2.17
1964	2.37	2.28	1.98	2.23
1965	2.43	2.36	2.06	2.30
1966	2.52	2.49	2.13	2.40
1967	2.64	2.66	2.23	2.52
1968	2.80	2.83	2.38	2.67
1969	2.95	3.00	2.54	2.83

Source: Progress in Food Distribution, National Association
         of Food Chains, Washington, D. C., August 1970,
         Table 5. Reprinted by permission.

Demands now being circulated by the Amalgamated Meatcutters and the Retail Clerks unions include a 4-day week of
32 hours, triple time payments on Sundays and holidays,
12-days guaranteed sick leave (which can be taken whether the
employee is sick or not) in addition to substantial increases
in wages, pension and health plan benefits. The emphasis on
shorter hours and a shorter workweek reflect the growing
interest in our society for more leisure. The impact of this
trend upon costs in the food industry can be particularly
serious because the hours of the typical food store have been
lengthening, not shortening, as more and more families choose
to shop evenings, weekends, and even on Sunday.

At the beginning of this section a parallel was drawn
between the retail food industry and the construction industry. The similarity goes deeper. Neither industry is in a
position to withstand excessive union demands. Strikes in
the construction industry can bankrupt a builder who is rendered incapable of meeting contractual obligations with
respect to cost and delivery. Food stores cannot long resist
a strike because of the overcapacity which exists in retail
food outlets in every city and town in the nation. Food
business cannot be deferred like the purchase of steel or
automobiles; once the doors close and the picket line forms,
the losses start and the customer turned away may never be
regained.

The result is that in both industries the wage structure

more and more is coming to reflect raw union power rather
than worker skill. On the West Coast girls working as cashiers
in supermarkets earn more than mechanics servicing jet planes.
A checkout job requires no previous experience and the skills
can be acquired in about a week of training. Yet the position
pays $13,000 per year.

Such high rates in the retail food business result from
bad settlements. In many cities of the nation there are one
or two supermarket firms who will not take an extended strike.
Union strategists know this and are able to pick off the
weakest targets. Then through a domino process, other companies fall in line, spreading the bad settlement throughout
an industry.

Not only is there a tendency for settlements to spread
within a given geographical area, but also of late there is
some indication that the Meatcutters' and the Clerks' unions
are attempting to widen the areas of uniformity of wages and
extend to lower wage southern areas and smaller towns the
bargains made in higher wage metropolitan areas. Such uniformity, if achieved, would add still another dimension to the
wage escalation.

For the reasons enumerated, retail food operators anti-
cipate wage adjustments in the coming years of a magnitude
quite unprecedented by past experience. The consequences will
unquestionably be a substantial increase in costs and prices

and a major spur to introduction of improved methods and
equipment. However, the retail food industry was not
successful in fully offsetting wage increases by improved
productivity even when the size of such adjustments was more
modest, so it is hardly likely that they will be able to do
so in the future in the face of such a wage explosion unless
there is a major change in the pace of technological innovation in the industry. Never in the history of the food
industry in the United States has there been as urgent a
need for acceleration in the rate of productivity improvement
as confronts the industry today.

The escalation in wages in the food industry has a
special significance for inflation. When wages get out of
line in the shoe industry, domestic plants close down, and
consumers buy imported shoes. When construction costs get
out of line, fewer housing units are built and families stay
on in crowded quarters. But the food industry is a "pass-
through" industry. Higher wages will not put it out of
business and people must eat food. Nor are foreign imports
likely to offer any respite. The result is clear: the
American consumer will pay for higher wages in the food
industry. The American consumer therefore should have a deep
concern about productivity developments in this industry.
Barriers to productivity improvement pose operational problems
to executives in the industry, but in a very real sense they
take money out of the pocket of every American consumer.

The Concept of Productivity in
the Individual Firm

In Chapter I we considered some of the problems which complicate the definition and measurement of productivity from the point of view of the economy as a whole. If productivity calculation is complex at the national level, it is positively confusing at the level of the firm. Management in many companies uses quantitative measurements as guides to efficient performance, but upon closer examination the clarity of the measurement disappears and the index becomes a figure seemingly capable of manipulation.

The ambiguity of definition is brought out by the conflicting answers provided at the national and the firm level to the fundamental question: Can we control productivity? On the national level, the answer is not clear. Perhaps changes in tax, labor, and antitrust policy can provide a more favorable environment for productivity development, but this is a far cry from any contention that productivity can be controlled by national policy. At the firm level, however, the answer surprisingly comes through loud and clear: "Of course we can control productivity. We do this all the time. It is one of the day-to-day tradeoffs in business."

Warehouse Productivity

Let us look at some concrete examples in the food industry to illustrate this point. Ask any warehouseman what he means by productivity. He will answer that it is his physical output

relative to his labor input. Ask him how he measures changes
in productivity. He will point to series of figures, usually
compiled in the form of cases per manhour or tons handled per
manhour, which show the interrelationship of manhour input
and physical output.

Now suppose the warehouseman is asked: Can you improve
your productivity by, say, 10 per cent next year? The answer
in most cases would be: yes. The explanation would focus on
the major trade-offs which are part of the everyday operation
of business:

1) Productivity at the warehouse level can be improved
at the expense of service to the stores. This can be done by
cutting down on the frequency of delivery to the stores, prohibiting all special orders, laying out the warehouse on a
movement rather than a family commodity basis, and restricting
hours for receiving and shipping so as not to interfere with
the routine of work within the warehouse.

2) Productivity at the warehouse level can be improved
at the expense of the merchandising flexibility of the enterprise. This would involve strict limitations on inventory,
limitation of special buy-ins which clog the warehouse, and
reduction in the number and variety of items carried.

3) Productivity at the warehouse can be improved at the
cost of higher depreciation and interest charges. There are
always machines, equipment, and various devices available which
would improve physical productivity. They are not all purchased

because management must balance the effect upon profit of the
increase in capital costs on the one hand versus the improvement in physical productivity on the other. However, if the
warehouseman were simply interested in physical productivity
without regard to a profit budget, he could easily improve
productivity by 10 per cent through the purchase of new
equipment.

These are the trade-offs that management makes as part
of the normal routine of business. A similar list of trade-
offs is found at the store level.

Store Productivity

Maximization of productivity measured in terms of physical
output per manhour is not the sole objective of management in
retailing, nor is it even a dominant one. In the food industry,
as well as in other industries catering to the consumer, merchandising considerations—giving the customer what he or she
wants—are the dominant motivating factors in business policy and
frequently conflict with the objective of maximum efficiency.
This conflict is clearly seen in the managerial decisions which
are regularly made in the retail food business.

Service Departments: In order to woo customers, many supermarket
operators are installing service departments which require more
personnel to man them but enable the customer to take home hot
food. For example, in 1969, among member companies reporting
to Super Market Institute, 21 per cent of bakery departments
in supermarkets had bake-off facilities as compared with

only 13 per cent in 1968.[15]   About 22 per cent of all super-

markets now maintain some department which provides hot carry-

out prepared foods.[16]   Since these are service departments, the

effect of their addition is to reduce productivity as measured

by the usual indices such as sales per manhour.

Product Mix: Probably as many as 50 per cent of the items on the

gondola of the typical supermarket today were not in existence 10

years ago. The merchandise mix in the market is constantly chang-

ing and many of the new products are more time-consuming to handle

than the old ones. For example, frozen peas require more labor

at the store level in handling and restocking than canned peas.

The supermarket has taken on all kinds of nonfood items which

pose special handling problems—charcoal, toys, grilles, plants,

etc. If productivity figures are compared for 1960 and 1970,

what does the comparison really mean? Are we really comparing

two different kinds of institutions? Can management complain to

labor about the slow rise in output per manhour if at the same

time the change in product mix made possible a steady rise in

gross profit? Management decisions aimed at satisfying the whims

of customers can reduce productivity just as surely as a contract

provision in a union agreement restricting technological change.

Both business and labor have been motivated by other than strict

considerations of maximum productivity!

_____

[15]The Supermarket Industry Speaks, 1970, Super Market
       Institute, Chicago, Illinois, p. 20.

[16]Ibid., p. 21.

Convenience: Productivity in the food industry must often be traded off against service, quality, variety, gross profit, and capital costs. There is another tradeoff that is important, particularly from the point of view of the consumer. That is the tradeoff against time. In an affluent society goods become increasingly less important in the scale of values and time becomes increasingly more important. If time is indeed so significant a factor in the minds of customers, then perhaps distribution procedures which are relatively inefficient in terms of handling cost but efficient in terms of saving time are more productive in a meaningful sense to the customer.

This problem is faced both in large markets and in the so-called convenience stores. Suppose the introduction of the automatic checkout makes it possible to reduce the labor complement at the front end of a market by 20 per cent. Store A makes such reduction and as a result its productivity measured in quantitative terms of sales per manhour increases. Store B does not reduce personnel but uses the excess labor to speed customers through the checkout. As a result customers are checked out of Store B faster than in store A. Is store B less productive from the point of view of the customer?

The fastest growing segment of the retail food business is the convenience store. Typically, prices are higher than in supermarkets and unit sales are small, averaging less than one dollar per customer.[17] If we use sales per manhour as an index of productivity, the convenience store will not measure up well in comparison with the supermarket. But the convenience store

---

[17]Data provided by National Association of Convenience Stores.

is very efficient in terms of inventory turns, averaging two to three times that of the average supermarket.[18] Moreover, from the point of view of the customer in a hurry to purchase a bottle of milk and a loaf of bread, the convenience store saves time. How do we compare productivity in institutions which have such different operating philosophies?

These are complex questions with no ready answer. As is so often the case in economic problems, for lack of a better way of measuring productivity, we shall have to rely on the data which are available. However, if we want to stimulate improvement in productivity, we will require additional research into the critical factors which affect the trade-offs referred to in the preceding analysis. If manhour output is balanced against capital purchases and merchandising considerations, how does it happen that the actual balance struck seems to result in a rather consistent net increase in productivity of about 3 per cent per annum? Why is not the increase more, or less? Perhaps sufficient research into the managerial decision-making process will give us an insight with respect to the factors affecting this marketing mix so that we can then better design public policy to stimulate productivity improvement.

Productivity on a Company-Wide Basis

Companies tend to measure productivity at various stages in the flow of product through a company where quantitative measurements can conveniently be made. Thus in the food industry, most retail chains measure productivity at the warehouse level by one set of data and at the store level by another. Few companies, however, have any concept of productivity for the company as a whole.

---

[18] Data provided by National Association of Convenience Stores.

This segmented view of the distribution flow produces com-
plications in the measurement of productivity. Take, for example,
the impact of a managerial decision to reduce direct deliveries
to retail stores. In some markets, as many as 120 separate deliveries are made each week by vendors delivering their products to the store door. In an effort to reduce the interrup-
tion to store routine and the possibility of pilferage which
such deliveries produce, many chains have been shifting such
deliveries to their warehouses where the merchandise is consolidated with other shipments to the stores. The result of
such action usually is an improvement in manhour output at
the store level and a reduction of productivity at the warehouse level. Many of these vendor-delivered items are light
or difficult to handle, so that conventional indexes used by
warehousemen, in terms of tons per manhour for example,
would register a decline as a result of the shift. Has there
been a decline in productivity in the firm as a whole? How
would this be measured?

Other Possible Indexes for Measurement of Productivity

It is evident that analysis of performance in individual
segments of a company's business can give a distorted view of
productivity change. However, companies in the food industry
as a general rule do not maintain any company-wide measurements
of physical productivity. If such measurements were to be made,
what definition would be useful and what kind of data would
be required for this purpose?

1. Physical Units In and Out

Theoretically in a retail food chain with its own warehouse one might look at the total number of physical units
of product brought into the warehouse, shipped to stores
and sold to consumers during a given period in relation to
units of labor required. Such figures are not collected by
retail firms in the food industry at present. Even if they
were available, it is questionable whether the improvement
in measurement of productivity would balance the additional
cost and effort required to compile such data. Although
such figures would avoid the problem of favoring productivity
in one segment of the business at the expense of another, the
continuing change in product mix would still raise questions
as to the value of productivity comparisons over long periods
of time.

At the manufacturing level, most companies do not maintain
records on a companywide aggregate basis for tons shipped or
pounds handled because of the variety of products which they
sell and because of their dissimilarity in nature. When we
consider that in food manufacturing the average life of new
products is only three years, it can be seen that there is a
continual change in the nature of the products making up the
physical mix. Therefore, a continuous series based on physical
movement, whether calculated at a particular point in the intra-
company distribution process, or calculated on some aggregate

firm basis, would still be misleading because it would be based upon a changing list of products with different physical characteristics.

2. Total Physical Distribution Costs as a Per Cent of Sales

Another possible viewpoint to adopt in looking at physical productivity would be to examine the changing relation between cost of goods and sales, or alternatively the relationship between physical distribution costs and sales. Although this kind of measure has the advantage of encompassing the entire operation of a firm, it reflects two factors which are quite unrelated to physical productivity. Obviously sales can rise simply because of higher prices being charged and if such a price decision were made, the immediate effect would be to make physical productivity appear to have increased since the ratio of costs to price would diminish. By the same token, a rise in the cost of goods purchased—as often happens in the food industry when agricultural prices fluctuate—would produce changes in the index in the direction of a decrease in productivity.

Furthermore, the margin of profit in the food industry is inextricably related to the mix of product. Margins have been steadily increasing because an increasing part of the overall mix of product at both the manufacturing and retail level is devoted to products with a high degree of built-in convenience. These products necessarily carry a higher gross

profit. If we are interested in physical productivity in
the ordinary sense of the word, we ought not to confuse its
determination by tying its calculation to gross profit and
price.

3. Reciprocal Productivity Ratios

As was pointed out in Chapter I, productivity is simply
a ratio between output measured in specific units and any
input factor, also measured in specific units. The fact that
productivity change is customarily reported in terms of the
increase or decrease of product output in relation to input
of labor is a reflection of the dominant importance of labor
input as a factor in most business operations. However, the
change in output could also be measured relative to the input
of capital, or land, or management.

While it is generally known that the increase in product
output depends upon the contribution of all of the factors of
production, the custom of stating the results in terms of
labor input has in fact created a measuring device for determining the rate of improvement in compensation for labor.
Reporting productivity change in terms of "labor productivity",
therefore, by conveying the impression that somehow labor is
entitled to the entire increase in total output, may itself
be a factor contributing to the generation of inflationary
wage demands. Labor leaders customarily start with the rate
of productivity advance as the floor of their demands, and then

go on from there.

An executive of a large retail food chain suggested to the writer that perhaps a more meaningful analysis of productivity change would result if the measuring device used were the reciprocal of the customary index. Thus, instead of looking at output per unit of labor, we would examine labor input per unit of product output. We could also look at equipment input per unit of product output, and so on. These various ratios of factor inputs could then be added or compared one with the other. Such a comparison might make it clear that the reduction in labor input per unit of product was in fact purchased at the cost of a large increase in equipment input as a result of mechanization of various operations. This kind of analysis would attempt to bring to measurement of productivity in the individual firm the concept of "total factor productivity" which is associated with the research of Professor John W. Kendrick.[19]

4. Total Factor Productivity

Although in the food industry individual companies usually compare total output with labor input to measure productivity performance, the concept of "total factor productivity" is gaining acceptance in many other industries.[20]   Total factor

---

[19] See John W. Kendrick, "Productivity, Costs and Prices: Concepts and Measures", in G. F. Bloom et al, eds., Readings in Labor Economics, (Homewood, Ill.: Richard D. Irwin, Inc., 1963), pp. 610-623.

[20] For case studies of utilization of this concept, see National Industrial Conference Board, Measuring Company Productivity, Studies in Business Economics, No. 89, New York, 1965.

productivity relates net output to the associated total factor

input, i.e. the input of both labor and capital. Only by re-

lating output to all associated inputs can it be determined

whether or not there has been a net savings of inputs per unit

of output. For example, output per manhour may rise as a re-

sult of the substitution of machinery for labor. In order to

ascertain the true economies effected by such a change in the

proportion of the factors of production, the increase in capital

cost must be subtracted from the saving in labor cost. Output

per manhour, therefore, provides only a partial picture of

productivity changes, whereas total factor productivity yields

results which indicate more clearly whether or not there has

been a savings in total inputs per unit of output.

Calculation of total factor productivity is not as simple

as determination of output per manhour, but the basic data are

generally available to most firms. In brief, this concept

requires, first, the calculation of gross output which is usually

done on a dollar basis and then deflated by a price index to

make it comparable with the base period. From this figure the

value of intermediate materials and services purchased from

other firms is subtracted. The resultant figure is then divided

by the sum of labor inputs and capital inputs. The former can

be calculated on the basis of hours worked times average hourly

compensation in the base period. The latter is perhaps the

most difficult concept to measure in total factor productivity

computation. One measure is net investment (taking account of

depreciation) multiplied by the before tax rate of return earned

by the company on its capital in the base year.

Although the calculation of total factor productivity is not simple, the resultant figure is much more meaningful in evaluating productivity advance in a firm or industry than conventional data based on output per manhour.

a) First, if productivity is to be a meaningful concept to the manager, it must be related to costs. Output per manhour gives only a partial picture of this relationship; the profit-oriented manager is interested in knowing whether or not his total costs of producing a given unit of output have decreased and labor productivity figures can not provide the answer.

b) Second, in most firms output per manhour figures have a built-in upward bias because over time suppliers tend to perform certain of the functions formerly carried on within the purchasing firm. In the food industry, for example, poultry is purchased prepackaged today from suppliers, whereas in years past it was prepared at the store level. To an increasing extent, the same process of prefabrication and prepackaging is occurring in the produce and meat departments. When such a development occurs, the cost of goods rises to reflect the built-in labor incorporated in the product by the supplier. A concomitant result will be that output per manhour in the purchasing firm will rise because fewer employees or manhours will now be needed to process the product for sale to customers. To say that there has been an increase in "labor productivity" in the purchasing firm distorts the change which has occurred. The total factor concept avoids this problem by subtracting from the total output of the firm the cost of all intermediate materials and services purchased from others.

c) Third, total factor productivity gives a truer picture
of changes in efficiency within the firm for use in collective
bargaining negotiations. Since in most firms capital input has
risen more rapidly than labor input, total factor productivity
will show a slower growth than output per manhour, since capital
has over time been substituted for labor.

d) Fourth, the use of total factor productivity calculations may be particularly important when a firm or industry
anticipates a period of intensive capital utilization. The
bias of conventional labor productivity indexes as measures of
changes in productive efficiency can vary from one period to
another, both in economy-wide calculations as well as in the
individual firm, when there are marked changes in the ratio of
capital to labor. For example, in the period from 1948 to 1957,
output per manhour rose somewhat faster than over the long period
1919 to 1957. But this did not mean that the rate of advance
in total factor productivity had accelerated. It simply reflected a higher rate of substitution of capital for labor due
to the relatively high rate of investment in the postwar years.
The fact is that the rate of advance in total factor productivity
was exactly the same in the postwar decade as in the longer
period 1919-1957.[21] This consideration can be of critical importance to the retail food industry at this juncture because the
advent of the automated checkout and automated warehouse will
require huge investments in capital equipment so that the ratio

---

[21] Kendrick, op. cit., p. 618.

of capital to labor is likely to be substantially altered.
The result is certain to be a substantial acceleration in the
rate of increase in labor productivity as conventionally
measured, yet it is conceivable that the rate of advance of
total factor productivity will not be markedly altered.

Calculation of productivity change on a total factor
basis would require the food industry to undertake considerable initial basic research and compilation of data until
statistical procedures could be tested and clarified. Nevertheless, the results might well be worth the effort. The
food industry needs to consider carefully whether or not in
an era when productivity trends are becoming the subject of
close scrutiny by management, labor, government, and the
public, it wishes to continue to rely on ratios which because
of underlying trends in the industry may become increasingly
unreliable.

The Need for Productivity Statistics

If we are really serious about making some major breakthroughs in productivity, then it is obvious that we shall
need reliable statistics to monitor our progress. It may be
that the figures presently utilized by wholesalers and retailers are adequate for these purposes. On the other hand,
it is equally possible that if the problem of data collection
and evaluation is given high priority by industry executives,
changes can be made which may at least in part provide answers
for some of the perplexing questions raised in the foregoing
analysis.

At the manufacturing level, the availability of productivity data is very poor, reflecting the conviction of most food concern executives that the diversity of products makes comparison between companies over time extremely difficult and of questionable value. Although the difficulties must not be underrated, the collection of data on a firm and industry basis to indicate general trends would seem to be essential in the long run in any concerted attack on productivity.

The paucity of productivity data in the food industry is typical of many other industries as well. C. Jackson Grayson, Jr., Chairman of the Price Commission, has observed that many companies asking the Commission for permission to raise prices did not understand the concept of productivity and had inadequate records to satisfy the Commission's requirements.[22] Perhaps one lasting benefit from industry's Phase II experience will be increased interest on the part of management in maintaining adequate productivity data.

A Perspective on Productivity

This brief analysis indicates that productivity in the context of the food industry can be approached from many points of view:

1) We can analyze productivity from the point of view of the entire economy. In this sense, utilization of the returnable bottle, for example, would be highly productive even though

---

[22]New York Times, January 20, 1972, pp. 59, 61.

its utilization would produce higher costs at the store
level.

2)   We can look at productivity from the point of view of
the customer. In this case productivity may be more meaningful if it takes account of the saving of time rather than mere
cost of distribution.

3)   We can look at productivity from the point of view of
the entire firm. In this view, productivity is simply one part
of the overall marketing mix and tradeoffs in varying amounts
reflecting changing market conditions must be made among efficiency, gross margin, quality, and sales appeal.

4)   We can look at productivity from the point of view of
particular segments of a business. Under this hypothesis, the
warehouse is looked at separately without consideration of
the fact that its productivity at a particular point of time
is not the maximum which could have been achieved by management
but represents the results of a tradeoff with other elements
of the business.

Finally, in understanding the role of productivity in
the food industry it must be recognized that neither manufacturer, retailer, nor consumer places a high priority on
productivity and efficiency in overall objectives.

The key objective of the manufacturer is volume and sales.
In order to generate sales and volume the manufacturer is will-
ing to increase variety, shorten production lines, cannibalize
old products, and use various promotional devices such as
cents-off packages, premium packs and other gimmicks which

obviously produce distribution problems but which are effective
methods of stimulating sales.

The focus of the retailer is to build up an image which
will differentiate his store from that of competition. To this
end he is ready to put in service departments, add carry-out
service, and carry his own private label even though its movement is much less than that of national brands. The retailer
is faced by a high breakeven point produced by tremendous
excess capacity. It is more important for him to buy sales
than to concentrate on efficiency at the expense of service
and volume.

The customer is of course interested in value and an
essential element thereof is the price. The success of the
discounter in most areas indicates that price is extremely
important in today's market because of the continual pressure
of higher prices on limited consumer budgets. Nevertheless,
the success of the convenience stores, the large sales of
national brands at high prices compared to private label
brands of equal quality, the fact that consumer replies on
why they shop at particular stores stress quality and service,
all indicate that there are other elements in the purchasing
decision and that if consumers could vote on productivity
and price as compared to better service, the chances are
that they would vote heavily in favor of the latter.

All this leads to the surprising conclusion that although
the food industry in America is often held up as an example
of the acme of distributive efficiency, the fact is that

efficiency is not the driving force in the industry. Furthermore the proliferation of retail outlets and the proliferation
of products, both indicative of other goals of manufacturers,
retailers, and consumers, will make the attainment of an
accelerated rate of productivity improvement extremely difficult to achieve in the industry.

CHAPTER III

MANUFACTURING AND PROCESSING

Because of the broad definition of "the food industry" which we have adopted, manufacturing and processing necessarily include such diverse operations as a packer of lettuce, a milling company, a meat processor, a soft drink concentrate manufacturer, a paper manufacturer, and a detergent manufacturer. These and other companies of equal diversity were interviewed by the writer in this study.

Is it possible to detect any meaningful trends in such a diverse group of companies with widely differing products? Obviously each company will display its own special problems reflecting not only the peculiarities of its own competitive position and management philosophy, but also the technology and economic trends relevant to its own product group. Therefore, generalization is indeed difficult—and perhaps dangerous. Nevertheless, as will become apparent from the discussion, some broad and significant trends do seem to emerge despite the heterogeneity of products represented by the varied group of firms.

The Changing Product Mix

The variety of products produced by each firm and the change in this product mix over time make calculations of physical productivity changes extremely difficult. Suppose a company produces three products: coffee, a packaged dessert and a snack chip. Obviously the shipping packs for each of these products differs considerably in weight, size, and value. Likewise

differing amounts of labor are required in the manufacture of each
product. If over time there is a change in the relative proportions of these products in total output, how can this be taken
account of in measurement of physical productivity? If management
uses an index such as cases per manhour it will get one result; if
it uses hundredweight of product per manhour it will get another.

The complexities caused by the ever-changing product mix in
food manufacturing as well as the changing relative importance of
various product groups introduce some measure of unreliability into
general indexes purporting to measure productivity changes in a
broad sector of food manufacturing. For example, the U.S.Department
of Agriculture publishes a series entitled "Output per manhour in
establishments manufacturing farm-originated foods, 1960-70" (See
Table II). Data are stated to be preliminary for 1964-1970. Output
estimates are based on value added indexes published by the Bureau
of Census projected for non-census years by physical output data
published by the U.S. Department of Agriculture.[1]

As can be seen from the Table, output per manhour in the industries included in the aggregative figure increased from 100 in the
base year of 1967 to 105 in 1970. However, during the same period
there was considerable variation in productivity trends among the
component industries studied. For example, in dairy products output per manhour increased from 100 in 1967 to 108 in 1970 while in
poultry and eggs there was a decline during the same period from
100 to 98. Grain mill products increased output per manhour from
100 to 117 while bakery products fell from 100 to 99.[2]

_____

[1]Marketing and Transportation Situation, Economic Research
      Service, U.S.Department of Agriculture,November 1971,p.12.

[2]Ibid., pp. 12-13.

Aggregative figures may thus conceal significant variations in productivity trends among component industries. Furthermore, in certain product lines available statistical data may not be sufficiently detailed to reveal the changing labor content of new products. In food manufacturing it is an observable fact that more and more convenience—and therefore more labor—tends to be built into many new products. Unless data collection is sufficiently detailed to reveal this trend, statistical techniques may tend to understate the actual rate of productivity growth.

TABLE II

OUTPUT PER MANHOUR IN ESTABLISHMENTS MANUFACTURING
FARM-ORIGINATED FOODS,   1960-1970*
(1967 = 100)

1960	79
1961	83
1962	87
1963	92
1964	94
1965	97
1966	99
1967	100
1968	105
1969	104
1970	105

*Establishments included are primarily engaged in manufacturing
shortening and cooking oils, margarine, macaroni and spaghetti,
meat products, poultry and eggs, dairy products, processed
fruits and vegetables, grain-mill products, bakery products,
sugar, and confectionery.

Source: Marketing and Transportation Situation, Economic Research
Service, U.S. Department of Agriculture, November 1971, p.12.

The Secondary Status of Productivity as a Management Objective

Because of the problems created by a continually changing product mix, a majority of companies included in the writer's survey did not maintain physical productivity figures for top manage-

ment perusal. Company executives preferred to rely on so-called
standard costs and exceptions therefrom as a control device rather
than to attempt to derive meaningful physical productivity figures.

However, even if physical productivity figures were more
readily attainable in such concerns, there is reason to believe
that they would not be accorded much importance. The reason is
that productivity as such is not a dominant factor in managerial
decision-making in food manufacturing and processing firms. An
exception to this rule is found in meat and produce processing
where brands are generally weak or nonexistent and market share
tends to rest heavily on relative advantages in cost and price.
In grocery and nonfood manufacture, on the other hand, advertising
and promotion are critical strategies while development of a
consumer franchise rather than the lowest cost production is the
goal of management. The name of the game is sales and volume
and variety, not maximum productivity and standardization.

Nowhere is this conflict between sales and efficiency seen
more clearly than in the area of product line proliferation. In
almost every company, whether the product is jams and jellies,
facial tissue, breakfast cereals, or pantyhose, the same expan-
sive development goes on, eroding manufacturing efficiency and
adding to inventory and handling costs. Colors, flavors and sizes
multiply as manufacturers battle to satisfy the heterogeneous
ever-shifting tastes and whims of the consuming public. Experience
in the pantyhose industry—a new food store item!—is indicative
of the problem. In 1965 when the industry was in its infancy,
one of the largest manufacturers produced one basic style, four
colors, and five sizes. In 1971 this same manufacturer produced

32 styles, 10-12 colors, and 2 to 5 sizes in each variety! Although
the speed of knitting machines increased enormously during this
period, the costs of physical distribution have mounted due to the
variety of product.

The problem of product proliferation will be considered in more
detail in Chapter IV. Suffice it to say at this point that although
plant managers and physical distribution executives complain about
the costs entailed by widening product lines and the peaks and troughs
in production created by various sales promotion events and salesmen
incentive programs, they are generally overruled by marketing and
sales executives. Manufacturers are ready to buy volume at the
expense of inefficiency; they will not buy efficiency at the expense
of sales.

It is possible that this managerial emphasis may change in the
next few years as increasing price consciousness on the part of the
consumer and rising costs of manufacture and distribution produce
pressure on profits which will direct more executive attention to
the area of productivity. On the other hand, developments in retail
trade—such as the growing tendency for chains to carry only one or
two lines of manufacturers who have the leading share of market in
certain product categories—may make manufacturers even more concerned with maintaining and increasing sales and market share.

Trends in Productivity, Wages and Unit Labor Costs

As a preface to a discussion of trends in this complex industry,
the caveat must again be repeated that products, physical facilities,
and competitive conditions vary so widely that comparison of data
from a small sample of companies is meaningless. All that can be
said is that certain broad trends seem to emerge from the limited
number of interviews conducted by the writer. These suggest the

following:

1) In direct production most companies have experienced
year-by-year growth in output per manhour for specific products
and expect such improvement to continue as newer and faster
machines are utilized. In a few companies, production has
already been so highly automated that as one executive put it,
"We are running out of operations to automate!" In this company
pounds per manhour produced stood at 84.5 in 1965 and 85.7 in
1970, indicating that productivity had tended to reach a plateau.

However, in general it seems likely that productivity in
manufacturing will continue to improve through the more extensive
use of automation, better internal engineering, new technology
and improved management techniques. Improvement in productivity
will also come about from the adoption of known developments
which take time to work their way into the industrial process
because of the fixity of equipment.

In many companies making various kinds of prepared foods,
the process of new product development itself brings with it a
natural improvement in productivity. When a new prepared food is
first introduced, its volume is naturally small and considerable
labor will go into its preparation. However, as the product
achieves increased sales, new volume production methods can be
utilized and manhours per unit come down. New product development, therefore, has a mixed effect upon productivity. Since
only a small percentage of products developed in the laboratory
are commercially successful (about 20 per cent according to some
statistics), a large number of hours of labor of laboratory,
production, and marketing personnel involved in this process are

basically unproductive. Furthermore, the continued introduction
of new products and variations of old ones tends to disrupt the
routines of production and make for shorter runs of product with
an adverse effect upon manhour output. However, the other side
of the coin is that the continued change in product mix which is
a continuing phenomenon in the American food industry provides a
growing source of production economies.

2) There has been relatively little improvement in the
utilization of indirect plant labor in functions such as maintenance, cleaning, security, and so forth. Little improvement is
expected in these areas in the years ahead because of increasing
governmental pressure for better housekeeping, sanitation, and
pollution control. Since in some highly mechanized manufacturing
plants as much as two-thirds of plant labor is indirect, the lack
of improvement in productivity in this category of work acts as
a drag on overall manufacturing productivity.

Despite this fact, it appears that output per manhour in manufacturing has steadily increased at the rate of about 3 per cent
per annum. No figures are available for "food manufacturing" as
broadly defined in this study. However the rate above cited can
be compared with the annual rates of change in manhour output published by the Bureau of Labor Statistics for six food manufacturing
industries, which are as follows:[3]

SIC Code	Industry	1960-70 (Percent)
203	Canning and preserving	2.5
2041	Flour and other grain mill products	5.5
206	Sugar	3.9
2071	Candy and other confectionery products	2.8
2082	Malt liquors	6.4
2086	Bottled and canned soft drinks	6.4

[3] Data from U.S. Department of Labor

3)   Warehouse productivity tended to accelerate for a number
of companies at various times in the past few years depending
upon when they commenced unitized handling of product on any substantial scale. However, the rate of increase in unitization has
now slowed down so that gains from this source—though still
available—have not been sufficient to offset the decline in productivity produced by continuing product proliferation.   The result
for many companies, therefore, has been a leveling out over the
last few years of physical output per manhour in warehouse
operations.

A typical example of this pattern of changes is afforded by
a company in the detergent business. As can be seen from Table III,
steady progress has been made in physical productivity in manufacturing, but warehouse handling remained on a plateau from 1967
to 1969. The drop in manhours from 1966 to 1967 was attributable
to the introduction of automatic palletizers and unitized shipment. The poor performance in 1970 was attributable to the
incidence of a truck strike.

Most of the manufacturing concerns included in the writer's
sample reported a different experience in magnitude of wage increases for manufacturing labor as compared with labor in distribution warehouses. In the former case, although rates were rising
faster than they had for most of the past decade, the average percentage increase was still in the 7 to 9 per cent range. By contrast,
warehouse adjustments were much larger and in one instance cited to
the writer will average 16 per cent for each of the next three years.

As a result of these trends, unit labor costs have tended

TABLE III

Productivity in Manufacturing
and Distribution

Company A

Physical manhours per 1000 pounds of product produced
(production only)

1966	3.63
1967	3.56
1968	3.32
1969	3.04
1970	2.88

Physical manhours per 1000 pounds handled in warehouse

1966	.83	
1967	.73	
1968	.73	
1969	.73	
1970	.82	(truck strike)

Physical distribution cost (exclusive of advertising and promotion) measured by dollars per hundredweight of shipments from
factory to customer

Year	Freight	Warehousing*	Total
1964	$1.09	.64	$1.73
1965	1.05	.66	1.71
1966	1.10	.70	1.80
1967	1.08	.72	1.80
1968	1.10	.74	1.84
1969	1.11	.83	1.94
1970	1.28	.93	2.21

---

*Warehousing part purchased; includes warehousing of finished
product at plant or warehouse

to remain relatively stable or rise only slightly in manufacturing
operations, while unit labor costs in physical distribution
operations have risen substantially. Total physical distribution
cost measured by dollars per hundredweight of shipments has risen
even more sharply because of the escalation in freight rates
in recent years.

One consequence of these diverging trends is likely to be
increased emphasis upon improvement of productivity in the
physical distribution area. For many companies, physical
distribution costs represent a larger percentage of the sales
dollar than do direct manufacturing costs. Yet in the past
most of the effort in time studies and industrial engineering has
been directed to the production line. Today many concerns are
establishing the position of Vice President in Charge of Physical
Distribution and giving such an executive broad authority in the
area of traffic, transportation, warehousing, inventory, and
other aspects of distribution. Manufacturers and processors seem
to be in general agreement that the major break-throughs and
real opportunities for innovative improvement in productivity lay
in the physical distribution sector.

Plant Size and Efficiency

The question of the relation of plant size to efficiency
has been a much debated and highly controversial issue in the
food manufacturing industry. Industry spokesmen have pointed to
the economies of size as a reason for mergers and acquisitions.
The Federal Trade Commission and the National Commission on Food
Marketing, on the other hand, have flatly denied that any

significant savings would flow from an increase in plant size in this industry. Thus, the staff of the Federal Trade Commission, in their Technical Study No. 8 for the National Commission on Food Marketing, concluded:

> Economies of scale, except for advertising and promotional activities, are generally insignificant in the food manufacturing industries. Often the largest companies do not operate the largest plants...the limited data which have been developed on costs of production by size of plant show that efficiency in plant operation is achieved at relatively small outputs. /4/

Whether or not this contention was substantiated by the facts in the past, there is considerable evidence to suggest that it will not be true in the future. Statements of a number of executives interviewed by the writer indicate that the need to improve physical productivity in production and distribution is spurring a consolidation of plant facilities into larger units. There are two major reasons for this trend:

Production Economies: In the first place, companies are finding that by combining production of several different products with similar raw material inputs and, a fortiori, consolidation of production of plants producing the same product, they can afford equipment to handle incoming materials on a bulk basis and use bulk handling devices which produce substantial savings in manpower. Such techniques are applicable to sugar, flour,

---

4
The Structure of Food Marketing, Technical Study No. 8, National Commission on Food Marketing, June, 1966, p.104. The FTC was, of course, directing its attention to food manufacturing in the narrow sense of companies producing edible products. The conclusion of the writer in the text seems to be applicable to such companies as well as to those producing various nonfoods which are sold in food stores.

shortening, and other ingredients which are used in a great many grocery products. Even if a plant has a large production of a finished product, its purchases of one of these ingredients may not be sufficient to warrant utilization of bulk handling devices. However, when other products are added to plant production, the resultant mix may create a sufficient demand for specific raw materials to make possible major economies in purchase price and handling methods.

Distribution Economies: In the second place, the proliferation of product variety is causing many companies to take a new look at their plant location and physical distribution system structure. As the variety of product line increases, individual production runs tend to shorten. In some cases, runs may not be long enough to last for an entire shift. When this occurs there is a substantial waste in manpower. A machine must be shut down, usually washed and cleaned, and set up for the next variety, color, or flavor. During the interim, employees go on a coffee break, smoke a cigarette, and the whole routine of production is lost. Executives agree that the ideal arrangement is to have sufficient output for a week's run of a product, but a day's run would certainly be the minimum. However, if production is fragmented among a number of plants, the result may be periodic shutdowns in all of them whereas if production could be consolidated, runs would be longer and more efficient utilization of manpower would be possible.

Product proliferation is adding its weight to increased size of plant in still another interesting manner. Many manufacturers used to ship carload lots of specific fast-moving

products direct to the warehouses of wholesalers and retailers.
As product lines broadened, manufacturers added other items
which did not move in as large volume and most buyers could
not purchase these in carload or truck load lots. As a result,
they were compelled to order them in less than truckload (LTL)
and less than carload (LCL) loads. This is very expensive
because of the differential in freight rates which apply to such
small shipments. Responding to the needs of the wholesaler
and retailer, manufacturers set up so-called mixing distribution
warehouses which collected various products of the manufacturer
from scattered plants. The manufacturer was then able to ship to
the buyer a mixed car or a mixed truckload of the various
products which would travel at lower rates than the LCL and LTL
previously applicable.

However, the utilization of an intermediate warehouse by
the manufacturer imposed a substantial cost upon his handling of
the product. One large canner, for example, estimated that the
cost per case of handling product through such a mixing warehouse
(exclusive of freight) amounted to 10 to 12 cents per case of
merchandise. Manufacturers realize that there must be an
assemblage point somewhere to combine shipments of various
products into carload and truckload lots. However, in view of
the rising costs of operating mixing warehouses and the
advantages already referred to in combining production of a
number of products in one plant, some manufacturers are now
considering the possibility of handling the assemblage function
at the plant and enlarging plant facilities sufficiently to

handle a number of products which could then be combined in ship-

ment direct from plant to the wholesaler's or retailer's warehouse.

This trend will not prove to be most economical for every

manufacturer; there are many other offsetting factors which

must be considered. Some manufacturers are concerned about the

vulnerability to strikes resulting from consolidation of pro-

duction in a few large plants. Others mentioned the difficulty

of handling incoming raw materials and supplies for a variety

of different outgoing products. For many companies the key

factor will be the impact of freight rates on such consolidation.

For others the major consideration is service to customers and

utilizing regional mixing warehouses reduces shipping time to

customers, thus enabling buyers to maintain smaller inventories.

Nevertheless, from the point of view of physical distribution

economy, it is obvious that the fewer times product has to be

rehandled, the greater will be the economies involved. Elimina-

tion of one warehousing step in the distribution process seems

highly desirable, provided that purchasers are still able to buy

mixed loads from the manufacturer.

In view of the foregoing trends, perhaps a new appraisal is

required of the desirability of mergers and acquisitions in this

industry. If in fact substantial economies can be effected in

production and distribution by consolidation of production of

smaller plants into larger facilities, then this factor should

be considered in the formation of public policy with respect to

application of the antitrust laws to mergers and acquisitions.

other hand would improve productivity of customers in unload-

such shipments.

Manufacturers in the food industry utilize three types of

:ized loading devices:

1) The first and most common is the wooden pallet which is

ied with tiers of cases and then moved by use of the conven-

nal forklift truck. One study has indicated that at the end

1965 motor carriers serving food distribution warehouses were

ing 45 per cent of their volume in unitized loads and 93 per

t of the unitized loads were on wooden pallets.[5] The pallet

a number of advantages as a handling device. The load can

handled from all four sides; two pallet loads can be handled

one load, thus permitting double decking in cars and trailers;

the pallet can be handled with conventional types of hand and

ered forklift equipment. On the other hand the pallet system

not without disadvantages. Pallets are bulky and take

ice—about 6 per cent of a 60-foot car.[6] They have to be

ored and returned. Pallets themselves are expensive, they are

clined to become dirty, and they must continually be repaired.

2) A second system uses fiber slip sheets upon which cases

merchandise are piled. The load is then moved by a forklift

uck with special attachments either as a "push-pak" or a

ull-pak". The slip sheet produces a negligible loss of weight

d space in a car or trailer and there are no problems of return,

change, or repair because the slip sheet is used only one-way.

---

[5] J.J. Strobel and W.B. Wallin, The Unit-Load Explosion in the Food Industry, U.S. Department of Agriculture Forest Service Research Paper, NE-121, Northeastern Forest Experiment Station, Upper Darby, Pa., 1969, p. 9.

[6] Ibid., p. 15.

Opportunities in Physical Distribution

Although in the production area the nature of char
necessary to improve productivity vary considerably dep
upon the character of the product and the basic technol
volved in processing or manufacturing, once the product
left the production or processing line the needs of imp
physical distribution fall into fairly common patterns.
interests of brevity these can be placed in three major
gories: (1) increased unitization; (2) better packagi
(3) the performance of various retail functions at an e
in the distribution process. A major problem running t
of these possibilities is that while actions of the typ
gorized will tend to reduce distribution costs over the
distribution process they may actually raise costs to t
manufacturer-processor or reduce his productivity. The
while the opportunities which are discussed below hold
great promise for improvement in productivity in food d
tion, the question still remains how such changes can b

Unitized Loads

It takes an estimated four hours to load or to unl
carload of merchandise which is a dead load (i. e. the
are simply piled one on top of the other with no effort
separate them into manageable multi-carton units) as co
with about 30 minutes for a unitized shipment utilizing
sheet or pallet. It is obvious, therefore, that increa
utilization of unitized shipment by manufacturers would
their productivity in shipping and warehouse operations

However, there are major disadvantages inherent in this system.
The load can be handled from only one side; two unit loads cannot
be handled at the same time, as in the case of the wooden pallet;
and special equipment must be used for loading and unloading.
Likewise, proper handling requires more care, and special training
of personnel is necessary to familiarize them with the specialized
equipment. Nevertheless, there has been increasing interest in
recent years in shipment on slip sheets, because escalating transportation rates have made it increasingly important to utilize
transportation cube effectively.

3) The third system uses the clamp truck, in which the entire
shipment is loaded in blocks with clamp-truck equipment. A major
advantage of this system is that it eliminates both wooden pallets
and slip sheets for a variety of products. However, there are
also substantial disadvantages. The product must be center-loaded
in a trailer in order to provide clamping space on both sides of
the load. This requirement raises the risk of the load shifting.
Furthermore, the clamp truck is heavy and there is reluctance to
use it on motor carrier equipment. The clamp truck itself requires
special skill and training if it is to be utilized properly without
damage to merchandise.

In the present state of our technology, it appears that broader
use of the wooden pallet can provide the most direct route to increased productivity in physical distribution. Although other types
of handling systems have some advantages in specialized situations,
the wooden pallet system is the only one which can be applied in a
total concept from the handling of raw materials through manufacture

and distribution, and then direct to the retail store.[7]

From the systems point of view, the most efficient use of pallets in physical distribution requires a pallet exchange pro-gram. Such programs operate in fourteen nations in Western Europe and an international pallet-exchange program is operating among Austria, Switzerland, and Western Germany.[8] Under such a system, a manufacturer would be able to take a pallet of merchandise out of stock, load it into a railroad car or trailer, ship it to the wholesaler or retailer who leaves the merchandise on the pallet and then places the entire unit load in his warehouse stock. For such a system to work, two prerequisites must be met:

1) There must be an agreement among the various participants in the distribution process that only a pallet of specified size will be used so that it can fit into racks, trucks, cars, and so forth in an efficient manner.

2) There must be in effect a floating pallet supply utilized in common by manufacturers, wholesalers, and retailers with an agreed upon basis for exchange.

The food industry has recognized the advantages which would flow from such a system and has attempted to obtain broad general acceptance of these two conditions. Despite some progress, the pallet system in the industry now seems to be headed for serious trouble. A brief look at the problem is instructive because it indicates how difficult it is to develop and maintain a viable system to improve productivity in a distribution system where the various members of the channel have different needs.

Standardization of Pallets: About 15 years ago there were

---

[7]Ibid., p. 56.
[8]Ibid., p. 3.

as many as 90 different pallet sizes in use in the food industry.
As a result of cooperative action taken by the Grocery Manufacturers of America, the National Association of Food Chains, and
other trade associations in the industry, this number has now
been reduced to two basic sizes in the dry grocery category. The
first is the so-called GMA pallet which is 48 x 40 inches in
overall dimensions and must conform to detailed specifications in
terms of strength, weight, type of material, etc. This is the
size pallet in general use by manufacturers for their in-plant
handling. It is best suited for items which move in substantial
volume.

The second size pallet in use in the industry is primarily
found in wholesalers' warehouses and, to some extent, in parts
of chain retailer warehouses. This is the so-called 40 by 32
pallet. This is a smaller pallet which is better adapted for
slow-moving items. Wholesalers customarily carry more items
in their warehouses than retail chains because they must cater
to the demands of the independent retail stores which they serve.
As a result they find they must maintain in stock many slow-moving
items. Naturally they desire to minimize the amount of inventory
tied up in such slow movers and therefore prefer to use the
smaller pallet. According to figures collected by the National
American Wholesale Grocers Association, about two-thirds of all
pallets in wholesalers' warehouses are the 40 x 32 size.

This diversity in needs reflected in a difference in pallet
size usage obviously detracts from the potential afforded by the
pallet exchange. When the wholesaler receives a car of mixed
products shipped on GMA pallets, he may find it necessary to unload

the pallets by hand in order to transfer some of the merchandise
to smaller pallets. Since it makes little sense to ship on
pallets which take space in a car only to have the load taken
off by hand, it is not uncommon to find warehouses receiving a
carload of groceries containing perhaps ten fast-moving items in
unitized loads and the balance of the items dead-piled at one
end of the railroad car.

Although the reduction in number of pallet sizes has been
of obvious advantage to the industry, serious questions are now
being raised by some retailers and wholesalers as well as by
physical distribution experts as to whether or not further
progress can be made under a two-pallet system. The logistics
of physical distribution are such that the real pay-off comes
from standardization to one basic pallet size. With two standard
size pallets in use, the wholesaler does not benefit from unitization when the manufacturer ships on a GMA pallet. On the other
hand, the manufacturer would reduce his efficiency if he had to
transfer product from the GMA pallet used internally in his plant
to the smaller pallet desired by wholesalers for shipment purposes.
Furthermore, two separate pallet pools would probably have to be
maintained.

Pallet size is only one piece of the entire distribution
system. What is needed is a compatible system in which, ideally,
carton sizes are modular and fit on a standard pallet which in
turn fits into containers, railroad cars and trailers. This is
the approach which is presently being taken by the American
National Standards Institute (ANSI). The latter institution is

also considering the possible impact of the metric system on various components of the physical distribution system. Their objective is to find a suitable sized pallet which could be generally adopted, much as the 31.5 by 47.2 inch pallet has become the standard pallet size in the European pallet pool. ANSI research personnel presently seem to prefer a pallet of 45 x 45 which their computer programs suggest is closest to optimum (although this size was discarded by some manufacturers years ago when they adopted the 48 by 40 pallet!).

The mere suggestion of starting all over again in the search for pallet standardization would surely stir up a bitter controversy in the food industry. Although there is a real question as to whether the existing system of two pallet sizes can produce the economies in distribution which the industry requires, it is also true that economies in shipping and inter-firm handling are only part of the problem. The wholesaler's inventory requirements with a multitude of products are different from the chain retailer's and the manufacturer's. Can one pallet size meet these divergent requirements? Perhaps another solution would be a module of cartons in a 16 inch dimension which could fit in multiples on both the 48 x 40 and the 40 x 32 pallet and could be overwrapped with film or a band to facilitate transference. In any case it is apparent that additional research is required to determine what size pallet can best serve the needs of the system as a whole, what economies can be gained through adoption of a single uniform pallet size, and also what diseconomies would be incurred.

For a system to change, some measurable costs must be imposed
at critical stages to make participants conscious of the need to
eliminate inefficiencies. Until recently the wholesaler who
directed a carrier to unload a palletized trailer of merchandise
by hand did not pay any more for the shipment than if it had been
taken off on a unitized basis. In 1971, however, the Interstate
Commerce Commission published a rule providing that the free time
allowance in connection with unloading of palletized shipments
via motor carriers was reduced to two hours whereas for dead
load shipments the allowance remained at five hours. As a result
of this ruling, if a palletized shipment arrives at a consignee's
dock and he elects to have it unloaded by hand, he may incur a
substantial detention cost.

   There is some unfairness in the rule as published which may
place upon the receiver the burden of providing mechanized equipment and a fork lift truck operator to unload the pallets mechanically in order to avoid detention costs; whereas such incidental
unloading costs should be included in the tariff. However, from
a systems viewpoint there is merit in imposing costs which make
it expensive not to utilize unitized shipments and unloading
procedures.

   The Pallet Exchange: In order for a system of unitized
shipment by pallet to work effectively with a minimum of rehandling, it is necessary for the pallet accompanying the merchandise to become an integral part of the receiver's warehouse stock.
Therefore, the concept has emerged of a "pallet pool" with an

obligation imposed upon the receiver to send back to the manufacturer an equal number of pallets of the same size and condi-
dion. When the manufacturer sends out GMA pallets he is concerned about getting back equivalent pallets because the pallet
float represents a considerable investment to him.

Unfortunately it appears that some retailers and wholesalers are not adhering to the spirit of the pallet exchange
agreement. Manufacturers allege that the pallets are not
being returned promptly and that retailers and wholesalers
are deferring their own replacements of old pallets by using
those belonging to the manufacturers. Also the complaint is
raised that the pallets returned are old and in need of repair,
so that the manufacturer not only ends up with poor pallets
but in addition must assume the burden of repairing them.
On the other side, retailers and wholesalers allege that some
manufacturers complain about pallets received but are actually
sending poor pallets to the buyer. These produce undue handling cost, breakage of merchandise and other problems.

The entire pallet exchange program, which took years to
develop and certainly has made a major contribution to efficiency in distribution, is now in serious trouble. One large
food processor has announced that it will no longer conform
to the GMA quality specifications and intends to utilize
cheaper pallets. Whether or not this move will be followed
by other manufacturers is not known at this point.

A possible solution to this problem might be the development of a cheap disposable pallet but at this time none is
available which would be generally acceptable to the industry.
Furthermore, a disposable pallet would create major problems
of disposal of solid waste. Another possibility would be a
plastic pallet which would be cleaner, require less repair and
possibly be more amenable to quality standardization than the
wooden pallet. However, such pallets, based on present technology,
would be considerably more expensive and would not really solve
the problem of the pallet float which is of such concern to
manufacturers.

Despite the problems alluded to in shipment of dry groceries
on pallets, this segment of the food industry has made much more
progress than others, such as produce. Despite the fact that
retailers and shippers of fruit and produce have been discussing
for a long period of years the necessity for unitized shipment of
produce, to this date the shippers have been unable to agree among
themselves as to the type or size of pallet or unit which should
be used. As a consequence, it is not uncommon to find that some
vegetables, such as lettuce, may be palletized in the field, unloaded into a vacuum cooler via pallet, but at the other end of
the cooler the pallet is unloaded piece by piece and box cars are
loaded with individual boxes by hand from a conveyor!

Other Forms of Unitized Loads

Although the pallet has many advantages in unitization—
especially in ease of handling—it does take up space in a car
or trailer. A dead load can fill an entire car or trailer body

whereas a palletized load loses the space taken up by the pallet itself and in addition pallet loads do not usually fill all the dimensions of the car. Therefore a manufacturer must weigh the additional freight cost per unit of product shipped versus the saving in labor at the shipping and receiving terminals. This trade-off will vary depending upon the nature of the product and the distance the carrier must travel. For example, a detergent manufacturer reported that about 50,000 pounds of detergent could be dead-loaded in a large trailer, compared to only 35,000 to 40,000 pounds on pallets.

This waste of space has led to the search for other unitized means of handling loads. One technique is to use a slip sheet as a substitute for the pallet, and then to overwrap the whole load with shrink film. The shrink film has the advantage of making the whole load more stable. As a consequence, there is less likelihood of damage resulting from shifting of the load in transit and in addition handling is facilitated by the cohesion imparted to the unit load by the overwrap.

However, there are problems blocking the extension of this kind of shipment. As we have already observed, from the retailer's or wholesaler's point of view, loads on slip sheets are more diffi-cult to handle and require special equipment at the warehouse. From the manufacturer's point of view, a shrink film overwrap—whether applied to a slip sheet or a palletized load—involves consider-able additional expense. The technique requires the purchase of shrink film tunnels for installation in the manufacturer's plant. Furthermore, it involves adding another operation to the line which requires additional handling and may in fact slow down the rate of flow from the production line. A large paper products manufacturer was interested in utilizing the overwrap principle because paper products are so light that a high pallet of cartons tends to fall apart. However, the manufacturer found that the cost of the film alone—without taking account of the investment in equipment—amounted to about fifty cents per pallet load. This manufacturer decided not to use the shrink process and instead developed a glue which could be used to hold the cartons lightly together.

Despite these handicaps, many physical distribution executives in the industry believe that the shrink film overwrap principle will gain greater usage in the future. It has even been suggested that for certain kinds of merchandise it might be possible to overwrap a whole carload of product and ship it on a flat car, rather than in a conventional railroad car. This technique has in fact been used on an experimental basis by a midwestern retail chain for shipment of paper bags. However, this technique would not be practical for most products because of problems of weather and pilferage.

Unitized Shipment to Stores

The idea of overwrapping a pallet or unitized load would have its greatest potential value in improving productivity if the entire load could move from the manufacturer direct to the floor of the retail store without the necessity for disassembling the load. Although this is a goal that all food industry executives dream of, it is not practical for most food items. The problem is that only a relatively few items move in volume in a retail food store sufficient to warrant unitized shipments direct to the store. The average grocery item moves less than a case— in contrast to a pallet load—per week per store!

The most advantageous time for a unitized movement of this sort to the store level would be when a manufacturer plans a major promotion for a fast-moving item and wishes large displays set up at the store level. Such displays not only sell merchandise for the manufacturer but also they develop excitement, interest, and sales for the retailer. However, to build mass displays of merchandise at the store level takes time, and time costs money, with the result that retailers are becoming less and less interested in this kind of activity. One solution would be a display set up by the manufacturer which is overwrapped and travels either direct to the store or via the retailers warehouse without disassembly. This kind of application has been used for such items as coffee, dog food, potato chips, and soft drinks. Although the technique has obvious merit, the great variation in availability of space in various retail stores makes the construction of a prefabricated display difficult for general application. Furthermore, many stores lack loading docks so that transfer of unitized loads is difficult.

Despite these and other problems, the concept of shipping certain fast-moving items in unitized loads direct from manufacturer to store level holds forth such promise of savings in distribution cost that it is worthy of continued research and experimentation by the industry. Over the next decade the growth in size of food stores plus the elimination of the need

for price marking which should follow from the introduction
of the Universal Product Code and the automatic checkout will
give additional impetus to such interest.

European markets are much further advanced than American
markets in this kind of development. A number of items are
customarily packed in movable cages which are shipped direct
from the supplier and then moved right into spaces provided
in gondolas. Master display cartons with a cardboard base and
a film overwrap are used for sugar and other items and move
direct from the supplier to the store shelf. In England, one
of the largest business enterprises has arranged for its
suppliers of private label merchandise to ship product pre-priced,
unitized with a shrink film over the individual retail packages
(see next Section) and delivered direct to the store.

In America, retail food chains which have captive integrated
manufacturing operations have not been particularly innovative
in devising new distribution methods. There are, however,
exceptions. For example, in the potato chip manufacturing operation of a large midwestern chain, the merchandise comes off the
line onto pallets and the pallets then move direct to the store.
Stores are required to order such merchandise in pallet loads,
and the merchandise never leaves the pallet from plant to store
until the customer buys a package.

Could a large retailer work out a similar arrangement with
an independent manufacturer of potato chips? The technology is
known, but the lubricant must be money. The retailer would
have to agree to require stores to order in pallet load lots

and to make large displays of the manufacturer's product;
the manufacturer on his part would have to ship in a manner
prescribed by the retailer at a substantial discount in
price. Unfortunately, the provisions of the Robinson-Patman
Act prohibiting discriminations in price erect an effective
bar to such innovative attempts to reduce distribution costs,
for, as will be discussed in detail in Chapter VIII, the Federal
Trade Commission has construed the cost-saving proviso of the
Act in such a manner that it is almost impossible for a manufacturer to justify the discounts that a retailer would require in the example cited.

Packaging

Shipping containers cost the grocery industry about
1 1/4 billion dollars a year. The kind of container which is
utilized has a direct effect upon the condition of the product,
damage in transit, ease of handling at the warehouse, ease of
opening and display, and disposal. The latter problem is becoming of increasing importance since the average supermarket
accumulates tons of corrugated material which must be disposed
of in some way.

The familiar corrugated carton gets fairly good marks for
ease of handling in shipment and protection of the product, but
it is difficult to open for price marking at the store, renders
it impossible to detect damage until the carton is opened, is
not designed for display purposes, and creates major problems
of disposal.

Several new techniques are now being tested or utilized in
the food industry. An overwrap of paper is now in general use for
desserts, roll tissue products, soup mixes, and some other products.
It is much less costly than corrugated, easy to open, and easier
to dispose of. However, it does not provide the protection of
corrugated and this deficiency will probably limit its use.
Corrugated itself is being refined through a process known as
wraparound corrugated. This is formed around a product and therefore results in a very tight pack in contrast to the knock-down
corrugated container which provides a much looser pack. The
wraparound pack is said to provide more protection because the
product and the corrugated in effect reinforce each other.

The most promising development in packaging involves the use
of shrink film, not as mentioned earlier in overwrapping an
entire unit load, but rather in overwrapping a group of packages
or cans. An innovator in this respect has been the Green Giant
Company which has been shipping canned corn and canned peas without a corrugated carton. The pack contains two corrugated trays
with a lip that extends about one-fifth up the side of the can.
Each tray contains a dozen cans and one tray is placed on top
of the other. This pack, containing two dozen cans, is then
enclosed in film and shrunk in a heat tunnel. Retailers report
that there has been negligible damage in shipment and the two
dozen cans can be placed on the shelf of the retail store as a
unit with the film being removed in seconds.

This method of shipment is commonly used in Europe where,
because of the shortage of pulp, corrugated is very expensive.

The executive of a large paper company indicated to the writer that the company's plants in Europe regularly shipped toilet paper from plant direct to stores with a film overwrap whereas in the United States the same product moved to stores via warehouses in corrugated cartons.

In the United States, there has been considerable enthusiastic talk about the shrink-film overwrap, but relatively little action, except for the Green Giant experiment. The railroads had initially viewed the innovation with concern on the grounds that the lack of corrugated protection might increase damage claims. However, experience has demonstrated that this is not so and the railroads have now published a tariff for shrink film overwrap shipments.

From the point of view of manufacturers, there is little benefit in converting to such packaging except for goodwill gained from retailers. The use of the shrink film is expensive and the application of the film can slow down a production line at a manufacturer's plant. Retailers view the overwrap principle as a useful process for a limited number of products. One problem is to find a multiple of packages for specific products which is generally suitable for retailers for direct stocking on gondolas. In view of the diversity in store size and merchandising practice, such agreement is difficult to obtain. Nevertheless, despite these problems in application, it is to be hoped that in the near future more manufacturers will experiment with shrink film. It does provide real labor-saving possibilities at the store level.

Performance of Retail Functions at Earlier Stage
in Process of Distribution

The retail store is basically ill-adapted to the performance
of certain functions. Among these are price marking and prefabrication of product. Unless night crews are utilized, the
price marking function is typically subjected to all sorts of
interruptions in a congested store with a resultant high level
of inaccuracy. Prefabrication of meat and produce cannot be
performed efficiently because of insufficient volume to warrant
mechanization. Furthermore, it is difficult to control and
maintain adequate standards of sanitation and refrigeration in
widely scattered retail outlets as compared with a centralized plant

For the reasons discussed, retailers have been interested
in moving these functions further back in the distribution process.
Developments now underway seem likely to accelerate this process.

Pricing

Prices for a particular branded product may vary regionally,
by city, by chain, and even sometimes from store to store within
a given company. Therefore, it is not practical for manufacturers
to pre-price most food products.

A more efficient system of pricing would involve the application of a symbol bearing a code to the product by the manufacturer,
or processor. The code would identify the product by manufacturer,
kind of product, size, promotional characteristics if any, and
other features. It would not state a specific price for the
product. However, if an optical scanning device were available
at the retail store checkout which could read the code and convey

this information to a computer, the computer could then relay to a terminal at the checkout the information as to the price for the product in effect in that store at that particular time.

This system, which relies upon what has been called "The Universal Product Code" (UPC), is now under active study by manufacturers, wholesalers, and retailers in the food industry. If implemented, it could represent the most important breakthrough in distribution costs in the industry since the development of the self-service system. Net savings to the industry by 1975 after all costs,are estimated to range from 100 million to 250 million dollars depending upon the extent of participation by retailers and the extent of source coding.[9]

Implementation of the UPC can give a major impetus to productivity at the store level—as will be pointed out in more detail in Chapter VII—but may reduce productivity and increase costs for manufacturers and processors. The latter would have to shoulder the full costs of the program, but would derive little or no benefit from the operation. These circumstances raise the question as to whether or not in a private enterprise system certain channel members will in effect assume a tax for the benefit of other channel members.

The interests of manufacturers and retailers clash in a number of specific areas involving implementation of this project. For example, the least cost route for manufacturers in application of the symbol is simply to add it to the product label. It is

---

[9]McKinsey & Company estimates. This organization has been retained by the Grocery Industry Ad Hoc Committee to study the feasibility of the universal code and checkout automation.

estimated that this would cost about 12 million dollars per
year.[10] However, this would be the least satisfactory method
of application from the point of view of the retailer since it
would greatly complicate the problem of accurate scanning at
the checkout. The best location from the point of view of
the retailer is the bottom of the can or package, but this is
the highest cost method for manufacturers. Costs for this kind
of application, if lithography is not possible, could run as
high as 51 million dollars per year.[11] Furthermore, account
must be taken of the fact that application of an additional
code to the retail pack will tend to slow down the production
line and thus reduce manufacturer productivity.

Will manufacturers assume these costs? Present indications
are that they will. An important consideration may be the
possibility that if manufacturers of national branded products
do not implement the system, retail food chains will arrange
for application of the code to private label products and this
will put branded items at a further disadvantage in retail
stores.

It is to be hoped that the UPC can be developed on a
voluntary basis by the food industry. Should this fail to
develop, however, it may be necessary for government to step
in and subsidize some of the costs of establishment of the
project, perhaps by agreeing to purchase some of the information
as to product movement which could be generated by this system.

---

[10] McKinsey & Company estimates.

[11] McKinsey & Company estimates.

The benefits to the industry and to the consumer are too large to permit too many years to elapse without effective utilization of the technology and concept. The UPC is only one of a number of codes which are now being developed in this country. The National Association of Wholesalers is instituting a code which will be used to identify products in seven different industries. Government should be aware of these developments because potentially the availability of codes identifying merchandise movement can pave the way to a much more accurate system of government forecasts, productivity figures, cost of living indexes, and other statistics.

Preparation of Produce

According to Produce Packaging and Marketing Association, somewhat less than half of the 55 billion pounds of fresh produce is pre-packaged today before delivery to the store, compared with about 20 per cent in 1955.[12] This percentage is likely to rise sharply in the next few years for a number of reasons.

In the first place, if the UPC is adopted, it will require the packaging of produce to facilitate scanning and recording of movement data. Therefore, prepackaging will become much more common at retail level. However, with wage costs rising, retailers will be unhappy about placing an additional burden upon store help and will seek methods outside the store premises where such packaging can be applied. To some extent this can be done at produce warehouses, but the cheapest and fastest locus for prepackaging is the processor's plant which very often may be in the fields.

---

[12]"Produce Probes New Forms", Modern Packaging, June, 1970, p.58.

The fewer times a perishable product such as produce is rehandled, the better will be its quality. Ideally, therefore, produce should be cleaned, trimmed, and packed at the field under controlled conditions and then shipped in containers which are suitable for transshipment to the store. Adoption of such a system will obviously require much more mechanization at the processing level. This in turn will require larger aggregation of facilities and more capital.

Vegetables and fruit for shipment to distant markets are typically produced under contract. The grower is responsible only for bringing the crop to harvest. The shipper does the harvesting, handling, trimming, grading, and packaging. This phase of the business is now becoming a focus of interest for large companies which are interested in selling branded products of dependable quality which will be picked and packed under optimum conditions. The result is bound to be an improvement in productivity in the entire process of distribution of such products.

Prefabrication of Meat

The potential for saving in prefabrication of meat is enormous. One does not have to be a physical distribution expert to understand that there is considerable waste involved in shipping bone and suet halfway across the United States only to have it discarded in the garbage can at the retail store. Out of every 1000 pounds of live beef, about 180 to 200 pounds end up as bone, fat, and suet in the primal breaking and final retail cutting process. On a typical shipment from Omaha to New York, if the 180 pounds of bone, fat, and suet were trimmed out at the packinghouse

instead of moving on through the system, the savings in packinghouse handling costs have been estimated to be about 15 cents per
hundredweight, and the savings in transportation costs in the
neighborhood of $1.75 per hundredweight. Together, these savings
would aggregate about 38 million dollars annually.[13]

Despite the obvious advantages of prefabrication of meat at
midwest packinghouses in the form of prepackaged retail cuts,
there is little indication that this possibility will become
commercially feasible in the near future. The fact is that although
there are large savings in transportation costs and handling,
the perishability of meat requires expensive technology to maintain its freshness and sanitation in transit when a carcass is
broken into retail cuts. If the product is shipped as frozen
retail cuts, the cost to the consumer can run as much as three
cents per pound over the cost of fresh meat, and in addition the
product discolors rapidly when exposed to light. About twenty
years ago, Swift and Co. attempted to market frozen meat in retail
cuts without success. There has been little movement in the
industry in this direction in recent years.

The most likely direction of the industry, already underway,is
toward processing of subprimal cuts and primals by packers who will
then ship to meat warehouses maintained by large wholesalers and retailers. The latter will in some cases ship primals or subprimals

---

[13]Wendell M. Stewart, "Cost Reduction Opportunities in the
Transportation and Distribution of Meats", Address at
NAFC-AMI Management Clinic on Meat, Hollywood Beach,
Florida, January 30, 1966.

to their stores and in other cases will ship retail cuts.   This development will be considered in more detail in Chapter VI.

Although the retailer is interested in economical distribution, he is also interested in maintaining the individuality of his perishable departments, and the meat department in particular.   Few retailers would be pleased to see meat prepackaged by packers in branded retail packages so that the customer could buy a steak like a can of peas, relying on the processor rather than the retailer.   This interest of the retailer happens to correspond with the interest of the consumer who it appears likes to exercise considerable discretion in size and thickness of cuts, which would be difficult to provide if the processor were to perform the packaging function.

Other items in the meat department, however, are more and more becoming prefabricated items.   Luncheon meats are prepackaged and sometimes price-marked by suppliers.   Poultry is also now available on a prepackaged basis from suppliers.

The Role of Manufacturers
in Productivity Improvement

Productivity can be improved in the food industry.   Whether or not such improvement will develop at a rate which is deemed satisfactory by American consumers depends upon two basic factors: the state of our knowledge, and the degree of cooperation existing between manufacturers and wholesaler/retailers.

There are some things we need to know before we can move ahead with major improvements in distributive efficiency.   As

will be more fully elaborated in the next chapter, this includes
the design of a modular system of distribution. What is the best
size of pallets? What should be the overall dimensions of shipping cartons? In these areas government can be helpful by funding the necessary research and providing leadership and assistance
in the setting of voluntary standards.

There are other areas in which the basic mechanism for improvement in productivity is known and the real problem is the
sharing of costs in the implementation of change. This is the
crux of the problem in the pallet exchange. It is the situation
with respect to the Universal Product Code. It is also the case
with new packaging methods, and many other improvements. In
most cases, the additional cost impinges on the manufacturer
in the first instance.

If manufacturers assume this burden, it will be a states-
manlike contribution to the cause of improved productivity.
Ultimately these initial costs are passed along through the
distribution process. Government cannot very well inject itself
into the complexities of this allocation process. The step forward depends upon the innovativeness of free enterprise. In the
food industry the chances that such progress will be made are
improved by the fact the constituent industries involved are
basically oligopolistic and that a relatively few large companies
account for the bulk of the volume. These large companies have
the financial strength to assume such cost burdens and can take
a leadership role to direct the entire industry to greater
productivity.

CHAPTER IV

THE NEED FOR STANDARDIZATION

Variety may be the spice of life but it can also be the bane of efficiency. The growing proliferation in the food industry—in size, shape, color, weight and variety—unquestionably adds a substantial burden to the overall cost of food in the consumer's budget. Greater standardization and reduced variety could save the industry millions of dollars per year in lower costs in manufacturing and at every stage of the distribution process.

But such action would necessarily limit consumer choice and impinge upon one of the most sensitive areas of the free enterprise system—namely the freedom to vary the product. The problem is complex and the benefits to be gained must be carefully weighed against the disadvantages and dangers inherent in restrictive measures affecting this critical area. We can buy efficiency in distribution—just as we can buy clean air; but the costs are substantial, and the trade-offs need to be weighed with care.

The advantages of standardization are well known to executives at all stages of the food industry but only lip service is given to its achievement. Manufacturers know that product proliferation shortens production runs, increases inventory costs, and complicates sales and merchandise plans. Yet manufacturers are always ready to add a new size, shape,

color, or weight to a product line if it gives promise of
increasing market share, or if a competitor has already done
so with even moderate success.

Wholesalers and retailers complain about product proliferation which requires new slots in the warehouse, additional
facings on the retail shelf, and more paper work at head-
quarters. Yet both retailer and wholesaler, in a continuing
effort to differentiate their own offerings of merchandise,
will put in an entire line of private label merchandise, or
deliberately select a packer's label not sold in a local market,
or attempt to offer for sale sizes, cuts, or weights of food
products somewhat different than those offered by competitors,
so as to make direct price comparisons by purchasers more
difficult.

Consumers—at least the vocal activists among them—complain
that the proliferation of product variety and package sizes and
weights has rendered the shopping task so difficult that value
comparisons can no longer easily be made even in the same store.
Yet, on the other hand, consumers foster proliferation by their
constant search for the new and different and by their willingness to pay more for special sizes and packages which meet their
own peculiar needs.

Variety promotes inefficiency; standardization would
lower distribution costs. But in the American lexicon, variety
is a good word and standardization is bad. Standardization

implies regimentation and drabness. To manufacturers,
standardization raises the spectre of grade labeling and
the weakening of brand loyalty. To executives throughout the
food industry, it raises fears of a system which might provide
some short-run advantages but in the long run, like the
building codes and zoning laws in the construction industry,
would stifle a business where change and variety have been
the keystones to growth.

Whether or not these fears are justified may depend upon
the particular kind of standardization which is sought to be
accomplished. In this chapter we shall examine in detail four
different areas where principles of standardization might be
applied: (1) product line variety; (2) size, shape, and weight
of retail packages; (3) overall dimensions of shipping cartons;
and (4) modularity in the distribution system.

Product Line Variety

This is the jealously guarded heart of the competitive
marketing system in America. Variety and its counterpart,
segmentation, are strategic tools in the continuing battle
waged by manufacturers for the consumer's dollar. If soup manufacturers could lawfully agree among themselves to restrict
production to five varieties of soup instead of the ever-
broadening line that now exists, they might achieve substantial
savings in production and marketing costs. But neither soup

manufacturers, retailers, nor consumers would necessarily
benefit. For the net result of reduction in this level of
proliferation would probably be a decline in the dollar volume
of soup sold with an undetermined effect on costs and prices.

Variety is a key component of sales promotion. A soup
manufacturer—like other producers—competes not only with
other manufacturers of the same product but also with all
other companies competing for the consumer's dollar. As
discretionary income becomes an ever-increasing share of
total consumer income, this competitive battle becomes more
intense and variety becomes essential to maintenance of
market share and profitable production.

Despite fears expressed by some oracles that science and
technology will convert us into a race of automatons, the
exact opposite seems to be now occurring. As Alvin Toffler
has aptly put it in his book, Future Shock: "We are moving
not toward a further extension of material standardization,
but toward its dialectical negation."[1] As a matter of fact,
Toffler sees us rushing toward a condition of "overchoice"—
a point at which the advantages of diversity and individual-
ization may be cancelled by the complexity of the buyer's
decision-making process.[2]

Because the purchase of food products is a daily task for
consumers in the American economy, the food industry must be in

---

[1] Alvin Toffler, Future Shock (New York: Random House,
    1970),p. 235.

[2] Ibid., p. 239.

a position to adapt quickly to changing needs and demands.
The food industry, therefore, more than any other single
industry in the United States, reflects the changing trends
in our underlying culture. Consumers vote daily for what
they want to see on the shelves. The growing variety of
food products is thus a direct response to the needs which
American consumers have communicated to the food distribution
system.

Restriction of product variety, even on a voluntary basis,
would seriously interfere with this sensitive decision-making
process and would necessarily substitute the judgment of a
few individuals for the collective judgment of the market
place. The needs and desires of American consumers with respect to product variety are too complex to be identified,
classified, sorted out, and evaluated by a group of manufacturers acting in unison under some voluntary procedure or by
a governmental agency. The dangers inherent in restriction
of free choice in the area of product variety seem so great
that they would probably outweigh any benefits which might be
achieved in overall efficiency.

Although product variety will undoubtedly continue to grow,
there is an increasing awareness among both manufacturers and
retailers of the costs which it entails and some indication of
positive efforts to keep it within bounds. One large manufacturer
indicated to the writer that his company was about to undertake
an experiment in a given geographical area where product line

would be pruned to determine the effect of such action on sales
and distribution costs. Retailers are reexamining movement
figures for many brands and products in an effort to increase
inventory turns and thereby improve return on investment. In
the coming decade an increasing number of retailers will rely
on sophisticated computer programs which will enable them to
make shelf allocations on a more scientific basis and to weed
out products which do not pay their way.

The problem of proliferation of variety in the supermarket
industry will be partially solved by a segmentation in the kinds
of retail outlets. There are consumers who appreciate variety
and are ready to pay for it. For this kind of consumer there
will evolve gourmet shops—food boutiques, if you will, which
will enable the consumer to select from a broad collection of
various categories of food products from both foreign and
domestic sources. On the other hand, for the consumer who is
interested in price, the retail food industry is already moving
in the direction of the stripped-down discount food store
offering a limited variety of brands and sizes but selling
at low margins. Between these two extremes will be various
combinations of the two principles of variety and efficiency
which will satisfy the needs of most consumers.

For the simplistic-minded efficiency expert the most
direct road to achievement of improved productivity in the entire American food distribution system would be to legislate

a reduction in variety. It is doubtful, however, whether this is a sound or acceptable solution in a society becoming more affluent and more segmented in its tastes and needs. Moreover, to the extent that it would require arbitrary interference by industry groups or government tribunals in the market system, it might introduce a factor of judgmental error which could ultimately bring with it even greater inefficiency and mis-allocation of resources.

Product variety is so inextricably related to new product development, growth, and profit in the food industry that it is unlikely that any program aimed at restriction would be generally acceptable to the industry as a whole. The question then arises as to whether a particular aspect of product variety—that relating to size, weight, shape and volume of retail package—might be more amenable to some sort of limitation with less adverse consequences to the competitive marketing system.

Size, Shape, Weight, and Volume of Retail Pack

This kind of proliferation has been the prime reason for consumeristic demands for unit pricing in the food industry. Weights do not come out to the even ounce; volume and package size vary from product to product, and sometime even within the same product category. The retail package aspect of food

distribution has grown like Topsy without any overall control.
The result is a proliferation of sizes, shapes, weights and
volumes which admittedly makes value comparisons difficult
among various products.

But while the packaging system may be complex, let no one
infer that it does not make sense. When it is taken apart,
item by item, it will be found that for the most part there
are quite valid reasons for various differences which exist
in package quantity. The problem is that the system evolved
as a result of efforts by manufacturers to respond to consumer
needs. These needs differ from product to product. Furthermore,
products in the same category differ in densities, so that
differing weights result in similar packages. A brief review
of some of the reasons for package proliferation creates a
healthy respect for the present system and indicates the major
problems facing any group of manufacturers or governmental
agency seeking to achieve some degree of standardization. One
fact is clear: it is impossible to have standardization in
weight if you wish to have standardization in package size. And
it is impossible to have standardization on either if the package is to contain the right amount of certain products in their
intended use.

Reasons for Packaging Proliferation

1) Certain products are use-oriented, that is the amount
in the package is determined by the end use to which the product

will be put. This is true, for example, of baking mixes
where sufficient product must be contained in a package to
produce a pie or cake in a standard pie or cake tin. The
weight of the contents will vary depending upon the kind of
ingredients contained. Likewise jars of baby food are designed
to provide one or two servings for a baby. The number of ounces
per jar will vary depending upon the kind of ingredients contained.

2) Certain products of the same type may look alike but
actually have different densities. This is true in the toothpaste field, for example, where one large manufacturer recently
marketed a paste with a different formulation and a different
density from other competing brands. The result is that if
standardization is sought on weight basis, the package for
this paste would be smaller than competition. In the canned
fruit category, a standard 303 can filled with fruit will
weigh 17 ounces if heavy syrup is used and only 16 ounces if
light syrup is used.

3) Certain products require odd sizes of cans because of
the nature of the product. Thus, asparagus spears require a
taller can than most other types of vegetables. The spears
could be cut down, but this would cause a loss to growers and
processors since the spears sell at a premium over chunks.
Likewise pineapple requires a can of a certain diameter to
accommodate the customary way of cutting pineapple. As in the

case of asparagus, the pineapple could be adapted to a standard
can but only at the expense of wasting part of the pineapple
which is now sold in slices and would otherwise have to be
sold as chunks at a lesser price.

4) Certain retail packs are designed for special groups
in the buying public who require small amounts of product. For
example, vegetables may be canned in a serving for one; or
toothpaste may be put up in a small travel size. Very frequently these specialty packs are relatively slow-moving and
therefore are not of much interest to large manufacturers who
are geared for mass production. However, they enable small
manufacturers to find a niche in the market. Formal standardization which would, in effect, limit package sizes to the
fastest moving categories would probably be most productive
in terms of cost savings but would seriously affect many small
producers in the food industry.

Under the procedure adopted for implementation of the
Fair Packaging and Labeling Act, standards have been agreed
upon by large producers accounting for the bulk of sales in
particular product classifications while small manufacturers
have been left free to continue sale of odd sizes. For example,
in the salad and cooking oil industry, the large producers
found that they were selling 15 package sizes which accounted
for about 95 per cent of the total sales in the industry. They
agreed to discontinue eight of these fifteen package sizes.

Four additional sizes were accounted for by a small manufacturer
who refused to go along with any curtailment because of the
serious impact it would have had on his business. Thus, in
this industry today, eight package sizes account for at least
95 per cent of the total sales while half as many sizes are
utilized in the remaining small fragment of the industry.[3]

5) Package size is an integral part of merchandising
strategy. Consider the problem faced by a manufacturer about
to market a new product. Because of competitive factors, a
decision has been made that the retail price should not be
more than 49 cents. The manufacturer then deducts the anticipated required retailer's markup and transportation costs to
get back to the manufacturer's selling price. The question
then arises as to the quantity of product which can be put
into the package and still leave the manufacturer a profit.
Thus, package size and contents become variables which are sub-
ordinate to merchandising considerations.

Manufacturers are concerned about suggestions to limit
flexibility in package size or contents because this would
tend to result in more and more competition on the basis of
price with cost increases being reflected in higher retail
prices. One has only to look at what has happened to the size
of candy bars to understand how closely related package size
and price are in merchandising policy. Inflation itself is a
cause of package proliferation. For many products there is a

_____

[3] Grocery Manufacturing, January 1969, pp. 6-7 .

psychological barrier above which price cannot go without
encountering stiff consumer resistance. This would occur with
many products at a dollar. As costs rise, manufacturers want
to retain the flexibility to bring out smaller sized packages
so as to keep the purchase price below the psychological
barrier.

In the case of canned products, limitations imposed by
existing can-manufacturing machinery tend to impose some
restrictions on flexibility of container size to meet merchandising considerations. Even so, however, there are about
75 different can sizes in common use in the food industry. Of
course, with products packaged in paper or cardboard, the size
of package can be varied more easily. Thus a manufacturer
may elect to combat the inroads of a competitor by bringing out
a package slightly less in weight than that of the competitor
at a lower price which will give the impression of a better
buy to the consumer. This ploy may well succeed, but the
result is proliferation of package size in the product category.

Experience under the Fair Packaging and Labeling Act

Under the Fair Packaging and Labeling Act (the so-called
"Truth in Packaging Law"),the Secretary of Commerce is em-
powered to convene industry committees to develop voluntary
standards for categories of products whenever he determines
that:

> there is undue proliferation of the weights,
> measures or quantities in which any consumer
> commodity or reasonably comparable consumer
> commodities are being distributed in pack-
> ages for sale at retail and such undue pro-
> liferation impairs the reasonable ability of
> consumers to make value comparisons with
> respect to such consumer commodity or
> commodities.

To date, using both formal and informal procedures, industry
representatives have agreed upon quantity patterns for packaged goods in about 40 product categories. These include
food and nonfood items ranging from adhesive bandages to
gift wrapping and hair sprays to tea bags and toilet tissue.
Taking edible food items alone, annual sales at retail of
commodities subject to voluntary agreements amount to about
$18.5 billion.[4] Such agreements have reduced the number of
package quantities 75 per cent in dry detergents, 37 per cent
in jellies and preserves, 52 per cent in breakfast cereals,
50 per cent in macaroni products, and 91 per cent in toothpaste.[5]

Criteria considered in adoption of standards have been:
(1) consumer needs; (2) packaging machine capability;
(3) distribution constraints; and (4) innovation.[6] Consumer
needs must take account of how the product is used. Therefore,
with different products, weight or measure or count of the
product had to be selected as the basis for standardization.

---

[4] Commerce Today, December 14, 1970, p. 6.

[5] U. S. Department of Commerce data.

[6] Grocery Manufacturer, January 1969, p. 8.

It is significant, however, that the main focus of standardization was the consumer—to develop packaging which would
make it easier for consumers to make value comparisons. The
fact that package size has a relationship to carton size and
ultimately to distributive efficiency was not an important
consideration either in the drafting of this legislation or in
its implementation. The fact that some improvement in efficiency
resulted from the reduction in package proliferation was incidental.

In the area of packaging, a national commitment to improve
productivity would probably require standardization of a type
which would conflict with goals set by consumerists. Improvement
in efficiency both in the individual firm and in the food industry at large requires standardization of package size, not
weight. Large food manufacturing companies are basically in the
packaging business. One large company visited by the writer
ships over six billion packages per year!   As this stream of
products comes off the production line, the highest level of
efficiency is achieved through the smallest variation in package
size. If packaging machines have to be adjusted for every change
in weight and density of the various products produced, the cost
can be substantial. Likewise, the real economies which can be
achieved in physical distribution in the industry lie in the direction of standardization of carton sizes. In this connection, it is
the dimension of the retail package which is the key module, not
the weight.

The Changing Balance in the Need for Regulation

Experience under the Fair Packaging and Labeling Act has proved to be a useful demonstration of what can be accomplished through governmental leadership and industry cooperation under voluntary programs, as well as the shortcomings of such voluntary procedures. Already there are complaints emerging about the lack of compliance with voluntary standards. Thus, in February 1971, a leading trade paper in the food industry pointed out that although the coffee industry had set sizes at 2, 4, 6, 8, and 10 ounces for soluble coffee, two major roasters still were marketing 5-ounce sizes.[7] Consumer spokesmen have complained that the supposed reduction in sizes is just a numbers game and largely illusory. For example, in the toothpaste industry, where much publicity has been given to the fact that the number of package sizes was reduced from 57 to 5, it is alleged that even prior to the reduction five sizes accounted for about 95 per cent of total production anyway. Few consumers have noticed any observable reduction in the number of sizes on the shelves of the markets they customarily trade at, although it is true that a comparison of various market areas may show some reduction.

Nevertheless, despite these shortcomings of the current voluntary program, it is the writer's opinion that at the present time government ought not to become more involved in setting standards with respect to the size, shape, and weight of

---

[7] Supermarket News, February 15, 1971, p. 6.

retail containers. Voluntary industry action should continue
to be relied upon to secure some degree of standardization
and reduction of proliferation in this important area of distribution policy.

But this judgment is not valid for all time. It depends
upon the relationship between a number of critical variables.
Among them are: (1) the extent of proliferation in product
variation existing at the time; (2) the level of wage rates;
(3) the rate of interest; (4) the rate of inflation in food
prices; and similar considerations.

Even if it were granted that the reduction in size
proliferation achieved under the Law is sufficient under
existing conditions, what happens if the number of items in
supermarkets increases—as some industry spokesmen predict
it will—from 7,500 items to 10,000 items before the end of
the decade? What happens if wage rates double, making the
cost of additional handling ever more costly? What happens
if interest rates soar to 9-10 per cent making the carrying
of additional inventories reflecting thousands of slow-moving
items prohibitively expensive? What will the tradeoff be
with respect to proliferation of size if the decision has to
be made against a background of runaway inflation?

One of the things we need to know is the magnitude of
savings which can be effected throughout the food distribution
system with a given curtailment of variation in package size.

This figure will obviously change over time and needs to be
monitored from time to time as wage rates, inventory carrying
costs, and other relevant factors change. At some point, it
is possible that as the critical variables change in magnitude
it may be in the public interest to impose governmental regulation of package size, if industry fails to respond with
adequate voluntary reductions.

If such a step is ever taken it is important that the
procedure involve adequate notice and an opportunity for all
parties to be heard in the drawing up of standards. More
important—and more difficult to implement—such standards
must provide for periodic review and amendment; for packaging
is a rapidly changing and innovative area in the food business.
It is a foregone conclusion that a regulation with respect to
package size drawn up in 1960 would be largely obsolete by
the end of the decade.

Would such regulation threaten the free enterprise marketing system? Any erosion of the system of free choice in
the market place is to be regretted. But inflation is also
a danger which poses serious threats to the free enterprise
system. Paradoxically, many manufacturers who are bitterly
opposed to any sort of regulation of package size are at
the same time applauding governmental control of wages and
prices as a means of controlling inflation. Is the governmental bureaucracy which such a system of controls requires

somehow more innocuous than that required to administer a
system of package standards?

⸦The setting of standards for industry to follow is a
government function which has proved to be of value in many
aspects of our marketing system. Moreover, consumers adapt
to such standards with relative ease. Few consumers complain
about the fact that liquor is sold only in a limited number of
bottle sizes. In Germany, beer is sold only in two bottle
sizes, but this has not apparently inhibited the consumption
of beer in that country!

Freedom to change package size is an extension of the
right to vary the product; the latter has long been viewed as
an essential, even "unalienable", component of the marketing
mix. Yet other parts of the marketing mix—pricing and
advertising, for example,—have been subjected to numerous
regulations and private enterprise has survived. Product
variation is justified only if it provides a service in meeting consumer needs. Today many consumer activists complain
that product variation has gone too far and has actually made
intelligent shopping more difficult. If in fact the net result of product variation is an economy of overchoice, if the
consumer is confused by proliferation and penalized by high
cost, then certainly there is cause for an evaluation which
would seek to determine what benefits might accrue from
standardization.

Size and Shape of Shipping Cartons

Still another kind of proliferation is found in the
size and shape of shipping cartons. This problem is rife
throughout the food industry whether the items are grocery,
nonfood, meat or produce. Indeed, more detailed examination
will indicate that this is a problem affecting a broad segment of American industry. Manufacturers try to standardize
containers within their own line of products so as to make
possible the use of palletizing machines and other automatic
equipment in their plants. But no concern is given to the
relationship between the carton sizes used by one manufacturer
and any other. The result is that the wholesaler and retailer
are forced to handle a plethora of sizes and shapes which do
not nest properly on pallets and which make it impossible
to utilize advanced materials handling techniques which require some degree of uniformity in carton size.

The degree to which such proliferation has spread is
shocking. A recent study made in a leading food chain's dry
grocery warehouse revealed 2,587 different sizes and shapes
of shipping cartons. The study further revealed that even
the same size case could come packed in as many as six or
more different sizes of shipping cartons.

Another study of cartons in a food chain warehouse revealed that in the packaged luncheon meat category there

were 168 items and 124 case sizes; in biscuit rolls and
cookie doughs, 18 items and 17 carton sizes; in frozen
poultry and meats, 47 items and 45 different case sizes;
in fresh vegetables, 76 items and 54 different carton sizes.
And so it goes through every category of food product.

In the fruit and produce industry, it is estimated
that more than 1400 different container sizes are used by
the entire industry. In contrast, European produce growers
have standardized on two pallet sizes and four carton sizes
for all fresh produce.[8] Needless to say, the problems of
transporting and processing produce are quite different
in the United States from those in Europe. Nevertheless,
the disparity in number of carton sizes used suggests that
there is room for considerable reduction. This problem is
under active investigation by the United Fresh Fruit and
Vegetable Association and government, carrier, grower, and
retail representatives.

The haphazard situation which exists in the American
food industry has developed because there are no guides for
manufacturers and processors to follow which indicate what
size cartons would be appropriate. The problem is highly
complex with a great many interdependent variables. Gains
and losses in efficiency must be measured throughout the
distribution system. It would be too much to expect that
standardization could be applied to all of the items carried

---

[8] "Produce Probes New Forms", Modern Packaging, June 1970, p.59.

in a typical warehouse in the food industry, but if standards
could be agreed upon for even several hundred of the fastest
moving items, a tremendous contribution would be made to the
cause of distributive efficiency.

The Concept of Modularity

Ideally, the standards adopted should embody a system
of modularity. The carton sizes agreed upon should be modular,
each being a direct multiple of the other, so as to permit
the greatest flexibility in unitizing shipments. Furthermore,
such modularity would insure interlocking for load stability.
The carton sizes should fit compactly onto a pallet and into
a truck, trailer, and railroad car with a minimum of overhang
and should fill carrier space without wasted area. Thus, a
system of modularity of cartons cannot be considered in
isolation from other components of physical distribution.

The concept of achieving modularity and standardization
in shipping carton sizes with a view to fostering economies
in distribution is no mere academic dream. As a matter of
fact, European countries are already putting various modular
programs into effect. For example, in Germany, textile
wholesalers and retailers, buyer organizations, cooperatives,
mail order houses and department and specialty stores have
agreed upon standardized dimensions for both consumer packages and shipping containers for a number of categories of
textile merchandise. The same program is being extended to

Switzerland and Austria and interest has also been evidenced

in France and the Netherlands. Sweden has published a pro-

posed program for modulation of shipping cartons for the food

industry which is presently under study in that country.

Benefits from Carton Standardization

Business executives at all levels of the food industry are

agreed that substantial reductions in marketing costs can be

achieved through the adoption of standard carton sizes. According

to an economist with the National Commission on Productivity,

standardization of pallet size is potentially more of a labor

saver than the electronic checkout.[9] The benefits to be gained

fall in the following categories:

1) Standardization would facilitate automatic handling of

merchandise. We are entering an era of the automatic warehouse

in which selection, palletization, depalletization, routing and

loading will be directed by computer and carried out with a

minimum of labor performing primarily supervisory functions.

The technology to accomplish this goal is known, but its imple-

mentation requires some degree of standardization of cartons.

In some highly sophisticated semi-automatic systems now in use

in food warehouses, merchandise is automatically selected from

racks and routed by conveyor to the loading dock to be placed on

the truck. However, instead of using a palletizing machine at

this point, the cases have to be loaded by hand onto a pallet.

The reason is that the proliferation of carton sizes makes it

impossible to use an automatic palletizer.

---

[9]See Sanford Rose, "The News About Productivity is Better
   Than You Think", _Fortune_, February, 1972, P. 190.

According to the officials of a large warehouse equipment manufacturer, if the fast-moving items in a food warehouse could be reduced to about 30 modules, a system could be designed which would permit all of the following functions to be performed automatically:

a)   partial unloading of truck or trailer at the dock;

b)   palletizing or de-palletizing;

c)   stock replenishment;

d)   order selection of the majority of such items;

e)   partial truck loading;

f)   price marking of contents.

Needless to say, if this degree of automation could be achieved, millions of dollars could be saved annually in food warehouses in the nation.

One of the most knowledgeable men in the food industry on the subject of warehousing, in a conversation with the writer, estimated that standardization of shipping cartons could save a cent a case in handling by making possible mechanical unloading of pallets, another cent a case by facilitating mechanical loading of pallets with a palletizing machine, and perhaps another half a cent per case through more efficient general warehouse handling and reduction of damage. These pennies multiplied by the billions of cases handled per year[10] could mean savings of millions of dollars to the industry and to consumers.

_____

[10]It has been estimated that about 15 billion cases of product are handled annually. See John J. Strobel and Walter B. Wallin, The Unit-Load Explosion in the Food Industry. U.S. Department of Agriculture Forest Service Research Paper NE-121, Northeastern Forest Experiment Station, Upper Darby, Pa., 1969, p. 4.

2) Standardization accompanied by modulation would
reduce shipping and storage costs. Adoption of a common
denominator module would permit all shipping containers,
pallets, transport equipment, facilities, etc. to be designed
in multiple units of given modules so that they would be compatible with one another. For example, Western Europe has
been attempting to standardize package dimensions based on a
module where width and length are in the ratio of one to the
square root of 2. The width of any given module is the same
as the length of the next smaller module so that the areas of
successive packages are related by the factor of 2. In other
words, one size is always contained twice in the next larger
size.[11]

At the present time, there is no necessary relationship
between the dimensions of a particular shipping carton and
any other carton with which it may have to nest. Likewise
there is no necessary relationship between the shape and
size of the carton and the size of the pallet commonly used
in the food industry. The result is that palletization becomes awkward. In some instances a substantial part of the
pallet remains unfilled as with some fresh fruit and vegetables; in other situations, as with groceries, cases frequently overhang the pallet and are exposed to damage. Since

---

[11] Donald R. Stokes, "Dimensional Standardization of Shipping
     Containers, Pallets, and Transport Equipment", Address
     at 11th Annual Meeting of Food Distribution Research
     Society, October 25-28, 1970.

shipment on pallets is becoming increasingly common in the
food industry, the lack of a good fit between case size
and pallet increases shipment and storage costs.

3) Standardization would reduce damage to merchandise
which does not properly fit on pallets. Packages that overhang pallets lead to damaged merchandise in every step of
handling—from the freight car, in the warehouse, in the
truck, and in the store. Modular cartons would assure that
merchandise fits pallets without overhang. Indicative of the
kind of savings which could be effected is the statement of
one large manufacturer who estimated that his annual losses
from damaged merchandise amounted to 2 1/2 million dollars.
He estimated that these losses could be cut in half if
shipping cartons were better adapted to fit the 48 by 40
pallet.

Carton Proliferation in the Produce Industry

The evolution of shipping cartons in the fresh fruit and
vegetable business in the United States dramatizes the complex
problems involved in attempts to standardize containers for
shipping merchandise. On the one hand, technological progress
has outrun governmental standards so that regulated container
sizes have little relevance for the industry. On the other
hand, the proliferation of types and sizes of containers has
led to uneconomic use of shipping space and raised questions

as to the acceptability of American shipping packs in other
nations which are moving towards standardization.

Although governmental policy in the United States has
for the most part avoided involvement in establishment of
container sizes on the theory that such action might stifle
initiative in developing improved containers, Congress has
enacted a number of laws regulating container sizes in the
fresh fruit and vegetable industry. These laws enacted in
1915, 1916, and 1928 applied to barrels, hampers, and baskets.
However, as technology advanced, these containers have tended
to be replaced by boxes and crates, which can be moved more
easily by forklift trucks and other motorized equipment.
As a result, the percentage of fresh fruits and vegetables
marketed in the United States shipped in containers governed
by federal standards has declined steadily.

With no voluntary or governmental standards applicable,
boxes and crates have proliferated in size and type. A study
made by the United States Department of Agriculture in New
York City and Los Angeles in 1965-66 found that for 49 different commodities, 371 different size containers were in use.[12]

Containers in the produce industry are too new to be
covered by prior federal legislation and too old to be fully

---

[12] Ibid., p.8.

compatible with modern unitized shipment. The size of these

boxes and crates was designed to fit into refrigerator cars,

reflecting an era when the practice was to load them by hand

and stack them in freight cars. As a result, most of the

containers now commonly in use in the industry do not have

the dimensions suited for efficient use of the 48 by 40

inch pallet which has been generally adopted as a result of

recommendation by the Grocery Manufacturers of America, the

National Association of Food Chains, the National American

Wholesale Grocers Association, and other food trade groups.

Table IV lists 14 commonly used shipping containers

and indicates the percentage of pallet coverage which is

used by the containers. Only two of these containers utilize

at least 90 per cent of the space on the 48 by 40 pallet.

Obviously use of close to 100 per cent of the space would

be the ideal, but use of 90 per cent is one of the basic

criteria specified by various European countries in select-

ing standardized containers.

Obviously we cannot market all fruits and vegetables in

the same size containers because of the variations in the

value of product, size, rate of turnover at the store level,

and other individual product characteristics. However, some

industry leaders believe that the hundreds of sizes of con-

tainers presently in use could be replaced by four different

size containers which would be designed for products falling

TABLE IV

Percentage of Space Occupied on Pallet by Type of Fruit

Commodity, Container & Tariff No.		Percentage of space occupied on 48 by 40 inch pallet (121.9 cm. by 101.6)
Apple, tray pack box	6146	82.5
Apricots, Brentwood lug	100	83.4
Apricots, face & fill box	591	75.0
Cherries, Campbell lug	610	77.6
Citrus, California fiberboard box	6490	82.7
Grapes, wood lug	1026	76.7
Grapes, TKV, box	1102	82.6
Grapes, sawdust chest	920	97.5
Plums, 4 basket crate	852	60.2
Peaches, California wood lug	1310	85.3
Peaches, wirebound box	3936	86.5
Pears, wood box	1375	91.8
Strawberries, tray carton	--	71.2
Tomatoes, wirebound box	4024	86.6

Source: Donald R. Stokes and Earl D. Mallison, International Standardization of Packaging, Agricultural Research Service, United States Department of Agriculture, p. 2.

into four categories of size: small, medium, medium large, and large. This is essentially what has been recommended by the Organization for Economic Cooperation and Development for European trade in fruits and vegetables. The United States Department of Agriculture has suggested that by using an 8-inch by 12-inch module as a guide to designing shipping cartons it would be possible to produce 100 per cent efficient utilization of space on the 48 by 40 inch pallet. This would not require major changes in present sizes of shipping containers, but it does require change—with the attendant costs of phasing out packaging equipment, inventories, and so forth.

The waste of up to 40 per cent of shipping space resulting from use of containers which have multiplied without relation to present shipping methods imposes excessive costs on the distribution process from point of origin to the retail outlet. As more of our fresh fruit and vegetables is palletized for transport in trucks, piggy-back trailers, railroad cars, airplanes and steamships, excessive loss of space in transport and in storage will become too expensive to tolerate. If we can design a sawdust chest for grapes and a wood box for pears to fit the 48 by 40 pallet with a high degree of efficiency, why cannot the same thing be done with the other products?

The answer is that it can be done—and probably eventually will be done—through voluntary action of producers and shippers.

This will undoubtedly take a period of many years because

various vested interests develop to prevent change.   It took

over 15 years to reach common agreement on the size of the

pallets generally used in the grocery industry.   Can we

afford to wait this long for action on standardized con-

tainers in the fruit and vegetable industry?   Conferences,

studies, and discussions have been going on concerning

this problem for many years, and thus far little has been

accomplished except a growing realization by all parties

that something must be done.   Voluntarism has the great

advantage of insuring flexibility and adaptability to

technological change, but it imposes a high cost on the

economy in terms of reduced productivity.   The challenge

is to devise a way to achieve standardization and maximum

use of shipping and storage space while at the same time

leaving flexibility for experimentation with new kinds of

shipping containers and methods.

Modularity in the Distribution System

As has already been mentioned, the problem of standards for shipping cartons cannot be considered in isolation from other aspects of the distribution system. What is needed is an overall view of the system which would integrate size of carrier, container, carton, pallet, case and possibly retail pack. Actually, most distribution experts believe that there is enough flexibility in the various variables so that the other components can be uncoupled from the retail pack. For example, if less space is required in a case in order to achieve uniformity in carton sizes, it is not essential to change retail package size. Another alternative is to vary the number of cans or packages in a case. As a matter of custom, it has been the practice to ship in groups of 24 to a case or 48 to a case. However, with more and more ordering being done by computer there is no reason why this number cannot be varied to meet other constraints. However, it must be recognized that changing the number of cans or packages in a case affects the manufacturer's shipping efficiency and also may have repercussions in terms of out-of-stock on the retail shelf.

The American National Standards Institute (ANSI) is currently studying the problem of modularity in physical distribution in the food industry. They are attempting to integrate pallet sizes, container sizes and inner dimensions

of carriers and containers for overseas shipment. Furthermore,
they believe that an American system should be compatible with
European standards or else shipments of American agricultural
products will be put at a disadvantage.

Opportunities Presented by Metrication

Any consideration of long run improvement in our distribution system must take into account the likelihood of adoption
of the metric system in this country. With England now in the
process of converting to the metric system and Canada likely
to follow, the United States is now being left with non-metric
allies of the stature of Botswana, Lesotho, and Western Samoa!
The realities of industrial competition in world markets, if
nothing else, will probably force our eventual transition to
the metric system, for the United States is now the only major
industrial power which has not adopted it.

Following the passage of the Miller-Pell Bill in 1968, the
National Bureau of Standards of the U.S. Department of Commerce
undertook the first full-scale investigation of weights and measures
in this country since 1817. After three years of investigation and
extensive public hearings, the Bureau concluded that the United
States should change to the metric system through a coordinated
national program. Secretary of Commerce Maurice H. Stans has con-
curred in this conclusion and has recommended to the Congress that
the United States change to the International Metric System; that
Congress assign the responsibility for guiding the change to a
central coordinating body responsive to all sectors of our society;
and that Congress after deciding on a plan for the nation establish

a target date ten years ahead by which time the United States
will have become predominantly, though not exclusively, a
metric nation.

If Congress decides that the nation should convert to the
metric system over some given transitional period, an unusual
opportunity will be afforded to introduce some reason and logic
into our entire packaging, containerization, and distribution
system. Since all of these various components of the physical
distribution system may have to be changed in dimension in order
to conform to metric measurements, there will be an opportunity
to take a new look at our system and introduce some order into
it. Thus for example, the convention already referred to of
ordering in dozens might be replaced by ordering in tens; package
sizes and container sizes could be realigned to provide greater
uniformity; and many slow-moving package, can, and bottle sizes
could be eliminated.

Adoption of the metric system would also provide a unique
opportunity to apply the voluntary industry group standards-
setting procedures utilized under the Fair Packaging and Labeling
Act in a broad undertaking to improve productivity in the food
distribution system. Industry committees could be convened to
review sizes and shapes of various containers and to determine
what changes would permit conformity with the metric system and
at the same time provide distribution economies.

But first the necessary research must be done by or for
government so that suggested standards can be laid on the table
for various industry groups to consider. The National Association

of Food Chains and other industry groups have considered the
problem of modulation of shipping cartons but it is really
too large a problem for any industry association to handle.
The Bureau of Standards, the Department of Agriculture, or
the American National Standards Institute would be in a better
position to adopt the broad overview which is needed for such
a study.

Such a study would have to identify and attempt to measure
the savings in cost which would be effected by standardization
and balance against them the cost and diseconomies which might
also be incurred. With the results of a thorough study of
the problem as a guidepost, the Central agency established by
Congress to direct the transition to the metric system might
then function as a focal point for securing agreements with
respect to container sizes, pallet size, and carrier dimensions
which would conform to an overall long-run plan designed to
improve productivity in physical distribution.

Dangers of Standardization

Although standardization can unquestionably assist productivity improvement, the goal of standardization needs to be approached
with caution. The benefits and disadvantages of any particular
program for standardization need to be carefully weighed. Standardization may produce economies in one industry or sector but induce
diseconomies in another. If, for example, pallets were to be
standardized to conform to the GMA 48 x 40 inch pallet, wholesalers
would be compelled to carry large inventories of individual products
and to change their warehouse layouts, racks, and captive pallet

sizes. This would impose a considerable cost burden on one

sector of the food distribution system. Careful inquiry is re-

quired to determine whether or not the system economies are

sufficient to warrant such a change.

Likewise efforts to achieve standardization in product size

must be considered in the light of the restriction it necessarily

imposes upon consumer choice. Furthermore, restriction of sizes

may have a serious impact upon the viability of small business.

Standardization implies that certain sizes, shapes, or varieties

will be deleted from an industry's production. Frequently odd

sizes, small packages, and unusual varieties are fabricated or

processed by small enterprises. If large producers are permitted

to dictate standards, there may in the long run be a further

tendency to oligopoly since standardization tends to facilitate

volume production which usually confers advantages on large

producers.

Finally, caution must be exercised that standardization does

not lead to the establishment of inflexible rules and specifica-

tions which inhibit technological change. The building codes of

our cities and towns are classic examples of standards which were

set with all good intentions but which have become frozen through

the influence of vested interests and have imposed a barrier to

technological progress in construction. Standards should not

be sought nor agreed upon without some system also being devised

whereby orderly change in the future is possible.

CHAPTER V

TRANSPORTATION

The American food industry has often been called a marvel
of distribution. The American housewife is likely to have on
her table pineapples from Hawaii, lettuce from California, beef
from Iowa, and coffee from Brazil. The variety of product which
we enjoy—and take for granted—is a tribute to the complex
transportation system which serves the food industry and makes
possible this abundance of food items at low cost.

The American transportation system is good—but it is not
good enough. Beneath this impressive facade lies a different
picture—of railroad cars that stand idle in railroad yards,
unused 90 per cent of the time; of trucks that congest our
highways yet carry no cargo; of railroad cars that are lost,
delayed, or arrive late with spoiled or damaged cargo; of
trucks that speed over miles of highways and then stand for
hours at warehouses waiting to be unloaded.

No other functional element in our production and distribution system consistently operates at such a low percentage
of actual capability as our transportation system. No manufacturing establishment could tolerate a system under which
major components of equipment were utilized only 10 per cent
of the year. Our transportation system is riddled with inefficiency which the economy can no longer afford to bear.

The malaise of the transportation industry is a national
problem cutting across industry lines and affecting the lives
of all our citizens. Transportation enters into the cost of
all products. The transportation bill for the economy as a
whole is equal to about nine per cent of the Gross National
Product.[1] The actual percentage of total costs attributed to
transportation expense will vary by industry depending upon the
characteristics of the product being transported. The percentage
is relatively small for high value items such as cameras, automobiles, and TV sets and relatively large for low cost bulky
items such as coal and iron ore.

The impact of transportation costs is of particular
significance in the food industry because most food items are
relatively low in price. For most food products, the percentage
which transportation cost constitutes of total cost is about
eight to nine per cent, or close to the national average of
transportation costs to GNP. The percentage of transportation
costs to wholesale price is obviously much greater. On canned
fruit shipped from the West Coast to Boston, for example,
transportation costs can be as much as 15 per cent of the price
paid by the retailer. On some items, such as lettuce, the
freight cost from the West Coast to East Coast can be as much
as the cost of the lettuce f. o. b. in California!

1 D. J. Bowersox et al., Physical Distribution Management,
   rev. ed. (Toronto: The Macmillan Co., 1968), p. 125.

The inefficiencies which exist in our physical distribution system affect not only transportation costs per se, but also the costs of carrying inventories. When transit time is undependable, receivers and shippers hedge by carrying larger safety stocks. Furthermore, at any one time, larger amounts are tied up in transit than would be the case with an efficiently functioning transportation system.

To be sure, not all inventory levels are transportation-sensitive, but nevertheless there is a definite relationship between efficiency of transportation and the level of inventory required to maintain a given sales volume. One physical distribution expert has estimated that out of 140 billion dollars of inventories in the United States about 100 billion can be classified as transportation-sensitive. He further estimates that a 20 per cent improvement in transportation dependability could enable manufacturers, wholesalers, and retailers to reduce inventories by 20 per cent.[2] Whatever the relationship may be, it is clear that literally billions of dollars of merchandise are unnecessarily tied up in the physical distribution pipelines of this nation because of the inadequacies of our transportation system. As a matter of fact, the term "pipeline" is a misnomer for the disjointed stop-and-start movement experienced by most commodities as they move from terminal to terminal and from switching yard to switching yard.

---

[2]Peter S. Douglas, speech delivered at Ohio Physical Distribution Seminar, Cleveland, Ohio, May 16, 1968.

Transportation Costs and the Wage Explosion

Unless major breakthroughs occur in the transportation
industry, it seems likely that transportation costs will
rise faster during the decade of the seventies than prices
in general. This judgment is based upon the present precar-
ious financial condition of the railroads, which will require
upward rate adjustments, and the inflationary nature of
recent wage adjustments in both railroad and trucking industries.

The upward trend in freight rates is already discern-
ible. Railroad freight rates have risen 43 per cent since
mid-1967.[3] Average truck rates have risen by about 25 per
cent since 1967 with over half of this increase occurring
since mid-1970.[4]

Transportation rates are significantly affected by
changes in wage rates because transportation is a highly
labor intensive industry. The ratio of labor expense to
total operating expense within major segments of the transportation industry ranges from 45 per cent to over 60 per
cent.[5] While wage rates in both the railroad and trucking
industries advanced steadily during the past decade, the
annual increments were modest compared to recent and projected adjustments. The 1970 Teamster settlement involves

[3] Third Inflation Alert, Report by the Council of Economic
    Advisers, April 13, 1971, p. 21.

[4] Ibid., p. 22.

[5] "Productivity Versus Inflation", Labor Information Memo, No.3,
    Transportation Association of America, Washington, D.C., p. 4

a 40 per cent increase in wage rates over three years. The
Council of Economic Advisers, in its First Inflation Alert,
predicted that this increase would raise labor cost per unit
of output by about 10 per cent over the life of the contract.
In the railroad industry, large settlements are also being
negotiated. The Brotherhood of Locomotive Engineers will
receive wage increases totaling about 42 per cent over a
42-month period.

The Need for a Productivity Review

The labor problems facing the transportation industry
in the United States will ultimately be translated into
higher rates which will increase the cost of all products
which are sold through food stores. But the pressures upon
carriers will also lead them to cut down on service wherever
possible without concomitant downward adjustments in tariffs,
and this kind of impact will have a much less obvious but
no less important effect upon productivity, costs, and prices
in the food industry. For example, motor carriers are
presently attempting to eliminate unloading of fresh meat
which has been a traditional responsibility of motor carriers.
Rail carriers are questioning whether or not pallets should
be entitled to a tariff-free return to manufacturer's plant.

Despite the importance of transportation costs as an
element in overall food costs, transportation has been the
neglected orphan of the food industry. Few food industry
executives would classify transportation costs as a "controllable
expense". Both manufacturers and retailers maintain so-called

transportation departments, but the functions of such departments relate primarily to routing and choice of alternative
modes of transportation, rather than urging upon carriers
the need for new and innovative ways of transporting
freight.

In a very real sense transportation has become a vast
wasteland, removed from the probing scrutiny of the management
officials whose products must ultimately bear the cost of such
hidden inefficiency. In part, this no-man's land has developed
because of the artificial barriers created by the legal tech-
nicalities involved in transfer of title. If, for example, a
retailer buys a product from a manufacturer on a delivered
price basis, transportation is already included in the total
price and there is not much that the retailer can do about it.
A further deterrent to action by manufacturer and retailer in
this complex area is the fact that if they could between them
convince a carrier to adopt a different form of transportation,
there is no way of knowing which party would get the benefit
of the cost reduction. It is understandable, then, that food
industry executives are more inclined to spend their time and
energy on problems more directly under their control where
solutions will contribute more directly to profit.

The result is that the initiative in improvement of
transportation has been left largely to the carriers themselves—
with consequences which might be expected. Whatever may have
been the rationale for this strategy in the past, the present
critical situation in the transportation business—and in the

railroads in particular requires a new look at the transportation system to determine whether programs can be adopted
which will contribute to major improvements in productivity.

Obviously such an inquiry undertaken in depth would
require many years of detailed investigation and should
encompass the entire spectrum of modes of transportation
including air, water, rail and truck.

The objectives of this brief discussion are much more
limited. We are interested in examining various possible
ways of improving productivity in the transportation system
which serves the food industry. In this connection, we shall
concern ourselves only with shipments by rail and by truck
and only with measures or programs which hopefully could be
implemented in a reasonable time so that the benefits ac-
cruing from increased productivity would be available during
the decade of the seventies to slow the projected rise in
rail and trucking rates.

The specific topics selected for discussion are:
(1) utilization of the unit train; (2) broader use of the
backhaul in trucking; (3) reduction of detention time of
trucks at warehouses; and (4) consolidation of small
deliveries. Although these problems will be discussed
within the context of the food industry, implementation
of the recommendations outlined would also provide a basis
for improved service at lower cost to other industries
served by truck and rail.

The Unit Train and an Intermodal Transportation System[6]

Reduction of transportation costs, whether by rail, motor
carrier, water or air, depends upon the development of systems
which will enable equipment to be more fully utilized, reduce
the number of times product is rehandled, and cut elapsed time
in shipment. These principles led to the development of containerized freight in overseas shipment and the piggy-back in
domestic freight movement. The next natural development appears
to be the unit train concept.

The Significance of Unitization

The evolution of physical distribution in this country has
witnessed a continuous enlargement in the size of the unit for
shipment. First, individual items were combined in a case and
shipped in case lots. Then the development of more sophisticated materials in handling equipment made it possible to combine cases into a larger unit on a pallet. More recently, the
introduction of the container produced an even larger size
unit—a group of pallets of merchandise combined in a sealed
container which is then handled and shipped as a single unit.

---

[6] Much of the data referred to in this section are derived from
two basic studies of the unit train made by A. T. Kearney &
Company, Inc. The first, entitled "The Search for a Thousand
Million Dollars", was undertaken by that organization in
1966 for the National Association of Food Chains. The second,
entitled "Highballing to Market in Unit Trains", was prepared
in 1968 for the National Association of Food Chains and was
sponsored by Del Monte Corporation. These two studies represent the most recent and most detailed analyses of the
applicability of unit trains to the food industry. The author
is indebted to the aforementioned organizations for permission
to quote from these studies.

The dominant factor motivating this development has been the high cost of labor. Just as it would be unthinkable today to handle individual packages or cans of a product as the unit for shipment purposes, so in a few years rising costs of labor will make the container an economic necessity for transportation of product by rail, water, motor carrier or air. Another factor which will accelerate the use of containers is the rising incidence of damage and pilferage in shipment. Enclosure in a sealed container of durable design can save shippers and consignees as well as carriers millions of dollars by reducing loss from these two sources alone.

Students of international trade are aware of the phenomenal growth of this mode of shipment in overseas traffic in a relatively brief span of time. In 1966 the first container ship sailed for Europe. Today approximately 34 steamship lines offer container service to over 100 ports throughout Europe and Asia. It has been estimated that container ships carry almost 50 per cent of all international freight.[7]

In domestic freight movement, the utilization of containers has been less spectacular but the same economies which led to its phenomenal growth in overseas service are likely to speed its use in domestic freight movement. Today there are 16 major domestic railroad lines using containers. The American Association of Railroads estimates that by 1975 as much

[7] D. H. Overmyer,"Future of Physical Distribution Intermodal Terminals, "Defense Transportation Journal", p. 88.

as 20 per cent of all carloadings will be piggy-back, of
which about 50 per cent will be containerized.[8] Truckers
and airlines are also making substantial progress in application of containerization to the shipment of product in
their transport modes.

The Unit Train

A unit train is a group of permanently coupled cars and
engines operating as a unit which would shuttle back and forth
continuously between specified assembly and distribution
points. Although a unit train can consist of conventional
freight cars, it is more likely that the unit train will find
its greatest advantage in carrying forward the concept of
unitization. In this context, the unit train would be the
unit which combines a large number of containers into a
single mode of transportation. The train would consist of
a number of very light skeletal flat cars designed specifically
to carry containers. Since such cars have no deck plate, they
cannot accommodate standard highway trailers. However, in
operation the lower profile of the containers which reduces
wind resistance and the lower tare weight significantly
contribute to reduced operating expenses.

The unit train would bypass conventional switching,
classification, and train make-up terminals and staging yards

----

[8] Burton N. Behling, "Factors in the Future Development of
Rail Piggyback", paper delivered to 1966 Annual Meeting
of the Highway Research Board.

and would move directly from one specialized terminal to
the other. Such a system would sharply reduce in-transit
time and would make possible fuller use of rolling stock.
Instead of cars being in use only about 37 days per year,
as is presently the case with conventional train movement,
actual usage under unit train operation could be raised as
high as 274 days per year.[9] Such increased utilization
should make possible, on the one hand, a sharply increased
return on investment for the carrier and, on the other hand,
a major reduction in railroad rates which would make railroads more competitive with motor carriers.[10]

The unit train can reduce costs in a manner which cannot be duplicated by truckers over long haul routes. The unit
train can haul up to 100 specialized cars with a total crew of
three men. It would require 100 double bottoms or 200 tractor
truck units to carry the same cargo which a 100-car freight
train can move. Movement by motor carrier would require 100
to 200 men depending upon the number of trailers which could
be accommodated by a single cab. Obviously, the railroads
have a considerable labor-saving capability which they should
exploit.

---

[9] "Highballing to Market in Unit Trains", op. cit., p. 10.

[10] According to one articulate advocate of the unit-train-intermodal
terminal system concept, "....rates will be substantially
below box car rates and far below truck rates...service will
be much faster than rail and equal to the fastest truck
service." D. H. Overmyer, "The Future of Domestic Freight
Transportation", Address before Little Rock Chamber of
Commerce, Little Rock, Arkansas , June 23, 1969, p. 10.

But the railroads have had much the same advantage
even with conventional trains and yet have lost ground to
the motor carrier. The reason is a strange one; the motor
carrier, despite the fact that it must operate on the public
highways and is therefore subject to all the unforeseen delays
produced by congestion, accidents, and other circumstances
familiar to every driver, has been able to schedule fast,
prompt, and reliable delivery of merchandise, while the railroads with their own private highway unencumbered with other
forms of transportation and slow-moving pleasure vehicles, has
become the prime example of slow, tardy, and unreliable transportation.

The unit train can provide the system whereby the railroads can once more capitalize on their own peculiar advantage and offer a freight service which is fast, efficient
and reliable. Moreover, with public concern mounting with
respect to highway fatalities, congestion on our roads, and
air pollution, the unit train can give the railroads an image
of a transportation system especially suited to meet the
needs of the coming decade.

The greatly increased rate of utilization of equipment
which can be provided by the unit train can help to alleviate
the critical shortage of freight cars which now exists. Moreover, the higher rate of equipment utilization plus the elimination of time spent in switching and staging yards can substantially increase the productivity of railroad workers

measured in actual ton miles of freight carried. From the
point of view of both shipper and receiver, the greater
reliability of service afforded by the unit train will
improve productivity both at the manufacturer's plant and
the retailer's warehouse. A West Coast canner reported to
the writer that shipments by rail were arriving at consignees'
warehouses on schedule only about 50 per cent of the time
compared to approximately 90 per cent for motor carrier shipments. Delays in arrival of 3 to 7 days are not uncommon on
some routes. Such delays create additional clerical work,
uneconomic handling when loads arrive late, and other inefficiencies. The unit train, therefore, has the great
merit of making possible an improvement in productivity
not only for railroad labor but also for labor in many segments of the physical distribution system.

The Roadblocks to Development of the Unit Train

The unit train is not a new concept on the American railroad scene. As a matter of fact, there have been a number of
unit trains in operation in this country over a period of years,
especially in the movement of coal, potash, sulphur, grains and
lumber. At the present time there are between 30 and 40 trains
in regular operation that can be truly described as unit trains.
An additional 50 unit train operations are being planned by
electric utility companies to serve new generating stations
that will be constructed over the next five years.[11]

---

[11] "Highballing to Market in Unit Trains", op. cit., p. 11.

In the food industry, however, they are for all practical purposes nonexistent, except for a unit train of 60 cars which runs once each eight days carrying orange juice from Bradenton, Florida to Kearney, New Jersey. Major canners on the West Coast as well as some large food chains have sought, without success, to induce the railroads to undertake unit train service in the food industry.

The reasons for the reluctance of the railroads to embark upon a unit train program in the food industry are complex. The major reasons seem to be the following:

1) The industry is so beset by financial problems and labor difficulties that it is simply not attuned to take on a new and risky venture which seemingly would take large amounts of freight moving at reasonably profitable rates and put it in a category of rates far below the present level. One is reminded of the reluctance of some of the large food chains to embrace the concept of discounting.

The secret of making a profit while reducing price is to increase volume and thereby utilize existing excess capacity. The discounters in the food industry invoked this principle and made money while giving consumers the benefit of lower prices. The railroads can do the same thing, opening up new markets which would be attracted by low rates and timely delivery. As far as excess capacity is concerned, the railroads have the potential for tremendous leverage because normally freight cars move only 10 per cent of the time, a mere 2 1/2 hours a day.[12]

---

[12] Interstate Commerce Commission, <u>Summary Statements on Major Problem Areas</u>, "Freight Car Shortage", p. 1.

Unit trains would average more than 40 miles per hour. They would be moving with revenue freight about eight times as much as box cars normally average today and would cover about nine times as many miles per day.[13] It is this high rate of equipment utilization—rates which railroad officials find difficult to believe are feasible—that protagonists say would make the unit train attractive to the industry even at sharply reduced rates. It is significant that the orange juice unit train referred to above runs back empty from New Jersey to Florida, but presumably is profitable to the railroads and economical to the shipper because of the quick turnaround of the cars.

2) The fact that large amounts of traffic would by-pass marshalling yards might impair the ability of the railroads to make up trains to move from one local destination to another. This concern may be well founded, but in the future the utilization of more sophisticated computer control devices should make it possible for carriers to keep better track of car locations and arrival times so as to overcome this problem.

3) The railroads do not have the necessary funds to purchase the equipment and to construct the terminals which are essential to effective utilization of the unit train concept. This is undoubtedly true, but should not delay the development of the unit train concept. The necessary rolling stock could be purchased by user associations, individual shippers, or the operator of the terminal facilities. The terminals could be built and operated by private interests. The railroads would merely have to provide train crews and lease the right to use roadbeds.

---

[13] D. H. Overmyer, "The Future of Domestic Freight Transportation", op. cit., p. 8 .

The Intermodal Terminal

The unit train is not merely a technological breakthrough
in the use of equipment. Its most important function is that of
an integral part of a new system of distribution. The unit train
will not work at maximum efficiency without use of the container
and without adequate assembly and terminal facilities. Therefore
the entire system requires the development of a series of intermodal terminals. These would serve as the point of coordination—
the place where containerized product could be transferred from
mode to mode: train to truck, truck to ship, etc. The terminal cou
also serve as a consolidation point for less than truckload lots.

Because of the large cost of such facilities and the expensive materials handling equipment required, probably only one
system of such terminals would be economically feasible. The
owner-operator, therefore, would probably have to be accorded a
semi-regulated status with rates subject to ICC supervision.

One of the prime needs of the next decade will be the construction of a national system of terminals adequate to handle
the flood of containers which will soon engulf our transportation
system. Most of our present warehouses are totally inadequate to
handle these large units and furthermore they are not located in
areas where transfers can be made easily from rail to motor
carrier and vice versa with a minimum of congestion.

The Impact of the Unit Train on the Food Industry

The unit train has a great potential for reducing transportation costs throughout American industry. Its benefits are not
limited to the shipment of food products; indeed its greatest
market may lie in the transportation of manufactured goods.

However, the food industry and the unit train represent a "marriage of convenience". The unit train needs the volume which the food industry can provide and the food industry will benefit from the improved service and lower cost which can result from utilization of the unit train concept.

An effective unit train system requires a balance of shipments from east to west and from west to east. Since most manufactured goods tend to originate in the eastern part of the United States, the movement of food products—particularly canned fruits and vegetables—from west to east can provide a convenient backhaul.

Canned Goods: About 1.7 billion pounds of canned goods are shipped annually from California to the 20 largest markets in the other 47 states (excluding Alaska and Hawaii). About 90 per cent of this product is packed in 47 plants in Northern California, all within a 150-mile radius of the Stockton-Oakland-San Jose triangle.[14] This area therefore would be an ideal site for an assembly terminal.

Of the total shipments above referred to, about 33 per cent are destined for the New York-Philadelphia area and 15 per cent for the Chicago-Milwaukee area.[15] It has therefore been suggested that two unit trains be operated, one to New York and the other to Chicago. Experts who have studied the problem believe that

---

[14] "Highballing to Market in Unit Trains", op. cit., p. 19.

[15] Ibid.

the unit train could depart Northern California on Friday

evening and arrive in New York 77 hours later.[16] By contrast,

a leading West Coast canner reported to the writer that

shipments by conventional rail to New York via numerous

switching yards required anywhere from eleven to twenty-one

days!

It has been estimated that in comparison with present

costs (figured at the lowest applicable rate), both unit

trains would make possible a reduction of over 17 per cent

in freight costs for movement of canned goods.[17] As freight

tonnage increased over the conservative figures used to reach

these estimates, further improvements would undoubtedly be

possible.

There are other savings which would accrue, though

their size cannot be easily quantified. One is the effect

of a reliable unit train system on the size of inventories

maintained by wholesalers and retailers in their warehouses.

At the present time, it is customary to maintain so-called

safety stocks to protect against erratic rail service. If

schedules could really be relied upon with confidence,

inventories could be reduced, warehouse turns would improve

and there would be a substantial saving by the food industry

in expense now reflected in interest cost on inventory.

----

[16]
      Ibid., p. 12.

[17] Ibid., p. 25.

Additional savings would result from reduction of damage in transit. A substantial amount of the cargo damage now incurred in transit results from the impact of car against car as they are switched and shunted around in classification yards. The unit train would by-pass such yards and therefore damage would be materially reduced. This would reduce insurance expense as well as the time spent by consignees, shippers, and carrier personnel in handling damage claims.

The Future of the Unit Train

If the unit train and the intermodal terminal concept holds promise for improving productivity in physical distribution, what is needed to bring it from the idea stage to actual implementation? There are a number of concerned groups who are ready to move ahead with this kind of project. It seems likely that the necessary funds, the management expertise, and the physical equipment and facilities can be provided within the private enterprise system without government subsidy.

What is needed is active encouragement by the Department of Transportation, the ICC and Congress to the railroads to go ahead with an experimental program and to use their existing authority to set attractive rates for this kind of transportation.

The danger is that because the unit train will adversely affect the interests of various groups, it will be investigated to death. Historical evidence strongly suggests that the rate of innovation in the railroad industry has been slowed by the regulatory process. When the Southern Railway developed specially designed hopper (Big John) cars with 100-ton capacity and offered sharp reduction in rates, the Interstate Commerce Commission sought to prevent the reduction with the result that the use of the cars was delayed for five years after the service was first announced.[18] It is to be hoped that a similar stance will not be taken with respect to the broadened use of the unit train.

The unit train deserves broader utilization in the railroad industry. It can be the catalyst for a host of innovative improvements which can produce a marked increase in productivity in physical distribution. The regularization of rail service on a rigidly controlled basis would make possible revolutionary changes in inventory control, ordering procedures, and other phases of both procurement and marketing. The system itself will require entirely new warehousing facilities and equipment and therefore will make possible experimentation with the most advanced technological developments in materials handling. The overall result can be a real breakthrough in productivity in physical distribution.

----

[18]Ann F. Friedlaender, The Dilemma of Freight Transport Regulation (Washington, D. C.: Brookings Institution, 1969), p. 93.

The Back Haul Problem

If a man from Mars were to look down on our truck transportation system with x-ray eyes, he would be surprised to find that a substantial number of all trucks on American roads and highways were empty. How high the percentage of nonutilization of trucking capacity is, no one can state with authority. However, some estimates run as high as 40 per cent of all trucks on the road.[19]

That this situation can exist in the midst of a national concern over highway congestion and air pollution and at a time when compensation of drivers in the trucking industry averages over $5.00 per hour is glaring evidence of the need for a systems analysis approach to the entire problem. Unfortunately the parameters are so complex and the data so sparse that it is extremely difficult even to envisage a system which would maximize usage for all types of carriers serving the food industry. On the other hand, the appalling waste in underutilization of manpower and equipment which exists in this field of transportation calls for some kind of an immediate program, even though it may fall short of the optimum.

The approach taken in this discussion deals with only one segment of the trucking industry. It examines the private trucking sector because data on utilization is more available and because concrete proposals can be made and implemented which will substantially improve productivity. It must be recognized, however, that there are shortcomings in such a partial approach and that to

---

[19] In 1966, only 56.7 per cent of all trucks and combinations carried loads on major highways. See <u>Motor Truck Facts</u>, Automobile Manufacturers Association, 1969, p. 52.

some extent the benefits conferred on the private carriers by
liberalization of the back haul privilege may be gained at the
expense of common carriers who may thereby be deprived of available traffic opportunities.

The fastest growing part of the trucking industry is the privat
fleet. Most large chains and wholesalers operate their own trucks
to service their stores or accounts. In most cases, these trucks
deliver loads to stores from the warehouse and then return empty
even though they may pass by supplier plants or warehouses which
will at a different point in time deliver their merchandise to the
warehouse of the retailer or wholesaler and then return empty to
their own plant.

This crisscrossing of empty trucks is so obviously inefficient
that buyers and sellers have sought to reduce such waste through
arrangements for back hauls. Under this procedure, the retailer's
truck, for example, delivers its load to the stores and then on the
way back to the warehouse stops at the supplier's plant or warehouse
and picks up a load which the supplier would otherwise have had to
ship to the retailer's warehouse. The retailer either pays for
the product f.o.b. the supplier's dock, thus saving the transportation cost, or requests a reduction from the delivered price equal
to the amount of the transportation cost which would have had to be
paid by the supplier to a common carrier if the merchandise had been
delivered to the retailer's warehouse. It is obvious that through
such a procedure the productivity of the retailer's trucking equipment and driver is greatly augmented, since the return trip is used
to carry a full load of merchandise rather than air!

Despite the fact that most manufacturers, wholesalers, and retailers in the food industry agree that more widespread use of the back haul procedure would make a major contribution to productivity improvement and reduction in distribution cost, back hauls account for only a small part of inbound freight for wholesalers and retailers in the food industry. Figures compiled by the National American Wholesale Grocers Association suggest that back hauls for its members accounted on the average for only 8 per cent of total incoming freight. There is considerable variation among firms in the amount of back haul usage depending in part upon the willingness of management to devote time and effort to arranging such pick-ups. One large chain, which has made maximum back hauls a definite objective of operational policy has succeeded in raising back haul freight to about 25 per cent of total incoming merchandise at its warehouse. The disparity between this figure and the average cited above may give some idea of the vast opportunity for back hauls which exists in the food industry today.

However, not all retailers or wholesalers have equal opportunities to avail themselves of the back haul. One of the most important circumstances affecting the extent of back haul usage is the location of stores relative to the location of supplier plants. The ideal arrangement, of course, is one in which manufacturers' plants are located near the stores but for many retailers and wholesalers this fortunate juxtaposition does not exist.

Nevertheless, it is apparent after even a casual investigation that much more back hauling could be undertaken than is currently

the practice. Since this would represent a major contribution
to improved productivity in the food industry, it is pertinent to
inquire into the impediments which deter such expansion of the
back haul arrangement. These barriers fall into three categories:
(1) legal impediments; (2) manufacturer resistance; and (3) retailer
and wholesaler reluctance.

Legal Impediments to Expanded Use of the Back Haul

Products purchased by wholesalers and retailers in the food
industry are sold either f.o.b. the supplier's dock, with the
transportation charge varying depending upon the distance of the
wholesaler's or retailer's warehouse from the manufacturer's plant,
or on a uniform delivered price basis, in which case the average
transportation cost to all purchasers in the particular zone
becomes a component of the overall price. There is no question
of legality raised in the situation where goods are sold f.o.b.
supplier's dock and the purchaser elects to pick up at the dock
rather than have the goods shipped by common carrier. However,
where a uniform delivered price prevails and the purchaser
desires to pick up at the supplier's dock and obtain a rebate
equal to the common carrier cost from the plant to its warehouse,
a serious question exists at the present time as to whether or not
such a practice would violate the Robinson Patman Act.

Section 2 (a) of the Robinson Patman Act, 15 U.S.C., Sec.13,
provides in relevant part:

> That it shall be unlawful for any person engaged in commerce,
> in the course of such commerce, either directly or indirectly,

to discriminate in price between different purchasers of
commodities of like grade and quality, where either or any
of the purchases involved in such discrimination are in commerce, where such commodities are sold for use, consumption,
or resale within the United States or any Territory thereof
or the District of Columbia or any insular possession or
other place under the jurisdiction of the United States, and
where the effect of such discrimination may be substantially
to lessen competition or tend to create a monopoly in any
line of commerce, or to injure, destroy, or prevent competition with any person who either grants or knowingly receives
the benefit of such discrimination, or with customers of
either of them: PROVIDED, That nothing herein contained
shall prevent differentials which make only due allowance for
differences in the cost of manufacture, sale, or delivery resulting from the differing methods of quantities in which such
commodities are to such purchasers sold or delivered. . .

The current uncertainty as to the legality of back haul

allowances under a delivered pricing system results from a Federal

Trade Commission Advisory Opinion issued in response to a re-

quest by the General Foods Corporation. By letter dated August 8,

1967, General Foods Corporation submitted to the Federal Trade

Commission a description of its delivered pricing system to-

gether with a proposal to permit back hauls and to pay customers

availing themselves of this procedure an allowance equal to the

amount General Foods would otherwise have to pay to a common

carrier to deliver the product to the customer. The corporation

requested an opinion from the Commission as to whether or not

General Foods might lawfully pay such an allowance to customers

who pick up product.

The Commission responded to this request by letter dated

October 2, 1967 (See Appendix) in which it stated its conclusion

that implementation of such a back haul allowance program would

probably result in a violation of Section 2 (a) of the Robinson-

Patman Act, even though the allowance given to the customer was

no more than the common carrier cost from the seller's plant to
the purchaser's warehouse. This strange result was reached by
the following contrived reasoning:

> This result would seem to necessarily flow from the use of
> a delivered pricing system, for in such case the freight
> factor included within the price is not the actual freight
> to any given point, but an average of the freight costs for
> all customers within the zone wherein the delivered price is
> quoted, or, at least, a figure determined by some formula
> apart from actual costs. If one customer is then given a
> 'back haul' allowance for the actual freight saved, it would
> seem that a serious possibility of discrimination would
> exist in any delivered pricing system and it is highly
> doubtful that the defense of cost justification, at least,
> would be available.
>
> While this conclusion may seem unreasonable from one point
> of view, since the allowance will be for no more than the
> actual freight saved, it would seem to be a necessary result
> of using a delivered pricing system. Whenever such a seller
> departs from his delivered prices for the benefit of one
> customer, he leaves himself open to a charge of discriminat-
> ing against his other competing customers who order in the
> same quantities and hence fall within the same pricing
> bracket because he failed to make allowances for the indi-
> vidual cost factors present in their situations. The law
> does not require that a seller pass on his cost savings to
> his customers, but where he elects to do so in one instance
> it does require that he not discriminate between his pur-
> chasers where such discrimination has the prescribed adverse
> effect on competition./20/

The legal validity of the construction of the statute adopted
in this opinion is doubtful. The Commission has read into the
statute a requirement that the saving in delivery cost which a
seller wishes to pass along to a particular purchaser must be compared with the cost of delivery to all customers as reflected in
the seller's price structure. The cost justification proviso contains no such comparison requirement; it simply authorizes a seller
to pass along to any customer a reduction in price equal to or less

---

20
   See Appendix ·

than any savings in delivery expense resulting from a different method of delivering goods to that customer.

An opinion of the Commission is obviously not the last word on an issue; the matter could be contested in court. But the various constituent firms in the food industry are loath to take on such a chore. Some companies with delivered price systems have worked out alternative plans which they believe are lawful, but others, including General Foods, have felt obliged to conform to the FTC opinion. The opinion, therefore, stands as an unfortunate barrier to the expanded use of the backhaul.

General Foods raised a second important question in its request for an advisory opinion, which was not answered by the Commission because of its negative response to the backhaul allowance itself. The second question requested an opinion as to whether or not the program for backhaul allowance could lawfully be offered under conditions which would limits its availability to large (truck-load) orders. This restriction was suggested by General Foods because of the limited loading dock space at the corporation's warehouses and plants. General Foods indicated that it intended to load purchasers' trucks itself and would impose uniform restrictions on the type of customer equipment that could be used. Anyone familiar with the congestion which typically exists at the loading dock of any warehouse or plant will understand the reasonableness of the announced policy of General Foods which would have forbidden the picking up of small orders at the supplier's dock.

It could be argued that such a policy discriminates against small purchasers who would not be able to use a full truckload of merchandise and who would not have empty trucks available to get the full benefit of the back haul. This is undoubtedly true and therefore an important issue in the back haul problem is whether or not a requirement of availability to all possible purchasers should be read into the law.

The requirement of availability is given statutory support in Sections 2 (e) and 2 (f) of the Robinson-Patman Act which provide that services, advertising allowances, and similar considerations must be available on a proportionally equal basis. The fog which surrounds the practical implementation of these abstruse provisions has been the subject of considerable criticism by members of the bar and the business community. As far as Section 2 (a) is concerned, however, the Commission, in dismissing the complaint against New England Confectionary Co. (Docket 5686, reported at 46 FTC 1041) and more recently the U. S. District Court, N.D. Illinois, E.D. in Chicago Spring Steel Co. v. U.S.Steel Corp. (254 F. Supp. 83) have indicated that delivery and delivery allowances are an element of price to be considered under Section 2 (a) and not to be considered under Section 2 (e) or 2 (f) of the Act. Therefore, they apparently do not need to be made available on proportionally equal terms to competing customers.

However, the question of whether or not back haul privileges have to be available to all purchasers on some basis remains a legal cloud which impedes the full development of this practice.

Clarification of this issue by the Commission would be most
helpful; for manufacturers generally cannot undertake a program
which would require them to service at the plant all possible
purchasers, regardless of size of order.

Although enunciation of a policy limiting back haul privileges to truck load buyers might seem to impose hardships upon
small buyers, in actual practice the impact of such a policy
would be limited, because most manufacturers in the food industry
service a relatively small number of large retailers and wholesalers from their plants and distribution warehouses. The small
retailer today does not buy direct from General Foods; he buys
from his wholesaler, and the latter is usually able to use the
back haul privilege as economically as the large chain retailer.
Here again is another example of the importance of interpreting
the Robinson-Patman Act in the light of competitive conditions
as they actually exist, rather than in some theoretical context
which bears no relation to reality.

The back haul concept is too important a factor in productivity in transportation to be eroded by legal casuistry.
Considerations of efficiency, practicability, and the intent of
the Congress in providing a defense to price discrimination in
the form of the transportation cost proviso all dictate a more
liberal view of back haul allowances than that embodied in the
Commission's General Foods opinion. The Federal Trade Commission
is presently reviewing the validity of its opinion rendered in
this case. In the interests of improving productivity in

distribution, it is to be hoped that the Commission will
rescind its earlier opinion.

Other Obstacles to Extended Utilization of Back Hauls

A reversal of the Commission's opinion in the General
Foods case will not necessarily result in a rush by manufacturers to institute a back haul allowance program. Many
manufacturers dislike customer back hauls because the pick-
up privilege creates additional congestion at loading and
receiving docks. As one manufacturer put it, "The back haul
can improve the retailer's efficiency at the expense of a
diminution in the manufacturer's efficiency." Undoubtedly
the need to service retailers and wholesalers who wish to
pick up can have an adverse effect on manufacturer's efficiency but this can be minimized by prescribing and adhering
to a strict rule of appointed times for pick ups.

Not all retailers and wholesalers are agreed that the
maximum amount of back hauls is a sound operational objective.
Some argue that emphasis on synchronization of trucking schedules
to comply with manufacturer appointment requirements will result
in a reduction of level of service to the retail stores.

Despite these problems, most manufacturers, wholesalers,
and retailers agree that expansion of back haul privileges
and use is a practical approach to improved productivity in
the food industry. Empty trucks, whether paid for in the first
instance by the manufacturer or the wholesaler-retailer, represent a luxury which the food industry can no longer afford.

Improving Back Haul Technology

A truck driver is adaptable. He can drive a tractor that is carrying milk, or groceries, or charcoal. But most trailers are not adaptable. The result is that the driver who delivers groceries to various stores cannot bring back milk or other products because his equipment will not handle it. So he drives back empty with a loss in productivity both for himself and his equipment.

A recent innovation—the development of a system of transporting bulk liquid food products in large, collapsible, reusable rubber-fabric bag tanks in closed trailer vans—has made possible substantial reductions in empty mileage and transport costs for some food products. For example, one food firm is reported as saving 2.4 cents per trailer mile, or $360 on a round trip of 866 miles, by delivering groceries to supermarkets in rural areas and on the return haul bringing 4,500 gallons of whole milk to a metropolitan area processing plant. Yearly savings on this one route are estimated at be $54,600.[21]

Research leading to the development of such adaptable equipment was fostered by the U. S. Department of Agriculture. Further improvements in technology are required to make possible maximum flexibility in use of equipment with a minimum of time and labor spent in conversion.

---

[21] Progress Report of the Transportation and Facilities Research Division, Marketing and Nutrition Research, U.S. Department of Agriculture, Washington, D.C., July 1, 1970, p. 11.

The Problem of Detention Time

All over the United States at the receiving doors of
food warehouses—as well as warehouses in other industries—
trucks are lined up waiting to unload their cargoes. Some
trucks may wait for hours; others may arrive and be turned
away; others may commence unloading and then be told to
come back the next day to finish unloading. Truckers and
receivers seem to have become accustomed to such ineptitude.
But to any unbiased observer interested in the functioning
of the system, the results are shocking.

The waste which the existing situation produces in idle
vehicle time, idle labor time, and/or redelivery costs is
enormous. There must be a better way to handle our warehouse
traffic. The failure of the carriers, shippers, and consignees
to improve the existing chaotic situation calls for an airing
of such inefficiency in the forum of public opinion.

It is obvious that warehouses cannot possibly handle unloading of trucks efficiently if the bulk of them arrive
within a few hours in the morning—or, for that matter, on an
unscheduled basis at any other time of day. Some kind of
appointment system is essential to orderly processing.

The Appointment Problem

Although the appointment system sounds like a logical
solution, it is beset by problems. Key issues are the
following:

1)   There is no uniformity among the various tariff areas
as to the treatment of the appointment requirement. Obviously
if a carrier and a receiver both voluntarily agree that a
delivery should be made at a particular time of day, there
is no problem.   But suppose that the receiver requires that
the delivery be made at an appointed time and the carrier re-
fuses or arrives late.   What   then?   The answer depends in
part upon whether or not the right to request deliveries at
an appointed time is in the tariff.

In the Middle Atlantic territory the detention rule states:

> Upon request of consignor or consignee, or others
> designated by them, carrier will enter into a
> reasonable pre-arranged schedule for arrival of
> the vehicle for loading or unloading./22/

In other territories a charge of $3.35 is made by the carrier
if there is a requirement of a telephone call for notification
before delivery.   In still other territories, such as the
Southeast, the carriers have taken the position that a requirement that a delivery be made at a time stated by the consignee
is a service not in the tariff and therefore is illegal.

This viewpoint has been supported by the Interstate Commerce
Commission.   Thus, in a letter written to a large retail food
chain with respect to the chain's practice of requiring appointments for delivery, the District Supervisor for the I.C.C.
stated:

22
  325 I.C.C. 336, 367 .

> Anyone requiring a carrier to withhold deliveries
> until a certain specified time is requiring the
> carrier to perform services which are beyond that
> contemplated by the Bill of Lading Contract and
> the carriers' tariff. In my opinion directives of
> this nature amount to soliciting of concessions
> contrary to requirements of Section 222(c) of the
> Act....

> ....It is my further opinion that the carriers
> condescending and conforming to the above outlined
> requirements would be in violation of Section 217(b)
> of the Act which makes it unlawful for a motor common
> carrier to provide service or make charges to shippers
> (or receivers) different from those published in its
> tariffs. /23/

The I.C.C. has suggested that the way out of this quandary is
to have the requirement of an appointment published in the
applicable tariff.

Whether or not carriers will acquiesce in such a procedure
remains to be seen. In view of the congestion problem at
warehouse docks, the requirement of appointments—at least for
truckload lots—would seem to be a sensible method of improving
productivity.

2) A substantial number of shipments arrive in less than
truckload lots. In some cases, a truck may make 15 to 20 stops
during the day, dropping a relatively small number of pieces at
each destination. Obviously, for very small deliveries the
appointment system breaks down, because the carrier cannot
possibly work such times into a multi-stop schedule. Most
warehouses recognize this difficulty and therefore for small
orders—which are variously defined as less than 100 cases, or

---

[23] From correspondence made available to the writer.

less than 300 cases, etc.—no appointment time is required.
Instead, one or two receiving doors are especially reserved
for this kind of delivery on a first come-first served basis.

The major disagreement which seems to be developing in
the industry relates to shipments of more than the excluded
minimum but less than a truckload lot. If a truck has four
or five stops, does the consignee have a right to require that
delivery be made only at a specified time or between certain
hours? Obviously such a requirement imposes a burden upon
the carrier, but on the other hand, from the point of view
of the whole system, unless such arrangements are made there
will be an excessive amount of waiting at the warehouse dock
due to the unscheduled arrival of too many trucks during a
particular interval of time.

In order to bring the necessary pressure to bear to
improve the system, it is the writer's opinion that the I.C.C.
should permit the requirement of appointments on less than
truckload lots where the delivery exceeds a certain minimum
number of pieces. What this minimum should be would have to
be worked out after appropriate hearings and discussions among
consignees, shippers, and carriers. Such a requirement would
stimulate better scheduling techniques by shippers and
carriers and might eventually lead to the utilization of
computerized models or information systems to collate information quickly as to the best loading pattern for trucks and
the optimum routing design.

However, it must be recognized that the system will not work unless consignees cooperate by communicating scheduled appointment times to trucking companies sufficiently far in advance so that the latter can have ample time to coordinate delivery times and to load trucks in proper sequence. A major element lacking in the present system is an adequate and timely flow of information among the concerned parties.

3)   Some consignees will receive merchandise only during certain specified hours. For example, it is not uncommon for a food warehouse to announce that deliveries will be received only between the hours of 7:00 A.M. and 3:00 P.M. This places an additional burden upon carriers in working out reasonable delivery schedules which will mesh properly with the varying requirements of receivers. As a consequence, even if the trucking company is prepared to deliver on an appointment basis, it may find it impossible to work out an economical schedule because of the limitation on receiving hours.

4)   The excessive length of time required to unload trucks plays havoc with the appointment system. Suppose a truck arrives on schedule with a twenty-ton dead pile load. Tariffs generally permit fifteen minutes to unload each ton of mer-chandise. Thus, this trailer could take five hours to unload. But some warehouses have deliveries scheduled on a four-hour "swing" basis. If the truck is not finished unloading at the end of the four hour period, the driver could be told to stop work and come back the next day. However, this is obviously

inefficient and would involve the receiver in a redelivery
charge. On the other hand, if the unloading is continued, the
trucks waiting for the next shift will be delayed and the entire
schedule comes undone.

If this hypothetical load had been delivered on pallets
and if the consignee were ready to accept the pallets on an
exchange basis, the trailer could normally be unloaded in
45 minutes to one hour. This example dramatizes the fact
that the problem of truck congestion at warehouse docks is
closely related to the problem of unitized shipment. If the
food industry could standardize on one pallet, and if
palletized shipments became the general rule, the savings in
unloading time would be enormous. The food industry has
standardized on two basic pallet sizes, but two sizes which
do not mesh accomplish very little. Truckers complain of
instances where a load is delivered on a 48-40 pallet and
must be loaded by hand onto a 40-32 which is the size most
commonly used by wholesalers in the industry.

Avenues to Increased Productivity

A substantial improvement in productivity could be
effected in the unloading operation simply by better coordination between consignees and trucking companies.
However, such an effort would require a high degree of cooperation and mutual trust between the parties which at
present seems to be lacking. Food warehouse operators resent
the fact that carriers are attempting to curtail certain

services, such as sort and segregate, which were historically
included in tariffs. Motor carriers complain about the high-
handed manner in which warehouse operators assign appointment
times and require unloading functions without regard to the
costs imposed upon the carrier. Both sides have tended to
engage in mutual recriminations and lose sight of the fact
that the system can only work through mutual cooperation and
interest in developing efficient patterns of operation.

Coordination is obviously easier when fewer carriers are
involved. It is not surprising therefore to find that some
supermarket chains and large wholesalers are requesting vendors
to ship via specified trucking companies. The latter are then
in a position to consolidate the shipments of a number of
manufacturers and deliver one truckload to the consignee.
Continuation of this trend may result in a smaller number of
large companies handling the bulk of the business in food
products. Such a trend may be decried by structural theorists
but would undoubtedly contribute to improvement of efficiency
in the industry.

Another possible avenue to improved efficiency involves
night deliveries and receivings. Congestion at food warehouse
docks as well as traffic congestion in the streets and air
pollution from trucks stalled in day-time traffic all compel
a searching examination by the food industry of the feasibility
of shifting more receivings to night hours. Obviously such a

changeover may raise difficult problems of premium pay for
both truckers and warehouse personnel. However, the benefits
would seem to be considerable.

One fact seems certain. The steady rise in pay of truck
drivers will soon make the existing situation completely
untenable. Carriers will press for higher detention charges
and the costs of transportation by motor carrier will increase.
This is an area where waste and inefficiency are obvious. It
deserves a major effort on the part of carriers, shippers and
consignees to find a better way which will improve productivity
in the shipment and receiving of merchandise.

Consolidation of Small Shipments

Reference was made in the preceding section to the advantages which can accrue from consolidation of small shipments
bound for food warehouses. This problem of small shipments is
encountered at every level of the food industry. Manufacturers,
wholesalers, retailers, and carriers are all seeking ways of
handling economically the growing number of small shipments
which result from product line proliferation.

Store Door Deliveries

The problem is particularly acute at store level. Supermarkets customarily receive part of their deliveries through
a warehouse which in effect consolidates shipments from various

vendors and then reships to the store quantities determined
by its needs. The balance of merchandise is delivered direct
to the store by the original vendor. Such items are usually
referred to as "direct deliveries". Typical items which would
fall in the latter category are milk, bread, cookies and
crackers, beverages, various kinds of processed meat, fresh
corn, and a variety of specialty products.

Companies vary considerably in the extent to which they
rely on direct deliveries, depending in part upon the nature,
size, and adequacy of their warehouse facilities. Thus, if a
chain has its own meat warehouse it will normally require that
all processed meat items be delivered to the warehouse, rather
than store door.

There are advantages and disadvantages to direct deliveries. Direct deliveries save warehousing and transportation cost
for the retailer. Furthermore, if permitted by union contracts,
many suppliers will unload merchandise and place it on store
gondolas and display racks, thus reducing store labor cost.
Suppliers also claim that they can provide faster service and
fresher merchandise by store door delivery than if the product
goes through the retailer's own or affiliated warehouse. However, retailers do not generally agree with this latter claim.

The disadvantages of direct deliveries are the exposure
to pilferage created by a stream of vendors coming into the
store, additional time required by store level personnel to
check in shipments, the clogging of parking lots and loading

docks by vendor trucks, added paper work at the store and head-
quarters office to process invoices for many small shipments,
and a tendency on the part of vendor salesmen to try to monopo-
lize shelf space for their product. Another consideration is
that direct deliveries normally carry a smaller gross margin
for the retailer than if the items were sold to and delivered
to the warehouse for redelivery to the stores.

Except for beverages, milk, bread, ice cream, cookies and
crackers and certain meat and produce items, most direct deliveries fall in the category of specialty items. Orders per store
are relatively small, the items are costly to handle, and very
often a perishable quality is involved.

One study conducted in 1964 found that stores having a
weekly volume of $40,000 had an average of 135 direct deliver-
ies per week of which about 88 were below $50 wholesale
value.[24] Despite the rise in prices which has occurred since
that date, a study made in 1970 found that 65 per cent of
deliveries were less than $50 wholesale value.[25]

The cost of handling this stream of small orders places a
heavy burden of cost on the retailer. One executive estimated
that the total cost—including handling of additional paper
work at store and office level—added up to about $5.00 per
direct delivery. When the unmeasurable losses from pilferage
and faulty checking of incoming orders is added to this total,

[24] Dale Koenig and Earl H. Brown, "Analysis of Store Deliveries",
Operating Results of Food Chains, 1963-64, New York State
College of Agriculture, Cornell University, 1964, p. 26.

[25] Supermarket News, May 11, 1970.

it is understandable why retailers consider direct deliveries
one of the most inefficient phases of the food business.

Direct deliveries are even more costly for vendors. In
the 1964 study referred to, delivery cost of direct deliveries
below ten dollars were found to average 10.3 per cent of wholesale value. The average delivery cost of direct deliveries
below fifty dollars wholesale value was 6.4 per cent.[26]
Since wage rates in the trucking industry have soared since
this study was made in 1964, the cost of making small shipments
to food stores is rapidly becoming prohibitive.

A bird's eye view of the present system would reveal
a stream of trucks, starting out from their respective vendor
plants in the morning and crisscrossing around the city
dropping off small orders at various stores which they each
in turn visit. Such a system—or lack of system—creates
congestion at store receiving docks, adds to street congestion,
pollution, and noise, and is grossly inefficient in terms of
use of both drivers and equipment.

There is an obvious need for a service or facility which
could take a substantial part of these small deliveries and
consolidate them into one large load per store. In the department store and specialty store field, the United Parcel System
provides such a service. What is needed in the food industry
is a facility in which small shipments for all supermarkets in
an area would be received from suppliers who would have the
merchandise segregated by store. The various items would then

---

[26] Koenig., op. cit., p. 30.

be consolidated on a store basis and delivered as one load.
The operator of the facility would render one bill for all of
the items delivered to a store and would pay the various
vendors out of the proceeds. The consolidating facility would
carry no inventory and would have to be connected with vendors
and retailers by up-to-date communication systems so that order
information could be processed quickly with little lead time.

Why has this kind of facility been so slow in evolving in
the food industry? There are two major obstacles. The first
is the barrier presented by existing union contracts with
vendors which in many cases provide that driver-salesmen are
paid on a commission basis, depending upon the sales to individual stores. If the vendor now delivers to a central facility
or to a retailer's warehouse, drivers claim they are still entitled to their commission if the product ends up in stores in
their particular territories. Obviously there would be no
incentive to vendors to utilize a central facility if they
were still required to pay the same commissions to drivers.

The second problem is that vendors fear that if their
driver-salesmen lose the opportunity to visit the retail store
each day or week, they will lose shelf space or display area.
Another concern for vendors of perishable products is that store
personnel will not rotate product properly. To most vendors in
this competitive industry, sales come first and productivity
second. Whatever may have been the merit of individual solici-
tation and in-store merchandising by drivers in the past, it is
becoming less and less important. In the years ahead, markets

will increasingly rely on sophisticated computer programs to
determine allocation of shelf space and are not likely to be
swayed by the views of a driver salesman.

Despite union resistance and vendor reluctance, consolidating facilities are now beginning to appear in the industry.
In New York a large chain requires that all processors deliver to
a particular distributor who then consolidates vendor items into
one load for each of the company's stores. In another area, a
large wholesaler is planning a facility for affiliated stores.
Plans call for orders to be made up by each store at 6:00 P.M.,
collated, and communicated to vendors by 9:00 P.M. through a
sophisticated data transmission system. Vendors would then
assemble orders at night, deliver to the facility in the
early morning hours, the merchandise would be assembled by
store, and trailers would roll to the markets in the morning.

Large chains and large wholesalers will have sufficient
volume and sufficient leverage with vendors to set up their own
consolidating facilities. Smaller chains and independents may
have to share facilities either owned and operated by an independent company or perhaps some will establish jointly owned
facilities to obtain similar advantages.

This kind of facility has been talked about in the food
industry for years. Soaring wage costs may now bring it to
fruition. Available evidence suggests that such consolidation
can make a major contribution to reduction of transportation
cost and improvement of productivity for both vendor and
retailer.

Consolidation by Processors and Manufacturers

Processors and manufacturers are also thinking in terms of consolidating shipments by sharing facilities with other producers. Meatpackers, food manufacturers, and other processors are actively exploring the advantages which might accrue from the pooling of shipments to save freight and other distribution costs. Such savings can result even when the destination of the merchandise is a wholesaler or retailer warehouse, since consolidation may permit shipment on a carload or truck load basis rather than the costly less-than-carload or less-than-truckload rate.

Frozen food manufacturers have historically warehoused product in public warehouses where loads are consolidated containing the products of a number of manufacturers. Consolidation was adopted early in the development of the frozen food industry because of the high cost of refrigerated transport, the large number of slow-moving items in the typical line, and the narrow profit margins earned by processors.

Public consolidating warehouses are now developing in the grocery industry. One such center handles the products of a dozen large grocery manufacturers. The latter ship to the consolidating center which then assembles full loads of mixed products for customers.[27] Consolidating efforts are also being undertaken by manufacturers without utilization of special distribution facilities. For example, McCormack & Co. and Noxcell Corporation have been pooling shipments to customers from nearby plants. They report a 25 per cent savings in freight cost. A trailer

---

[27] Distribution Worldwide, February 1971, p. 54.

loads up with Noxcell products and then shifts to the McCormack
plant for the balance of the load. Bills of lading are prepared
by one company one month, the other company the next month, and
so on in rotation. Whichever company prepares the forms also
pays the carrier in full and then bills back the other company
for its share.[28]

Consolidation efforts of various kinds will move ahead at a
quicker pace in the coming decade, reflecting the pressure on the
one hand of product proliferation and, on the other, the inflation
in transportation costs. Such efforts will probably evolve without
government subsidy or intervention. However, the key to many such
efforts will be a joint venture or cooperative agreement among
companies who are competitors, and here the fear of the antitrust
laws may retard developments which promise major improvements in
productivity. Many companies in the food industry operate under
consent decrees and are extremely "gun-shy" of further encounters
with the antitrust laws. Therefore, even though there is nothing
unlawful in a joint venture which does not seek intercompany agreements on price or share of market, company attorneys are inclined
to veto joint ventures which might cast suspicion on the motives
of participating firms. In an era when cooperative ventures of such
nature are likely to become increasingly essential to productivity
improvement, a change in attitude in antitrust enforcement could
make a substantial contribution to productivity in this industry.

---

[28] "Cooperative Distribution Pays Off", Traffic Management,
February 1971, p. 49.

<u>Appendix to Chapter V</u>

FEDERAL TRADE COMMISSION
Washington, D.C. 20580

Office of the Secretary

October 2, 1967

Albert G. Perkins, Esq.,
Law Department,
General Foods Corporation,
250 North Street,
White Plains, New York. 10602

In re: File No. 683 7026

Dear Mr. Perkins:

This is with further reference to your request for an
advisory opinion with respect to your proposal to grant
so-called "back-haul" allowances to customers who pick up
their own purchases at General Foods' warehouses.

You state that you presently sell dry (non-frozen)
grocery products on a delivered price basis with bracket
pricing and do not permit customers to pick up products at
warehouses or plants. Customers with trucks returning empty
to their warehouses along routes near General Foods' warehouses and plants are now demanding the opportunity to pick
up products and to earn an allowance by so doing. You further
state that you are now considering a program whereunder
customers would be permitted to pick up products and be paid
an allowance equal to the amount you would otherwise have to
pay a common carrier to deliver to the customer.

Assuming a favorable opinion as to this question, you
further request an opinion as to whether the program may
lawfully be offered under conditions which would limit its
availability to large (truck-load) orders. This restriction
is contemplated because of limited loading dock space at
your warehouses and plants and because you intend to load
orders on customer equipment. Hence you intend to impose
uniform restrictions on the type of equipment that may be
used and upon the size of the order that may be picked up.

In the Commission's view, this proposal is governed by
the provisions of Section 2(a) of the Clayton Act, as amended
by the Robinson-Patman Act, which, in brief, provides that it
shall be unlawful for a seller to discriminate in price
between different purchasers of goods of like grade and quality
where the effect may be to substantially lessen competition
or to create a monopoly and where none of the defenses afforded

Albert G. Perkins, Esq.

by the Act are present. It is the Commission's further view
that the proposal is also governed by the provisions of the
order under that Section in Docket 6018, issued against your
Corporation in 1956.

The Commission has given your first proposal its careful
consideration and has concluded that, assuming the presence
of all other elements necessary to a determination of a
violation of this statute, its implementation would probably
result in a violation of the Act and the order in Docket 6018.
This result would seem to necessarily flow from the use of a
delivered pricing system, for in such a case the freight
factor included within the price is not the actual freight to
any given point, but an average of the freight costs for all
customers within the zone wherein the delivered price is quoted,
or, at least, a figure determined by some formula apart from
actual costs. If one customer is then given a "back-haul"
allowance for the actual freight saved, it would seem that a
serious possibility of discrimination would exist in any
delivered pricing system and it is highly doubtful that the
defense of cost justification, at least, would be available.

While this conclusion may seem unreasonable from one
point of view, since the allowance will be for no more than
the actual freight saved, it would seem to be a necessary
result of using a delivered pricing system. Whenever such a
seller departs from his delivered prices for the benefit of
one customer, he leaves himself open to a charge of discriminat-
ing against his other competing customers who order in the
same quantities and hence fall within the same pricing bracket
because he failed to make allowances for the individual cost
factors present in their situations. The law does not require
that a seller pass on his cost savings to his customers, but
where he elects to do so in one instance it does require that
he not discriminate between his purchasers where such discrimination has the proscribed adverse effect on competition.

In view of this disposition of your first question, there
does not appear to be any need for the Commission to pass upon
the second.

By direction of the Commission, Commissioner Elman not
concurring,

                              (signed)   Joseph W. Shea

                                          Joseph W. Shea,
                                          Secretary

CHAPTER VI

WAREHOUSING

In a business which is consumer-oriented, the function of
warehousing is to serve the needs of the retail store. This
fundamental principle explains in part the lack of progress in
productivity improvement in food industry warehouses.

The Productivity Record

Warehouses in the food industry are operated by (a) retail
food chains; (b) wholesalers, who may be affiliated with,
independent from, or owned by the retail stores they serve;
(c) manufacturers; and (d) independent parties who operate public
warehouses which serve as storage facilities or consolidation
points for frozen foods, groceries, and other items. Statistical
data with respect to performance are available with respect to
the first two classes of operations, but are practically nonexistent with respect to the latter two.

Despite improvements in mechanical handling equipment and
construction of new facilities during the past decade, the
available evidence suggests that there has been little increase
in productivity in retail food chain or wholesaler-operated
warehouses during the past five years.

In the retail food chain industry, comparable figures are
available for selected measures of efficiency from December, 1966
to December, 1970 (See Table V). As can be seen from this tabulation, tons per manhour of direct labor were actually less in
1970 than in 1966. Cases per manhour of direct labor have shown
an even more marked decline.

TABLE V

SELECTED MEASURES OF EFFICIENCY, 1966 to 1970

	Tons Per Manhour Direct Labor	Cases Per Manhour Direct Labor	Tons Per Manhour Total Labor	Cases Per Manhour Total Labor	Cases Unloaded Per Manhour R.R. Cars	Cases Selected Per Manhour	Pieces Selected Per Manhour	Cases Loaded Per Manhour
				Medians				
December 1966	2.13	161	1.33	103	247	186	210	508
December 1967	2.19	154	1.53	104	262	177	203	537
December 1968	2.03	150	1.37	105	229	169	203	496
December 1969	2.04	144	1.37	100	212	155	191	518
December 1970	2.08	144	1.36	103	214	169	179	525

Source: Data provided by Professor Earl Brown, Cornell University,
from food chain grocery distribution efficiency reports
maintained in cooperation with National Association of
Food Chains. Reprinted by permission.

A somewhat similar trend is evidenced by figures compiled
by the National American Wholesale Grocers Association (NAWGA)
which represents most of the wholesale grocery operators of the
nation.   NAWGA maintained a figure exchange on warehouse efficiency
on a continuous basis from 1961 to 1966 for a fairly constant group
of about 20 to 30 companies.   The statistics for tons per manhour
of direct labor handled in and out of these warehouses for this
period are as follows:[1]

1961	1.38
1962	1.52
1963	1.61
1964	1.86
1965	1.79
1966	1.44

NAWGA also maintains warehouse operating efficiency ratios
for groups attending annual seminars on warehousing.   These statistics represent the results of performance in a changing group of
about 50 wholesalers from all over the United States.   The statistics for tons per manhour of direct labor handled in and out of
the warehouse (dry grocery) are as follows:[2]

1963	1.43
1964	1.82
1965	1.75
1966	1.61
1967	1.54
1968	1.62
1969	1.69
1970	1.55

---

[1]
Data from files of National American Wholesale Grocers
Association.

[2]
Data from files of National American Wholesale Grocers
Association.

Both sets of statistics suggest that about the middle of the
past decade physical productivity in food warehouses began to
level off and diminish and that this trend has continued to date.
Manufacturers have also encountered similar problems, although
productivity has been spurred in some cases by increased unitization of shipments and the use of automatic palletizers. Nevertheless, the continued escalation in wage rates for warehouse
personnel in the face of little or no improvement in physical
productivity has caused a sharp upward trend in warehousing costs.
Figure 1 indicates the trend in warehousing costs for a large
diversified food products manufacturer and incorporates the expected impact of wage increases already agreed upon for the period
to 1973.

The Reasons for Poor Productivity Performance

The reasons for these trends are complex. Not all of the
following causes are applicable to all warehouses. Nevertheless
operators suggest that the following are some of the critical
factors which have contributed to the lack of productivity advance:

1) Increase in Variety: Although variety is a major problem
at the store level, in many respects its full impact is felt at
the warehouse level. A retail chain will have stores of many types.
Some may be in areas requiring the stocking of certain ethnic foods;
some may be in areas of apartment dwellers requiring small sizes
of canned products; others will be in areas where large families
predominate and large sizes must be carried, and so on. Each

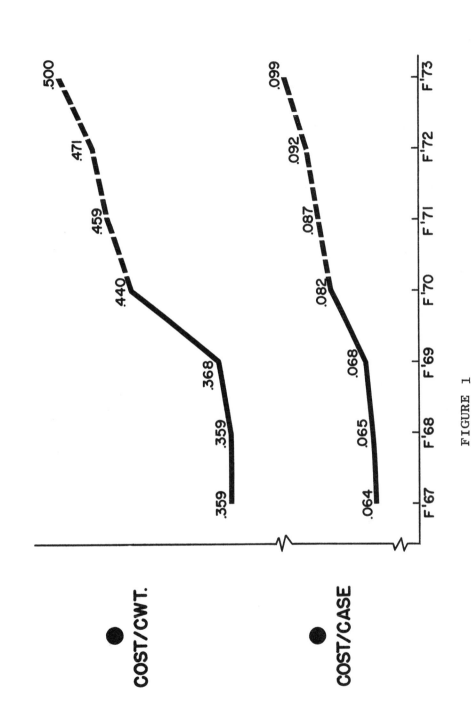

FIGURE 1

store can adapt its product mix to serve the needs of its customers, but the warehouse must stock all of these items (or
rely on direct deliveries) if it is to properly serve its stores,
which are its customers.

Retail food chains can exercise some control over the extent
of proliferation of product offered by their stores. But a
wholesaler serving independent markets cannot exercise such control and must carry the product which his customers want if he
is going to stay in business. As a consequence, wholesale warehouses customarily carry more items than chain warehouses, their
product movement is slower, they have to rely on smaller pallets
for a large proportion of their inventory, and their tons per
manhour performance will be substantially less than that achieved
by chain warehouses.

The number of items carried by wholesaler warehouses has
skyrocketed over the past two decades. In 1950 wholesalers
carried about 2,479 items; in 1960, 5,100 items; in 1970, 7,300
items.[3] Furthermore, the variety in type of customer served
has also increased. While chains have been closing smaller
stores and attempting to concentrate on fewer larger retail units,
wholesalers have been faced by an explosive growth in the so-
called convenience stores. This is one of the fastest growing
segments of the entire food business and such stores look to the
wholesaler as the source for their merchandise. About 63 per cent
of wholesalers now supply convenience stores, compared with only
55 per cent in 1967.[4]

---

[3] _Progressive Grocer_, April,1971, p. 91.

[4] _Ibid_., p. 95.

2) Change in Nature of Product Mix: Not only have warehouses added variety but also the type of product added has
frequently been more difficult to handle than conventional
products, or bulkier and lighter in weight so that its inclusion
has tended to diminish the usual measuring figure of tons handled
per manhour. In recent years, warehouses have added such products
as health and beauty aids, candy, housewares, toys, and similar
items. A good example of the problems presented by new items is
the difficulty encountered in handling charcoal. This has become
a major warehouse item as a result of the trend to outdoor cooking, particularly in the suburbs. Charcoal bags are bulky, break
and tear easily, and are relatively light. The result is that
considerable time can be consumed on this one item during summer
periods with a resultant reduction in warehouse efficiency.

3) Reduced Employee Effort: This reflects the combined
result of a number of factors—union restrictions on pace of work,
longer work breaks, less competent employees. Many operators
report it has become increasingly difficult to hire warehouse
personnel despite the relatively high pay offered. Union restrictions vary but in many parts of the country the number of
pieces which employees may select per hour is regulated by an
unwritten union agreement. The Teamsters Union has generally
resisted the introduction of incentive pay systems in warehouses
because of a fear that this would lead to an excessive pace of
work. One wholesaler who is about to invest in an expensive
highly automated warehouse told the writer that he would not do
so if he could put his workers on a piece rate basis.

4) Assumption of Additional Functions: In an effort to give better service to the stores, warehouses have been assuming functions which may actually reduce warehouse productivity but will improve store efficiency. For example, many warehouses today apply a label to each case of merchandise giving the description of the product, the number of retail packages in the case, and the suggested retail price. The latter expedites the pricing function at the store level since the employee doing price marking does not have to pause to look up price in a price guide but can simply use the price information contained on the case. Some warehouses have changed their layout to approximate more closely the way retail stores are laid out in categories of merchandise. This makes the checking of incoming loads easier for store personnel and also facilitates loading shelves, but it may reduce selection speed at the warehouse. The most efficient manner in which to lay out a warehouse is on a movement basis. In one warehouse visited by the writer, the fastest moving 10 per cent of the items accounted for 42 per cent of all cases shipped. Obviously selector time is saved if these items can be placed together in an area with the least amount of walking for the selector. But this procedure may require breaking up of so-called family groups.

5) A Temporary Slackening in the Rate of Technological Progress: Progress in warehousing seems to proceed in a series of steps, and the industry may now be in a period preceding another major breakthrough. The great improvements in grocery warehousing occurred during the period from the end of World War II

to the beginning of the decade of the sixties. During this
period wholesalers moved out of multi-story structures into
large one-story buildings in which a freer flow of merchandise
was possible with a minimum of rehandling. Coupled with this
development came the application of the computer to inventory
management and the use of various kinds of mechanical handling
devices such as forklift trucks, conveyorized lines, and so
forth. The increasing use of palletized shipments by manufacturers also facilitated the handling of incoming merchandise
at warehouses.

Now another kind of breakthrough seems possible, as will
be discussed below in more detail. The problem is that many of
the new automated techniques which are now available require an
entirely different kind of warehouse structure to be used to
optimum advantage. Because of the fixity of investment, the
replacement of conventional warehouses by such new facilities
will undoubtedly be gradual so that the improvements in technology in most warehouses for a number of years in the future will
be rather minor in impact.

The Importance of People

Despite the substantial progress which has been made in
mechanizing various functions in grocery warehouses, 86 per cent
of warehousing costs are still "people" costs and only 14 per cent
are attributable to the cost of machines, building, land, and non-
human resources.[5]

---

[5] Data provided by National American Wholesale Grocers
Association.

In these simple ratios we see both the problem of, and the potential for, improved productivity in the food industry. Unless more mechanization can be applied, the high people quotient in food warehousing will tend to pull down productivity over the next decade. Better personnel policies, utilization of motivational techniques, and possibly even profit-sharing to spur incentive may in part counter this trend, but the fact remains that lugging cases around a warehouse, even with the aid of a conveyor belt, tractor, or forklift truck, is hard work. Warehouse operators are unanimous in their opinion that it is becoming more and more difficult to obtain competent help to perform such work. The composition of the labor force today is unlikely to change this trend.

On the other hand, any business in which labor costs constitute 86 per cent of total operating costs still has a long way to go in applying mechanization and automation. Warehousing can be automated; techniques are now being experimented with which hold forth the promise of substantial reductions in labor costs. The problem, however, is that the dream of the total automated food warehouse is unlikely to be realized in the food industry without a greater emphasis on an overall industry-wide systems flow approach which results in some standardization of carton sizes and a higher degree of unitization of product.

The Trade-Off in Management Objectives

The warehouse is a focal point for the resolution of a number of conflicting management objectives. Every company would like to operate the most efficient warehouse in the industry, but this objective may not coincide with other important

goals. For example, inflation itself impedes productivity at the
warehouse level. As prices of manufacturers' products rise, there
is an incentive on the part of retailers and wholesalers to buy
ahead, particularly when there is a deal announced by a manufacturer
for a limited time. Purchasing such large lots helps to build up
gross profit, but it may substantially reduce productivity at the
warehouse which frequently has no room to store extra merchandise
and therefore must rehandle it from slot to slot until it is needed.

Some companies are ready to trade off return on investment
against a decrease in labor efficiency. A rough rule of thumb
in grocery warehousing is that it takes one square foot of warehouse space to move a case of merchandise per week. Thus to ship
400,000 cases per week will normally require 400,000 square feet
of space. But one warehouse in the industry ships about twice
the number of cases per square foot of space as the average of
the industry. Its turn on merchandise, therefore, is about double
that of the industry's, reflecting a tremendous saving in capital,
both in merchandise inventory and in building investment. On the
other hand, its labor productivity is below average.

Warehouse productivity is tied in with service to the stores
and with the kind of stores a retail chain wishes to operate.
One operator cut 1,800 items out of warehouse inventory, reduced
variety at store level, and went on an active discount policy in
his retail stores. The result was a tremendous increase in the
shipments of specific individual products to stores with a significant improvement in productivity at the warehouse level.

The New Warehouse Technology

New equipment, which is now technologically known and commercially available, promises to make possible major improvements in warehouse productivity. Analysis of the various functions in warehousing will help to place these improvements in proper perspective.

Receiving

The major savings here depend upon unitization of loads. If wholesalers continue to have to transfer by hand to a smaller pallet the merchandise shipped by manufacturers on the 48 x 40 pallet, there will continue to be a major waste of manpower. The receiving function requires about 10 to 15 per cent of total labor in a warehouse and a significant portion is clerical, relating to checking of incoming loads and adjusting to inventory. It is in this area that considerable savings are foreseen through a more direct interface between the receiving platform and the computer. With a visual display unit on the dock and with computer access for interrogation and a data entry terminal, a receiving clerk could query the computer by vendor number for a display of order information, commodity code number, description of pack and/or layer configuration, etc. As product is compared to the information displayed, quantities could be imputed directly into the computer and inventory could be priced and updated.

Storage

This function, which presently absorbs about 20 per cent of total labor requirements can be almost completely mechanized.

Stacker cranes can automatically transfer full pallet loads from the receiving dock to computer-selected storage slots.

Selection

The major focus of new technology has been the selection function because it absorbs the most labor in the warehouse—about 35 per cent of the total. Various techniques have been applied to this task. One is to separate the job of picking from that of replenishment. In a conventional warehouse, forklift operators and selectors ordinarily work in the same aisle; in newer systems these operators are separated so that each can work at higher speeds. Picking vehicles are becoming common so that the selector can reach merchandise more easily. These include picking platforms which enable the selector to easily reach merchandise at the top of a rack. A number of new systems involve batch-picking in which the selector picks not for one store but for a number of stores at once. Take-away conveyors are being used to transfer merchandise from the selection point to the assemblage and shipping dock. Finally, the most sophisticated approach involves a computer-controlled, wholly automatic ordering system where cases are automatically released from live storage racks through computer operation onto take-away conveyors which direct them to the proper loading vehicle.

The productivity of a selector can be enormously increased by these and other techniques. The average selector today using conventional equipment will pick about 145 cases per hour. However, he normally picks onto a pallet which is then conveyed to the loading dock and put on a truck. More sophisticated automated devices can increase the selection rate to 400 and even 500 pieces

per manhour. However, under such systems the cases are normally
put on a conveyor. They then have to be loaded by hand onto
a pallet for shipment to the stores. The reason is that the
proliferation in carton size is so great that automatic palletizers cannot be utilized. Therefore, where shipments to stores
are palletized, the productivity of the selector under an automated system must be divided by a factor of two because another
man is normally required for the palletization function.

Other problems resulting from automated selection systems
include high product damage rates, considerable mechanical down
time, and rejects and missorts in the batch selection systems.
Cases frequently go where they are not supposed to go. They
then either end up in a reject chute and have to be put back
in warehouse stock or they go to the wrong store, in which case
they impact service and sales. In some warehouses the fluctua-
tion in volume from the beginning of the week to the end of the
week has detracted from full utilization of the efficiency of
such systems. A selector may work for four hours and because of
the capability of the system be able to pick all of the merchandise which is necessary for that day's shipments, but he has to
be employed and paid for eight hours.

Replenishment

This function, which absorbs about 20 per cent of total
labor at the warehouse can be semi-automated. Stacker cranes
can carry out this function mechanically and the computer can
automatically signal when a slot is open.

Shipping

This function takes about 15 to 20 per cent of the total labor and is still one of the bottlenecks in the entire operation. Furthermore, there is little likelihood that automatic palletizers will be available to function effectively for this purpose until some degree of standardization is effected in carton size. Some operators are loading onto movable cages which can then go directly to the store floor, and these vehicles must be loaded by hand.

The High Risk of Progress

The new technology in food warehouses depends upon two components which have been used in other industries for a number of years. The first is the process computer; the second is the stacker crane. Together they make possible an automated storage and retrieval system. However, for the stacker cranes to operate to optimum advantage, a new kind of warehouse has to be constructed. A stacker crane cannot operate effectively in the conventional 21 foot high warehouse; it requires about 50 feet for optimum efficiency. Thus the new technology which is now in process of introduction in food warehousing will not measurably assist productivity in existing facilities. As new warehouses are constructed specifically designed to utilize the new techniques, there will be a substantial improvement in productivity in food warehousing, but this will be a slow process.

The new type warehouse is an expensive undertaking with a high risk factor. Construction of a building 50 feet high involves risks because the facility is less adaptable to other uses. Construction of a higher building actually saves cube and to this extent reduces costs per cubic foot of space, but it also entails

expensive layering of sprinklers because of the enhanced danger
of fire. The specialized equipment required for the semi-
automated warehouse may raise the cost of the facility by one
or two million dollars over a conventional facility depending
upon its size. However, equipment manufacturers project savings
which should pay back the original investment in three to five
years. The continued escalation in wage rates of warehouse
employees will make the cost-saving potential of such facilities
even greater as the years pass.

However, many potential users of such systems have been
delaying a decision because of concern resulting from the amount
of down-time experienced by some of the new installations. Furthermore, wholesalers in particular have to weigh the risk of losing
accounts if mechanical failures interfere with prompt and reliable
delivery.

There are a number of different automated systems now on the
market. It is doubtful that any one technique will become the
norm in the industry. Even today there is a great diversity in
layout and type of equipment utilized in mechanized warehouses.
The great variation in type of customer served, size of store,
product line and other factors makes it unlikely that any new
technology will suddenly move the industry to a new level of
higher productivity. Change will come slowly and productivity
is unlikely to show any substantial upturn for a number of years.

The Meat Processing Warehouse

A development which is progressing more rapidly than the automated grocery warehouse is the partial shift of some meat processing

from the retail store backroom to a central facility operated

by a wholesaler or chain retailer. An increasing number of

such distribution and processing warehouses are commencing

operation. One recent survey found that 21 per cent of chain

organizations had meat distribution centers in operation, 11

per cent has begun construction of a center, 42 per cent had

developed plans for a center, and only 10 per cent had no plans

for such a facility.[6]

Central processing of meat has many advantages. It is

impossible to control efficiently numerous small butcher shops

in the back rooms of retail stores. Mechanized equipment cannot

be used effectively in such departments because runs are not

long enough on store volume. Refrigeration and sanitation vary

considerably,depending upon store facilities and the caliber of

supervision,with a resultant loss in shrink. Furthermore, the

anatomy of a side of beef does not necessarily conform to the

demands of customers. Some stores can sell only cuts from the

hind quarter with the result that much of the animal is wasted,

whereas a central facility could send these cuts to other stores

where customers are more likely to buy them.

The labor-saving potential of the centralized processing of

meat is tremendous because cutting and wrapping fresh meat accounts

for about 67 per cent of total manhours in a store meat department.[7]

If both of these operations can be removed to a central facility

_____

[6]K. V. Flood, "Meat Distribution Center Developments", The
    National Provisioner, February 6, 1971.

[7]The McKinsey Meat Study, A Study Sponsored by the American
    Meat Institute and the National Association of Food Chains,
    February 24, 1964, p. 29.

where they can be performed on a controlled volume basis, both

the overall savings as well as the savings in labor at the store

level are likely to be substantial.

The extent of the saving will depend upon whether the central

facility cuts, wraps, and ships retail packages or whether it

simply ships primals or "knife-ready" beef. In the latter case,

there would still be a significant amount of cutting and wrapping

left to the retail store meat department.

A study conducted by the U. S. Department of Labor in 1963

estimated that a central facility processing retail cuts with a

weekly volume of $75,000 would have an annual labor cost of

about $217,000. Included within this figure was the labor force

that would be needed in the stores' retail meat departments. The

Department estimated this would vary between one to two men per

store who would be needed to service displays and provide special

orders for customer convenience. The study further found that

the labor costs at the store level under conventional operation

would amount to about $373,000, so that the savings in labor alone

would aggregate about $156,000 per year.[8] Since this study was

made, wage rates of meatcutters have almost doubled so that the

savings potential in terms of labor costs is even greater today.

In addition to the savings in labor, back rooms of meat

departments could be made smaller and the needless duplication

of expensive equipment in numerous locations could be eliminated.

Other savings flow from the fact that companies can salvage

several cents a pound more for fat in a central facility, because

---

[8] Centralized Processing of Fresh Meat for Retail Stores,
U.S.Department of Agriculture, Marketing Research
Report No. 628, October, 1963, p. 26.

with a federal meat inspector on the premises fat can be rated
edible as compared with inedible when trimmed at the store.

Although in theory the largest savings from a central
facility are achieved when retail cuts are shipped to the store,
relatively few companies are shipping retail cuts to their outlets. A more common practice is the breakdown into primal or
subprimal cuts. This is in sharp contrast with European procedure where for many years boned-out retail cuts have been shipped
to markets from central facilities.

One of the problems slowing the transition to central
processing of retail cuts is union contract restrictions. Although
the International Office of the Amalgamated Meatcutters Union
has not opposed central meatcutting, various locals have sought
either to retard its rate of introduction or to block its application to retail cuts. This can be done quite effectively by
requiring that a certain number of journeymen meat cutters be
on duty in the store at all times. Such a provision reduces the
labor-saving potential of the centralized facility since labor
has to be maintained on the retail premises whether required by
the work load or not.

Another major problem involves maintaining the condition of
the meat in a retail package from central facility to store door.
The longer the distance which must be traveled, the more bleeding
occurs and the greater the possible discoloration. Some companies
are entering the retail package stage gradually by shipping only
those cuts which are low-bleeder items and which maintain their
bloom in transit. Because of the perishability of meat in retail

packages, expensive refrigerated trucks must be utilized for shipment to the stores. Some companies have found that increased transportaion costs eat up a large part of the savings effected in labor, since unless the volume of shipments is very large the trucks cannot be utilized fully and cost per pound shipped becomes excessive.

Avenues to More Efficient Distribution

If we focus our attention on beef, which represents the most important single component of the product mix in retail meat departments, the most logical and economical way to handle the flow of this product from packer to consumer would seem to be in the form of frozen retail cuts prepared by the packer. Swift and Company lost four million dollars some years ago attempting to educate consumers to the logic of this kind of distribution. It is quite unlikely to materialize in the near future, because consumers quite illogically dislike frozen beef!

The next most economical route would involve shipment by the packer of fresh unfrozen retail cuts to retail stores. However, this is unlikely to occur in the near future because of the problem of maintaining bloom during long periods in transit and because cutting practices vary so much in different parts of the country that a packer would have difficulty in adjusting his cutting, labeling and packaging to the needs of various localities.

The third logical avenue would require the packer to ship primals to a central facility which would then cut and package into retail cuts. However, as has already been indicated there are major problems—both institutional and operational—which will slow this development.

The fourth possibility involves shipment to the store, either by the packer directly, or from a central facility, of primal or block-ready cuts in cartons. This procedure achieves economies in handling, cutting and general operation while avoiding some of the problems encountered in processing retail cuts. It seems to be the direction in which most companies will proceed during a transition stage to the eventual processing of retail cuts. Although the savings are not as great as those which in theory can be effected by central processing of retail cuts, nevertheless they are substantial. One chain estimated that in a store with a meat volume of about $10,000 per week there would be a saving of 20 per cent in manhours as a result of the adoption of this procedure.

Productivity Trends in Warehousing

The warehouse is a service facility. Improvement in productivity of the warehouse is normally of less concern than improvement in the productivity and service level of the retail stores. Warehouses vary so much in their function, product line, kind of customer, and physical facilities that it is difficult to forecast or derive any meaningful general trends. If we look at the entire distribution process in the food industry, it seems evident that during the decade of the seventies, major improvements in productivity will be felt primarily at the store level, but these changes may be bought at the expense of a slower rate of improvement and perhaps even a decline in productivity at the warehouse level.

CHAPTER VII

RETAILING

A discussion of productivity in food retailing must
focus primarily on operation of the supermarket. If we
define a supermarket as a food store having sales in excess
of $500,000 per year, then in 1970 75 per cent of all food
store sales were handled through supermarkets, although
this category of outlet represented only 18 per cent of all
food stores.[1]   Although efficiency is of obvious concern to
any business with a low margin of profit, the small food
store is primarily a convenience outlet and therefore both
the motivation as well as the opportunity for improved
productivity is often lacking.

The Problem of Variety

The supermarket in America is suffering from a bad case
of marketing schizophrenia. It does not know whether it is
in fact a small warehouse intended to distribute food to
consumers at the lowest possible cost or a merchandising
establishment in which the most sophisticated techniques of
display, departmentalization, decor, and equipment utilization
are combined to induce consumers to buy what the operator
wants to sell.

---

[1] Progressive Grocer, 38th Annual Report of the Grocery Industry,
April, 1971, p. 66. The definition of "supermarket"
adopted by Progressive Grocer differs from that utilized
by Super Market Institute. The latter requires a minimum
sales volume of one million dollars per annum.

This conflict is seen clearly in the struggle over shelf space. It is obvious that as more and more individual items are displayed on gondolas, the cost of stocking and refilling slots will increase. Efficiency dictates minimizing variety to concentrate sales and improve productivity; merchandising dictates expanding variety to increase sales and gross profit.

Experience demonstrates that variety has been the winner in this struggle. The number of items carried by the average supermarket increased from about 6,000 in 1960 to about 7,800 in 1970.[2] Since sales in the average market were about $1,850,000 in 1960[3] and about $2,300,000 in 1970,[4] it is apparent that dollar sales per product item have remained relatively constant. But during this same period food prices advanced over 20 per cent while store labor costs rose from 7 per cent of sales to over 8 per cent.[5] It is not surprising then that supermarket profits have continued to erode. For example, profits after taxes for food chains as a percentage of sales fell from 1.26 per cent in 1961 to .86 per cent in 1971.[6]

---

[2] Ibid., p. 65.

[3] The Supermarket Industry Speaks, 1961, Thirteenth Annual Report of Super Market Institute, 1961, p. 9.

[4] Data from Super Market Institute. The sales figure for 1970 is based upon a median while the 1960 figure is an average. Item figures are not strictly comparable with the sales figures because the former are derived from Progressive Grocer compilations which define supermarket in a manner different from Super Market Institute. It is believed, however, that the two sets of figures reflect the trend in sales per product item during this period.

[5] The Supermarket Industry Speaks, 1970, Twenty-second Annual Report of Super Market Institute, 1970, p. 13.

[6] Operating Results of Food Chains, 1970-71, New York State College of Agriculture and Life Sciences, Cornell University, Ithaca, N.Y., 1972, p. 11.

From 1960 to 1970, sales per manhour increased from
$24.84[7] to $36.37.[8] However, when this increase in dollar
sales is adjusted for the change in retail food prices,
productivity as measured by real output per manhour increased
at an average annual rate of only 1.5 per cent. Moreover,
from 1969 to 1970, sales per manhour rose only about 5 per cent
while prices rose 6 per cent so that there was an actual decline in physical productivity.[9] This is hardly an example of
productivity improvement for a marketing institution which is
supposed to be an example of efficient operation.

Nor is there any sign of let-up in the future. It is
generally assumed that before the end of the decade many markets will be carrying in stock over 10,000 items. An executive
of one of the largest food chains recently reported that his
company had been adding items at the rate of about 400 net
per year.

Increasing variety can be handled up to a point, but
beyond certain critical limits it threatens the nature of a
distribution system. The supermarket may well be approaching
these limits. The choice is narrowing to filling gondola
slots item by item by hand or cutting variety and putting full
cases of merchandise on the shelf.

[7]The Super Market Industry Speaks, 1970, op. cit., p. 12.

[8]The Super Market Industry Speaks, 1971, Twenty-third Annual
    Report of Super Market Institute, 1971, p. 2.
    These figures are available only from Super Market Institute
    and therefore are based on a different classification than
    previously cited Progressive Grocer figures. However, they
    are believed to be indicative of the trend.

[9]Ibid., p. 8.

The confrontation with variety will be resolved by different operators in different ways depending upon their basic philosophy of the business. One executive told the writer he believes in variety but not in duplication. He believes that the consumer has a right to a blue facial tissue but not to a blue facial tissue made by three different manufacturers. Many retailers in the coming decade will take this route and concentrate purchases on the fast selling brand in a particular category. Others may cut all variety sharply. Still others will stress variety and use it to draw sales even at the expense of efficiency.

The same kind of split personality exists in the area of special service. Some markets are adding service delicatessens and service bakeries while other operators are throwing them out. Some stores are cutting down on baggers and carry-out personnel while others are adding them. One thing, however, all executives agree upon. The supermarket business cannot be operated solely on productivity principles. It is, in the last analysis, a service business and there are certain critical limits below which service cannot fall without an immediate adverse effect upon sales. This critical limit occurs, for example, in waiting time at the checkout. Customers tend to exaggerate in their own minds the time elapsed waiting in a line at a ticket counter at an airline, or at a bank teller's window—and of course at the checkout in the supermarket. All markets, whether they view themselves as low-cost, low-price outlets or merchandising vehicles must recognize this basic fact and provide ade-

quate service at the checkout. It is for this reason that
the advent of the automatic checkout has aroused so much
interest in the industry.

The Front End

No other department in a supermarket offers as much
opportunity to reduce operating costs as does the checkout
operation which involves about 40 per cent of the man-hours
needed to run an average market. Checker productivity
typically varies widely from company to company and even
from store to store reflecting differences in proficiency
of cashiers and baggers, the length and quality of training
given to personnel, the nature and age of equipment, and
the level of customer traffic. In order to adapt service to
fluctuating customer demand, store operators customarily rely
on part-time workers to provide a substantial proportion of
front-end hours. Many of such employees are young, have
only a transient interest in their job and in the company,
and are apt to be careless in their work. The front-end,
therefore, is a function where automation is extremely
desirable to improve productivity and reduce error.

The Automatic Checkout

The food industry is now on the threshold of a major
breakthrough in technology which can revolutionize the
checkout operation and together with the Universal Product
Code can provide a flow of information which may substantially

improve the entire process of management decision-making
in this industry. Because of the high cost involved in
installing the automatic checkout system, it is likely to be
utilized only in large markets for some time until technological progress permits reduction in the prices of
necessary equipment.

The automatic checkout depends upon a scanning device
at the checkout and the application of a code on the
merchandise. Various techniques have been developed by
different companies to scan the merchandise, but the overall
system generally involves the following components: an
optical pattern recognition scanner, a high speed printer,
teletype machine, tabulator, and a computer. The scanner
reads the code and the price is shown immediately on a
lighted bar above the tabulator in the customer's view. One
such system requires the operator at the checkout to pass
a wand over a symbol on the merchandise in order to read the
relevant product identification code. Another company's
device requires that the merchandise be pushed over a slot
in the checkout stand where a laser beam hits the symbol and
reads the relevant information. In each case the price information is maintained in the "memory" of the computer and is
activated by the scanning technique. When the customer's
order is completely checked out, she receives an itemized list
of all purchases with the package price -- and under some

systems with the name of the product and unit price—

alongside. Since the cashier has no control over the pricing

function, ring-up errors are eliminated as long as each

piece of merchandise is exposed to the scanning device.

The potential savings of the automatic checkout in a

store with an annual sales volume of 4 million dollars and

with almost complete source coding is illustrated in Table VI.

The savings estimates are the result of a study[10] (hereinafter

referred to as the "USDA Study") conducted at Indiana State

University under the auspices of the Agricultural Research

Service of the United States Department of Agriculture.

In view of the fact that net earnings after taxes for the

year 1970-1971 for all retail food chains reporting to the

figure exchange of the National Association of Food Chains

amounted to only .86 per cent of sales,[11] a possible savings

of one per cent before taxes makes this one of the most

exciting developments in the history of the food business.

The savings potential derives primarily from the

following areas:

Increased Checkout Productivity: According to findings

---

[10] H. S. Ricker and H. F. Krueckeberg, "Computerized
Checkout Systems for Retail Food Stores", Management
Information Bulletin No. 3, School of Business, Indiana
State University, Terra Haute, Indiana, April, 1971.

[11] Operating Results of Food Chains, 1970-1971, op. cit.,
p. 11.

TABLE VI

Estimated Potential Savings With An Optical Scanning Computerized
Checkout System for a Store with a $4 Million Sales Volume:
1/   Customer Unloading the Shopping Cart

| Type of Savings | Dollars | Annual Savings | |
		Percent of Operating Costs 2/	Percent of Sales
Increased Checkout Productivity	$17,424	2.09	0.44
Reduced Checkout Error	14,200	1.70	0.36
Reduced Checker Training Costs	700	0.08	0.02
Eliminate Price Marking and Repricing	3,075	0.37	0.08
Inventory Reduction and Ordering Efficiencies	10,200	1.22	.26
TOTAL	$45,599	5.46	1.16

Estimated Potential Savings With An Optical Scanning Computerized
Checkout System for a Store with a $4 Million Sales Volume:
1/   Split Checkstand With Checker Unloading the Cart

| Type of Savings | Dollars | Annual Savings | |
		Percent of Operating Costs 2/	Percent of Sales
Increased Checkout Productivity	$16,200	1.94	0.41
Reduced Checkout Error	14,200	1.70	0.36
Reduced Checker Training Costs	700	0.08	0.02
Eliminate Price Marking and Repricing	3,075	0.37	0.08
Inventory Reduction and Ordering Efficiencies	10,200	1.22	0.26
TOTAL	$44,375	5.31	1.13

1/   Excluding the cost of implementing the system.

2/   Operating costs represent 20.87 per cent of sales or $834,800.
     Operating costs differ from gross margin (21.3 per cent) due to
     exclusion of net operating profit, (0.44 per cent).

Source: H. S. Ricker and H. F. Krueckeberg, "Computerized
          Checkout Systems for Retail Food Stores", School of
          Business, Indiana State University, April, 1971, p. 26.
          Reprinted by permission.

made in the USDA Study, optical scanning improved checkstand throughput 18 per cent. A 19 per cent improvement in productivity was realized when the shopper unloaded the cart.[12] It was found that individual grocery items could be scanned and recorded 52 per cent faster than they could be rung up using conventional cash registers and techniques. The 19 per cent increase in productivity would result in a savings of over 17 thousand dollars annually in a store doing four million dollars per year (See Table VI).

It must be emphasized that the substantial improvement in productivity observed in the USDA Study resulted when all items were premarked with the appropriate symbol. If the operator at the checkout must stop and manually enter the code for items which are not marked, the benefits described could be substantially reduced.

The extent to which the potential for improved productivity presented by the automatic checkout will result in a quantifiable measurable change in store productivity depends upon the objectives of management. Some companies will utilize the savings potential inherent in the new system to reduce the number of hours of checkout personnel at the front end. To the extent that this is done with no change in sales, there will be an increase in sales per manhour. On the other hand, other companies will use the new system to improve customer service. For example, by maintaining the same number

---

[12]Ricker, op. cit., p. 17.

of checkout hours and utilizing the automatic checkout it
may now be possible to reduce the average number of persons
in line at any checkout from three to two.

Thus in a customer-oriented business such as the food
business, the impact of productivity changes sometimes is
clouded by management decisions which are customer-oriented.
Of course, the end objective of improving the level of service is that such action will increase sales and ultimately
be reflected in higher sales per manhour.

Reduced Checkout Error: In a business in which profit
is measured in decimal points, the possibility of loss through
cashier error poses serious problems.   Studies which have
been made by various market operators reveal that cashier
error almost invariably results in a net under-ring rather
than an over-ring.   The causes of this circumstance are known
but difficult to control.   Most error at the checkout arises
either from cashier carelessness or inability to read the
price on a package or can.   When the cashier is in doubt as
to a particular price, she is instructed to stop checking the
order and signal for assistance.   As a practical matter, a
cashier under pressure with long lines of customers waiting
is more likely to guess than to go through the procedure
recommended by company policy.   Furthermore, when she makes
a guess she is likely to guess on the low side.   Inflation itself increases the incidence of under-rings, because cashiers
when in doubt tend to remember the older, lower price.

There are no reliable figures as to the amount of loss in supermarkets attributable to cashier error. Obviously this figure will vary considerably among companies and even among various stores in a given company depending upon the caliber of supervision, the degree of care given to price marking, and the ability, conscientiousness, and training of cashiers. The USDA Study estimates that the loss due to cashier error varies from about 3/10 to 8/10 of one per cent of sales. The figure used in Table VI of .36 per cent of sales seems to be a fair approximation to an industry norm. This loss would be almost completely eliminated by the automatic checkout provided each item is brought into contact with the scanning device.

Some underrings may be deliberate. For example, a friend comes through the checkout and the cashier simply does not ring up the full amount of the order in the register. The automatic checkout may make such action more difficult but it cannot eliminate it completely. If the merchandise is not exposed to the scanner, its cost will not enter into the final tabulation. Dishonest employees have a way of finding deficiencies even in the most sophisticated equipment!

Reduced Checker Training Costs: Since a substantial portion of front end personnel in a market are part-time workers, there is a high degree of turnover. This necessitates a continuous training program for new personnel, in addition to the normal periodic retraining for old employees. The USDA Study estimated turnover at about 60 per cent per year and the cost of training a new checker at from $42 to $75.   At

an average cost of $60 per employee, the automatic checkout

would save about $700 per year in a store with a four million

dollar volume.   In addition, the automatic feature of the

operation would make it possible for stores to hire less

competent applicants and thus would alleviate the hiring

problem for this category of personnel.

Elimination of Price-Marking: A four million dollar

volume store will handle about 10 million units of product

through the checkouts each year.   Not all of these items

have to be price-marked in the store, but the price-marking

function represents an important segment of total in-store

labor.   Furthermore, after merchandise has been price-marked,

there are often price changes due to cost changes, promotions,

and competitive moves.

In the USDA Study it was assumed that about 30 per cent

of the total items were meat and produce items which would

continue to be price-marked in the store.   Another 19 per

cent were assumed to be vendor-delivered and pre-priced even

under existing procedures.   Therefore elimination of price-

marking would be applicable to about 51 per cent of the items

handled.   The savings applicable to such items could amount

to as much as $3000 per annum.   In addition, if centralized

packaging of meat and produce develops so that price and

code can be affixed at the warehouse, there would be an

additional savings of about $1660 annually.

Inventory Reduction and Ordering Efficiencies: Since

the automatic checkout and Universal Product Code would make it
possible for a company to know on a day-to-day basis precisely
what items had been sold from stock, ordering could be put on an
automatic replenishment basis. It has been estimated that this
could save as much as $4000 per year. In addition there is the
possibility of less quantifiable savings through better inventory
control. The USDA Study has lumped all of these possible benefits
together and assumed an overall savings from automatic ordering,
reduction in interest and taxes on inventory, and related economies
of $10,200.

The Economics of the Automatic Checkout: The precise costs
of store level equipment to implement checkout automation are
not known since no manufacturer is presently producing such equipment for the trade. However, industry sources estimate that the
necessary equipment for installation of the automatic checkout in
a store with an annual volume of four million dollars would
cost in excess of $150,000, while for a store doing about two millio
dollars, which is closer to the industry average, the cost would
be about $100,000. Savings before capital costs have been estimated
at about $36,000 per annum for a store with an annual sales volume
of two million dollars.[13] This would give the operator a reasonably
attractive return if he could be sure that the savings would be
forthcoming. The problem is that the cost-saving capacity of
the automatic checkout depends primarily upon the extent to which
the symbol bearing the code is applied at the source by manufacturer, processor, and packer. Application of the symbol in
the store is estimated to cost in excess of $5.00 per thousand
items compared to 33 cents per thousand at the manufacturing

----

[13]
    McKinsey & Company estimates.

level.[14] If the symbol had to be applied at the store level
to a large proportion of the products, it would eliminate most
of the attractiveness of the proposed system.

The industry therefore was faced by a dilemma: how do you
get the system started? Since the major cost of implementation
of a Universal Product Code (UPC) must be borne by manufacturers,
they were naturally reluctant to move ahead with a program from
which they would derive no direct benefit unless they were
assured that their customers would buy sufficient equipment to
utilize the code procedure. Retailers, on the other hand, were
reluctant to make specific commitments (other than that they
supported the program in principle) until they knew what percentage of product would be source marked. Furthermore, there was
a natural hesitancy on the part of retailers to commit themselves
to the first models of a new technique since it seems likely
that experience in the field will elicit improvements. And
equipment manufacturers were loath to get into mass production
until they had sufficient orders to make it worthwhile to tool
up for manufacture of the specialized equipment necessary for
operation of the system.

Still another unknown has been the attitude of the customer.
What will be her reaction to the elimination of all price-marking
on cans and packages? Prices will, of course, be displayed on
markers on gondolas and the customer will receive an itemized
list of prices for products purchased at the checkout. It has
also been suggested that in each aisle of a store a scanner

---

[14]McKinsey & Company estimates.

could be installed so that a customer could apply the scanner to
a product and determine the price.

There is no logical reason why customers should not accept
the new system, but, then, consumers are not always logical!
Shoppers have resisted frozen meat even though they frequently
buy meat out of a case and throw it in the freezer when they
get home. In many parts of the country consumers will not buy
prepackaged produce because they like to "feel the merchandise".
Will customers trust the computer more than the girl at the
checkout? This unanswered question poses another uncertainty
in the path of retailer purchases of automatic checkout equipment.

Despite these problems, remarkable progress has been made
in obtaining industry agreement and support for the basic elements
required to implement the concept of the UPC. At this writing,
the industry, through the cooperative efforts of trade associations representing all sectors of the food industry—chain
retailers, small grocers, grocery manufacturers, and wholesalers—
has taken the following steps:

1) A code has been agreed upon. This will take the form
of a 10-digit, all numeric code with the first five digits used
to identify each manufacturer and the second five to identify
items within each manufacturer's line.

2) A company has been selected to manage the code—that is,
to assign manufacturers identification numbers, provide an inquiry
service, and administer guidelines for manufacturers to follow
when they assign item numbers. Supervision of this entire process
has been assigned to a Board of Governors Council whose 21 members
are drawn from all segments of the industry.

3)   One million dollars has been raised by the industry
to start up the code management agency.

4)   Grocery manufacturers have agreed to assume the costs
of applying the code to their particular products.

5)   Work is now in process by a special industry subcommittee to establish symbol standardization guidelines. The
symbol is the machine-readable representation of the code.

In some respects this last step represents the most
difficult decision of all.   The subcommittee representing food
industry leadership has been discussing the technical problems
of code design, application, and scanning with approximately
thirty equipment manufacturers, both American and foreign.
These companies have expended millions of dollars in research
and development in the hope that their particular equipment
will be favored by food retailers for use at the checkout
counter.   Choice by the subcommittee of a particular kind
of symbol may give certain manufacturers an advantage over
others.   This results from the fact that most major equipment
manufacturers are not pursuing compatible scanning approaches.
Companies are working with everything from voice entry to
holography.

The subcommittee is presently wrestling with the sensitive
issue of how to designate a particular form of symbol as the
only one acceptable to the industry and yet assure fair entry
by all equipment manufacturers into the lush market which the

UPC will open up in the retail food industry. Perhaps some
form of licensing arrangement will have to be utilized to solve
this problem.

The experience of the food industry thus far in developing
and implementing the UPC provides some instructive insights into
the problems of attempting to apply a systems approach to an
entire industry:

1) Tremendous savings can result to an industry from successful application of the systems approach. In the food industry it
has been estimated that by 1975 with 7800 stores participating and
with 75 per cent source symbol marking, the UPC will generate net
savings after account has been taken of all costs of approximately
$149,000,000 per year.[15]

2) Savings are not necessarily distributed in relationship to
costs. Food manufacturers will receive relatively little benefit
from the new system yet their costs will amount to approximately
30 million dollars per year as a result of the expense incurred
for new labels and other costs incidental to application of the
code at source. On the other hand, the major benefits will accrue
to retailers who will no longer have to price merchandise and who
will gain other advantages as well.

3) Leadership by chief executives of large companies can avoid
the problems which might otherwise accrue from the lack of correspondence between costs and benefits. The need for the UPC was
acknowledged and the burden accepted by the large food manufacturers
in a true gesture of industry statesmanship. It is doubtful if this
project could have been launched if the industry were fragmented

---

[15] McKinsey & Company estimates.

among many small companies.

4) Agreement by industry leadership with respect to the nature of industry technological needs spurs research expenditures by equipment manufacturers. Once the concept of the UPC was taken out of the talking stage and the industry agreed on the broad outlines of the system which was needed, equipment manufacturers poured millions into research where before there had been only minor activity. Industry committees can perform a real function in crystalizing needs in concrete form so that supporting companies can afford to take risks inherent in research and development of new apparatus.

5) Every step of the foregoing process is fraught with anti-trust problems. Technically there is no law against efforts by an industry to achieve standardization. As a practical matter, there are substantial risks involved. One of the problems is that there are no guidelines for such action and an overzealous govern-ment attorney could certainly raise questions about decisions and procedures at each step of the process. It is to be hoped that will not be so in the case of the UPC. Nevertheless, it seems clear that the process of standardization necessary to implement a systems approach on an industry basis could benefit from Congressional action which would clarify the procedures which can lawfully be followed.

Food industry leaders expect that by mid-1972 many manufac-turers and retailers will already have underway the administrative changes necessary to convert to the UPC. March 30, 1973 has been set as the deadline for symbol selection. Thereafter various types of scanning equipment will have to be given operational tests in stores. Although it is hoped that the automatic checkout will become a significant factor in the industry by 1975, it is possible that its adoption by retailers will be slower than expected. The capital equipment required to implement the system at store level is extremely costly and retailers may be reluctant to be pioneers. Eventual adoption of this or some comparable system seems almost certain, however. The rapidly rising rate of wages paid to food store personnel will expand the labor-saving potential of the system year by year and therefore make its introduction even more attractive.

The Electronic Checkout

The Jewel Companies, a midwest diversified retail food chain, has taken a different approach to the front end problem. Rather than attempting to attack the whole problem in all its complexity, as does the automatic checkout, Jewel has sought merely to substitute an electronic terminal for the cash register. There is no scanning device nor coding of merchandise. The results, however, are a major improvement in productivity with only a modest increase in cost.

Under this system, terminals at each checkout are connected to a series of minicomputers located in the store. The terminal not only enables the customer's order to be checked out faster but also provides information which would otherwise have to be tediously compiled. Thus all manufacturers' coupons and company-issued coupons are collated by department through the terminal. A complete breakdown of cash, checks, and coupons can be obtained at any time by the manager at a

control terminal. A coding device is available so that the
movement of particular products can be monitored to determine
the extent to which they are being pilfered.

Since the use of this device is still relatively new, it
is too soon to determine the full amount of the productivity
increase generated. However, from the writer's own observation
it was apparent that the terminal was considerably faster than
a register for checking out an order and in addition would save
considerable clerical time through its ability to collate information which normally had to be prepared by hand. Furthermore, it appears that the cost per checkout would only be
slightly more than that of a conventional register.

Bagging

The bagging function is likely to be the focus of major
efforts aimed at increasing productivity. If the automatic
checkout is generally adopted, the increased speed of checkout will enable the operator to bag while the order is being
recorded. Other approaches involve automatic unloaders and
automatic baggers. Thus far the latter have not been successful because of damage to fragile merchandise.

Another source of "increased productivity" is to have
the customer assume the bagging function. Throughout Europe,
customers customarily bag their own orders. Increasing labor
costs in this country may compel the adoption of a similar
policy. Customer bagging is already being utilized in the

so-called warehouse stores in various parts of the country.

Improvement in Other Store Functions

The retail supermarket will be the beneficiary during the coming decade of a wide range of innovations. Many of these will shift labor input to an earlier stage in distribution, but the major advantage from their introduction will be felt at the store level. To an increasing extent the store will become a distribution mechanism with little or no fabrication carried on in the premises.

Meat Department

As was pointed out in Chapter VI, the retail meat business is undergoing a fundamental change as an increasing percentage of meat is delivered to stores with some processing already performed. A recent study found that about 80 per cent of stores operated by large and small chains receive some or all of their fresh meat via warehouse distribution centers.[16] Productivity is improved at the store level since less labor is required for cutting. Furthermore, sales may actually increase because the personnel are better able to keep the case full.

Produce Department

The produce business is also going through a transition stage with large public companies becoming involved in the

---

[16] Chain Store Age, November 1970, p. 33.

growing and marketing of crops. Such companies are keenly
interested in applying modern cost-saving distribution
methods to the movement of produce to market. As a result,
in the next few years an increasingly large portion of produce will be trimmed and prepackaged at the field. The
savings resulting from this shift of labor input can be
huge. One study found that the trimming and prepackaging of
lettuce in the field could save the retailer from a minimum
of ten cents per carton to a maximum of 35 cents per carton.[17]
Other savings will accrue to the retail store from the
establishment by some companies of produce warehouses which
prepare retail packages for shipment to the store.

The Grocery Department

The most important breakthrough in the grocery department
will come about from the use of the automatic checkout which
will eliminate the need for price-marking. Little change is
foreseen in shelf stocking except that a number of fast-
moving items will be packed in traypack or in shrink film
overwraps so as to facilitate placement on the shelves. The
basic problem inhibiting more effective materials handling
in this area is the fact that the grocery business even in a
large market deals with very small units of individual products.
For example, a recent study found that of the 6487 items of
groceries and nonfoods in a modern A & P super market, 5884

---

[17] The Search for a Thousand Million Dollars, A. T. Kearney
& Company, Inc., Report prepared for the National
Association of Food Chains, 1966, p. 8.

or almost 91 per cent moved less than a case of 24 units per
week. Only 56 items in the store moved more than the equivalent of four cases per week.[18] These figures reflect
graphically the impact of variety on product movement. High
volume markets which restrict variety will be able to
increase substantially the number of items which move on
a case lot basis and this will bring with it real economies
in handling costs. In addition, computer programs such as
COSMOS (Computer Optimization and Simulation Modeling for
Operating Supermarkets)[19] may   enable stores to make more
scientific allocations of shelf space which take account of
the handling costs associated with shipping, storing, and
display of specific items. This may result in a product
mix which will bring labor costs into a more favorable
balance with gross profit.

The receiving function will also become more mechanized
in the years ahead with greater utilization of movable equipment such as cages to move product from the warehouse
directly to the store floor for easy access to shelves. It
is also possible that more experimentation will be undertaken
in this country with methods used in Europe which involve
movable segments of gondolas which can move from the supplier

---

[18] _Progressive Grocer_, September, 1970, Part I, p. 59.

[19] This system, sponsored by 19 manufacturers under the
guidance of the National Association of Food Chains,
is in operation in a number of retail food chains.

or from the warehouse direct to the display on the store floor.

The Advent of the Super Supermarket

There is general agreement among executives in the food
industry that the decade ahead will witness the development of
high volume markets, many doing $100,000 to $200,000 per week.
Already in 1970 more than 11 per cent of new stores reported
sales per week in excess of $100,000.[20] The medium-sized market
will rapidly be driven out of business. It is too large to be
convenient and too small to enable the operator to be efficient.
Two factors have led to this situation. On the one hand the
spread of discounting has so narrowed profit margins that the
break-even point in volume has substantially increased. On
the other hand, wage rates have risen so precipitously that
the only markets which can survive are those which can afford
to automate and to utilize modern material handling techniques.

Of course, stores have been getting larger year by year
since the inception of the supermarket, and therefore it is
easy to think of the new development as simply a continuation
of this natural evolution. But some of the most knowledgeable
operators feel that what is now happening is more than an
evolution in size—it is a breakthrough in distribution technique which ultimately may make possible major improvements
in productivity. For with the super supermarket will come
significant changes in product handling techniques. Among

---

[20] The Supermarket Industry Speaks, 1971, op. cit., p. 13.

the most important of these are the following:

1. There will be much more warehouse to shelf movement
in full case lots. Stores doing volumes of over $100,000
per week already have found that even slow-moving items will
turn over a case of product in a month. Since it is likely
that labor costs will rise considerably faster than interest
costs, market operators will stock many more items on a case
lot basis, preferring to tie up money in inventory rather
than to incur extra labor cost.

2. With case lot movement to the shelf possible on a
broader (though still limited) scale and with the need for
price-marking obviated by the automatic checkout, operators
of large markets will press for shipments from manufacturers
in traypacks and film overwraps so as to minimize rehandling.
Bulky items such as charcoal, potato chips, toilet paper, and
similar products will move on pallets direct to the store
floor and will remain on pallets for display purposes.

3. The volume of a large store will make it economic
to maintain expensive equipment at the store level. This
will range all the way from minicomputers for use in connection with the automatic checkout to sophisticated materials
handling equipment for handling incoming loads.

4. Large stores will be able to purchase in sufficient
quantity so as to receive a full truckload of mixed merchandise. This may include frozen foods shipped together with
grocery items. One large wholesaler has found that by
freezing frozen foods to 30 degrees below zero and insulating

the pack, they can be shipped with nonfrozen products and
arrive in good condition at about 10 degrees below zero.
The advantage is that the truck door is opened only once;
loss through pilferage is eliminated and loss of trucking
time through waiting at stops is eliminated. Consolidation
of such loads will encounter some resistance from Teamster
local unions which in many areas have exclusive jurisdiction
based upon a specific product carried by a truck.

    5. Orders for direct deliveries are substantial enough
to warrant consolidation through a distributing warehouse
which will be operated or controlled by the retail food
chain or an affiliated wholesaler.

    6. High volume stores have a direct impact on pro-
ductivity and handling techniques at the warehouse level.
For example, chains with high volume markets are able to
utilize the GMA pallet exclusively since merchandise turns
rapidly. Selection productivity is considerably higher when
a selector is picking merchandise for stores doing $100,000
per week than for stores doing $30,000. High volume at the
retail level makes an entirely different approach to product
handling attractive and viable through the entire distribution system.

Is the Supermarket Obsolete?

    Many years ago Professor Malcolm P. McNair developed
the concept of "the wheel of retailing" to explain the

pattern of retail evolution.[21]   His hypothesis was that new

types of retailers generally enter the market as low-margin,

low-price institutions, but gradually acquire more elaborate

facilities, equipment, and promotional gimmicks so that they

end up as high-cost, high-margin outlets. They then become

vulnerable to newer types of marketing ventures which again

enter as price cutters, and so the pattern of evolution

continues.

Is the supermarket in danger of such displacement by

new concepts in retailing? Despite the spread of discounting

in the food industry, the modern supermarket is an elaborate

and expensive facility. Can food and related products be

delivered to the consumer in a cheaper manner?

There will, of course, always be variants of the super-

market concept which will be able to shave costs by elimin-

ating certain services and thus appeal to customers who are

very price conscious. Thus in some areas of the country

there are so-called warehouse stores where merchandise is

sold off pallets and the customer price-marks the merchandise

and pays 10 per cent over "cost." However, this kind of

outlet has limited acceptance and probably can operate profit-

ably only in certain types of neighborhoods.

Some observers believe that the continual rise in the

---

[21] M. P. McNair, "Significant Trends and Developments in the
Postwar Period," in A. B. Smith, ed. Competitive Distribution in a Free, High-Level Economy and Its Implications for the University (Pittsburgh: University of
Pittsburgh Press, 1958), pp. 17-18.

gross margins of supermarkets will ultimately make it profitable to by-pass the store entirely and deliver to the customer direct from the warehouse. At first glance this would seem to be the ultimate in efficiency since it would eliminate one complete rehandling of merchandise and thus make possible substantial reductions in cost. Moreover, advocates of the potential of such a system point to the fact that food shopping is becoming a chore to many people, that the credit card now eliminates the need for a deliveryman to take cash, and that telephonic computer connection may make possible semi-automatic ordering.

The next decade may well see this kind of service set up within the food business, but it will not be a low-cost service and it will operate primarily as a convenience for a small segment of the population. One such venture, called "Telemart," recently went into bankruptcy after a short and abortive career. Telemart was set up to deliver supermarket items to customers who ordered by telephone from a catalogue. A computer was supposed to keep track of orders, inventory levels, and to specify the most efficient delivery routes. It opened with some 2600 orders received in the first two days and was unable to handle these efficiently through its warehouse space and shipping facilities.

However, there is a real question whether this or any other kind of system can serve the mass market at a lower cost than the supermarket. The advantage of the supermarket

concept is that three of the most time-consuming functions in
purchasing -- selection, assemblage, and delivery -- are
handled by the customer herself without charge. Thus, the
supermarket by its very operation involves a high degree
of labor-saving which other kinds of outlets will find difficult to duplicate.

Delivery of orders to homes is rapidly becoming uneconomical
unless a large fee is charged.With the labor cost of a union
driver approaching six dollars per hour and the cost of equipment rising, an operator would have to charge over one dollar
per order to break even, assuming that a driver in a metropolitan area could only deliver five to six orders per hour.
If the average order is $20.00, the delivery cost alone to
the consumer would be in the neighborhood of five per cent.
Furthermore, no telephone order system can possibly handle
the variety of items that is on display in the supermarket.

Another variant which has often been discussed is the
completely automatic supermarket in which the customer
inserts a numbered magnetic card into various display windows
and then receives her order through a conveyor system at the
cashier's station. Such a facility consisting of a warehouse
over a 2,663 square foot sales area is said to be under development in Tokyo, Japan.[22] Such facilities, or various types of
vending machine operations, may find a place in down-
town neighborhoods where land is scarce and also in

----

[22] Supermarket News, April 12, 1971, pp. 1, 24, 26.

apartment house projects. It is quite unlikely that they
will replace the supermarket.

It is the writer's opinion that there is no new kind
of outlet on the horizon which is likely to replace the
supermarket as the primary source of mass distribution
of food in the coming decade. The supermarket itself will
undergo a major transformation by reason of the developments
already referred to and will demonstrate new capabilities
in delivering food at low prices to the American consumer.

The Problem of the Ghetto Supermarket

The increasing minimum size required for optimum
efficiency in supermarket operation will further increase
the gap between prices paid by ghetto residents and more
affluent residents of the suburbs. Numerous studies have
substantiated the validity of the contention that "the
poor pay more."[23] However, these studies have also indicated
that the primary cause for the differential in prices is the
fact that ghetto residents concentrate a much larger share
of their total purchases in small markets which customarily
charge more than large supermarkets. Few large markets are
now being constructed in ghetto areas and the growing lot
size required makes it even less likely that there will be
any significant expansion in such neighborhoods. The failure

23
      See, for example, "Prices in Poor Neighborhoods",
         Monthly Labor Review, October, 1966, pp. 1085-1090.

of the food industry to meet the needs of such residents stems
from a variety of causes including cost and availability of
land, labor problems, pilferage, high insurance rates, risk of
violence and riot damage, and similar causes.

The gains of increasing productivity ought to be evenly
distributed in our society. The nature of the continuing
evolution of the supermarket is such, however, that the
primary beneficiaries will tend to be those who least require
it. Without some kind of governmental subsidy to business—
in the form of tax relief, payroll subsidy, rental abatement,
or other incentive—the ghetto resident will be unaware of
the advent of the super supermarket.

Productivity and the Consumer

The decade ahead can be an era of marked improvement in
productivity in food marketing because of the confluence of
a number of significant trends and innovations referred to
in the foregoing discussion. The rate at which these new
concepts and systems are applied can vary considerably and
such variation will have a major effect upon the rate of
increase in labor costs in the industry. If the automatic
checkout can raise productivity at the checkout stand 18
per cent, its contribution to the rate of productivity
improvement will be nominal if the innovation takes six
years to be generally applied, whereas its contribution can

be highly significant if the application becomes general
in three years. The same can be said for centralized
meatcutting.

To some extent the rate of introduction of such innovations can be influenced by government policy, but in the
last analysis it will be the customer who will determine the
rate of productivity improvement in the industry. If she
casts her vote for price and patronizes the discount stores
heavily, the emphasis will shift to productivity and the
pace of application of the various improvements mentioned
will accelerate. If, on the other hand, she votes for
variety and service, the rate will be slowed.

It is quite possible that there will be no consensus
and no clear direction. We are becoming more diverse in our
values and in our needs as a people. It seems likely that
the decade of the seventies will see a proliferation in
the kinds of food stores available: discount markets, convenience stores, boutiques, super supermarkets. In such a
case productivity will be even more difficult to measure and
will be less consistently sought as a management objective.

CHAPTER VIII

PRODUCTIVITY AND THE LAW

Essential to any national program to improve productivity is a critical review of the legal framework within which business must operate. The antitrust laws, including the Robinson-Patman Act, were enacted to implement specific objectives of public policy. The question must now be asked: Has the impact of such laws on business activity tended to inhibit the development of new and innovative methods of distribution which would improve efficiency and productivity? An affirmative answer to this question does not necessarily mean that the laws should be repealed or amended. It does mean that the purpose and effect of such legislation should now be reviewed in the light of our current national priorities and particularly with our current problems of inflation and inadequate rate of productivity improvement in mind.

The antitrust laws and the Robinson-Patman Act in particular have been the subject of continuing investigation over the years by various Congressional subcommittees, special commissions, bar association groups, and practitioners and experts. Most of these inquiries have been concerned with all phases of this legislation and its impact upon a number of variables, such as effectiveness of competition, industry structure, price rigidity, small business, and efficiency.

The scope of this chapter is much more limited. The discussion will focus upon the effect which the antitrust laws have had and are likely to have in the future upon productivity and efficiency in the food industry. The emphasis will be directed to the impact of such laws upon the development and utilization of new techniques, new forms of organization, and new methods of distribution rather than upon the ultimate structure of industry. Whether or not an oligopolistic industry is less efficient or more efficient than an industry with many small businesses is a subject which has been hotly debated in the literature and about which there has been more emotional rhetoric than substantive proof. Constraints of space preclude an examination of this issue.

The antitrust laws are "old" laws. It is hardly necessary to make the point that our economic and social system has changed radically since 1890. Even more radical has been the change in the technology of manufacture and distribution, the transformation of distribution outlets, and the change in the functions, size, and character of the middleman and the retailer in our distribution system. All of these changes call for a reevaluation of the impact of these laws which were enacted in a different milieu.

The Robinson-Patman Act

The Robinson-Patman Act was conceived in the social ferment of the Great Depression as a means of protecting the small businessman. The decade of the twenties had seen the chain stores pioneer the integration of various functions in order to achieve various economies and in the process eliminate reliance on various independently owned businesses which performed the functions of wholesaling, brokerage, and retailing. As a result of the economies achieved by this integrative process, the large chains were able to sell cheaper and also to bring increased pressure upon suppliers for price reductions.

The enactment of the Robinson-Patman Act represented the successful culmination of the struggle by the less efficient but more numerous and politically more potent small enterprises in our society against the innovations in distribution techniques introduced by large corporations. The judgment was made amid the staggering unemployment of the thirties that it was more important to maintain the livelihood of the small businessman than to opt for greater cost reduction and price reduction for the ultimate benefit of consumers. In retrospect, it is understandable why society made this judgment at this particular juncture in our history. The possible benefits of cost and price reduction flowing from improved efficiency could not have been accorded much importance in

a period when government through the NRA was actually
committed to stabilizing and raising prices.

Today, however, the control of inflation is a major concern of public policy. Maintenance of the viability of small
business is still a priority, but the balance between this
objective and the goal of improving efficiency may well be
different in the inflationary seventies from what it was in the
deflationary thirties. Recognition of this fact has led to
critical comment on the impact of the Robinson-Patman Act
at the very highest levels of government. Thus, for example,
the Council of Economic Advisers, in the <u>Economic Report of</u>
<u>the President to Congress</u> on January 16, 1969, observed that
the Robinson-Patman Act

> may conflict with the development of more
> efficient methods of distribution such as in-
> tegrating wholesale and retail functions or
> dispensing with independent brokers. By re-
> quiring proportionally equal treatment in certain
> promotional practices, the Act has discouraged
> experimentation with marketing techniques. /1/

Cost Justification

The section of the Robinson-Patman Act most closely
related to productivity and efficiency is the proviso relating
to cost justification. Section 2(a) makes unlawful a discrimination in price which may "injure,destroy, or prevent
competition with any person...." as well as a discrimination
the effect of which "may be substantially to lessen competition

---

[1] <u>Economic Report of the President</u>, January ,1969, p. 109.

or tend to create a monopoly...."   However, the proviso to
Section 2(a) adds that a price differential is not unlawful
if it makes

> only due allowance for differences in the cost
> of manufacture, sale, or delivery resulting from
> the differing methods or quantities in which such
> commodities are to such purchasers sold or
> delivered....

It seems evident from the clear language of the statute
as well as its legislative history that the cost-savings
justification was intended to afford protection to businessmen who pioneered in development of new distributive techniques.
However, the interpretation accorded this proviso by the
Commission has emasculated its effectiveness. Although in a
few cases the Commission has evidenced a liberal viewpoint and
permitted the cost savings defense to prevail where all but a
minimal amount of the alleged cost savings was proved,[2] in
general its requirements for cost savings documentation is
more rigorous than business can provide without undertaking
intensive surveys and undergoing substantial expense. The
Report of the Attorney General's National Committee to Study
the Antitrust Laws observed that "only the most prosperous
and patient business firms could afford pursuit of an often
illusory defense."[3] As a result of the Commission's demand
for certainty and exactitude where certainty and exactitude

---

[2] U.S. Rubber, 46 FTC 998 (1950); Hamburg Bros. 54 FTC 1453 (1958).

[3] Report of the Attorney General's National Committee to Study
   the Antitrust Laws, 1955, p. 173.

do not exist, businessmen in general have been wary of exper-
imenting with new techniques in distribution, tailored to the
needs of particular buyers, which would require a showing of
cost savings in order to justify their implementation.

Within the last two years, the reports of two White House
Task Forces—The President's Task Force on Productivity and
Competition (the so-called Stigler Report) and The White House
Task Force on Antitrust Policy (the so-called Neal Report)—
have both recommended revision of the Robinson-Patman Act in
order to make cost justification a viable and practical defense. The Neal Report recommended a specific amendment which
would permit differentials in price which make "appropriate"
allowances for differences in cost. "Appropriate" allowances
include those which (1) approximate the difference in consideration exacted; (2) are based on reasonable estimates; or
(3) are based on a reasonable system of classification.[4]

Although a specific amendment of the Robinson-Patman Act
would be a desirable means of clarifying the requirements of
the cost-saving defense, such action could also be taken under
the existing law by administrative procedure. The Act spells
out only the functional areas in which the savings are to be
demonstrated. It is the FTC which has determined the degree
of proof required. The FTC could eliminate much of the

---

[4] Hearings before Special Subcommittee on Small Business and the
Robinson-Patman Act, of the Select Committee on Small Business,
House of Representatives, 91st Congress, 1st Session,
Washington D.C., October 7-9, 1969, Volume 1, p. 282.

criticism directed against its administration of this aspect
of the law and make a major contribution to the fight against
inflation by bringing its accounting methods into line with
general business accounting practice.

Specifically it is recommended that the FTC adopt the
following measures as its contribution to a national program
to improve productivity in industry:

1) Promulgate an administrative interpretation of "due
allowance" under Section 2(a) substantially equivalent to the
definition of "appropriate allowance" adopted by the Neal
Report;

2) Issue a set of guidelines with accompanying examples
to clarify the kind of accounting support which will be required in future proceedings involving the cost-savings
defense;

3) Establish a committee to work with the National
Institute of Accountants in further clarifying appropriate
accounting techniques which may be used in justifying cost-
saving as a defense under the Act.

Liberalization of the cost-savings defense would be of
significant advantage to the food industry in developing new
arrangements and procedures which could cut costs and ultimately
result in lower prices to consumers. The preoccupation of
the FTC with savings in cost which can easily be measured has
tended to put the cost-saving efforts of the industry into a

straitjacket. The FTC can see the cost-savings to the industry in a carload lot versus a less than carload lot; it can rationalize a quantity discount on a store-door quantity basis. But with respect to arrangements such as annual discounts for quantity purchased, where savings are admittedly more difficult to measure, the FTC has in effect closed the door on experimentation by the industry. And yet even the man in the street would agree that there must be a savings in distribution costs when a firm can plan on continuing purchases from a large buyer.

The Robinson-Patman Act and Incentive Arrangements

Concentration of volume with particular customers makes for efficiency. The Robinson-Patman Act does not accept this fact, except in very limited circumstances, but every businessman will attest to its validity. A major complaint of executives in the food industry is that the interpretation accorded the Act has effectively barred manufacturers from developing incentive arrangements pursuant to which manufacturers could pass along to purchasers in reduced prices part of the savings which flow from concentrated purchases or from conformity with certain practices which assist the manufacturer in improving productivity.

Suppose that a retailer approaches a manufacturer of paper bags with the following innovative suggestion:

> I want to reduce my buying expense and you want
> to reduce your selling expense, and even out
> fluctuations in production. I don't care when
> you deliver bags to me or in what amounts pro-
> vided that at all times my inventory of bags
> does not fall below x bags nor exceed y bags.
> You can schedule production of my bags when con-
> venient to you and ship when convenient to you.
> You will be responsible for maintaining my in-
> ventory; billing and notification will be handled
> automatically. I will concentrate all my pur-
> chases with you. Now what kind of a discount
> can you give me?

Under existing interpretation of the Act, the manufacturer

would probably have to answer: None! In the first place,

he would have difficulty in proving cost-savings to the

satisfaction of the FTC. In the second place, the buyer

is really looking for a discount reflecting the fact that

his incremental orders can be filled during slack times

from excess capacity. But the law makes it clear that the

incremental buyer cannot be permitted the full advantage

of the benefits flowing from capacity operation since such

benefits could not have accrued had not all other buyers

added their purchases to the volume of the business. And

yet arrangements such as that outlined above ought to be

encouraged because they do make possible improvements in

productivity. Certainly where there is a difference in

timing of purchases and there are substantial peaks and

troughs in demand and production, cost distinctions should

be permitted on a marginal cost basis if they are to be

meaningful to the business community.

Flexibility of the pricing mechanism is needed in our economic system to induce purchaser and seller to enter into mutually advantageous arrangements. But the rigidity of the Robinson-Patman Act forecloses such possibilities. Suppose a manufacturer wants to reward buyers for increasing purchases over the previous year as a base. He proposes a scale of discounts based on how much the retailer is able to increase his business over the preceding year—2 per cent for a 20 per cent increase; 3 per cent for a 30 per cent increase, and so on. Concentrating volume reduces costs. But the FTC says that such a proposal is unlawful and discriminatory.[5]

Take the case of a manufacturer who sells his goods on a delivered price basis. He finds that on the average he can save about 5 per cent in freight costs if customers will take merchandise in truck load quantities. So he offers a discount of 5 per cent to all purchasers who will buy in such quantities. We have already seen in Chapter V how the Commission has obstructed the use of the back haul where manufacturers sell on a delivered price basis, so it should not be surprising that the Commission adopts a similarly unrealistic view in the case of a flat discount. In an advisory opinion the FTC has taken the position that such a uniform discount would violate Section 2(a) of the Act because it would not be uniformly cost-justified.[6]

---

[5] Advisory Opinion No. 153, December 19, 1967.

[6] Advisory Opinion No. 198, March 5, 1968.

Faced by administrative action of this nature, manufacturers, wholesalers, and retailers understandably have
been discouraged in their search for innovative and more
efficient distribution arrangements.

The One Big User Problem

In Wilmington, California, on San Pedro Bay, the United
Fruit Company (United) maintains a terminal facility for
handling bananas. Ships unload into the terminal and then
the bananas are shipped from the terminal to various purchasers by ship or rail. Harbor Banana Distributors, Inc.
(Harbor), a large banana wholesaler, maintains a facility
at Long Beach, California, also on San Pedro Bay. Harbor,
like other purchasers, had been picking up its bananas at
the United facility after they had been unloaded and temporarily stored in the United terminal. One day Harbor approached
United with an idea which seemed to make good sense from the
point of view of distributive efficiency. Harbor suggested
that United bring its ship alongside the dock of the Harbor
facility so that there would be no need for the rehandling of
the bananas through the United terminal. United agreed to do
so, but stated that it would have to make a charge for its
services. The arrangement was consummated and resulted in
substantial savings in handling costs and freight to Harbor.
United's action was motivated in part by a desire to serve a
good customer whose warehouse happens to directly abut the
discharge facility of United's major competitor.

The Federal Trade Commission has brought suit[7] against Harbor and United alleging, among other things, that the practice referred to violates the Robinson-Patman Act. The facts are that there are no other wholesalers in the Los Angeles area who have waterfront facilities adequate to accommodate the banana ships for direct unloading. Furthermore, Harbor allegedly controls 77 per cent of the banana business in the area and has acquired another banana company in a merger which the FTC seeks to upset. A FTC hearing examiner has ruled that Harbor must divest its interest in this acquired firm, but has dismissed the charge against United.

If, as seems likely, the Commission appeals the examiner's decision insofar as it affects United, then a basic issue of public policy will be presented which ought to be fully argued and resolved. The basic question is: If the big buyer is the only one with unique facilities, is the seller barred from working out arrangements which make the most efficient use of those facilities?

The rationale for an affirmative answer is that permitting such special arrangements for the benefit of the big buyer will make him more efficient and thus accentuate the tendency to monopoly in the market. The rationale for a negative answer is that we should not penalize efficiency; if permitting the large buyer to use his facilities so as to optimize efficiency creates a monopoly and if the monopoly does in fact operate to the detriment of the public interest, then—and not till then—should the antitrust laws be applied.

---

[7] *United Fruit Company, et al*, FTC Docket No. 8795.

Large buyers and sellers have the volume, the resources, the staff support and the motivation to work out innovative arrangements which can result in substantial improvement of productivity in their respective enterprises. If the nation is interested in accelerating the pace of productivity improvement it should encourage such arrangements. Large companies can afford to experiment and to fail. If such arrangements do in fact improve efficiency, smaller companies may be able to achieve similar objectives through joint ventures or cooperative enterprises. If the Robinson-Patman Act is used to stifle such plans even before they are born, then the whole economy will suffer—large companies, small companies, and the American consumer.

The Unproductive Promotional Allowance

Section 2(d) of the Act makes it unlawful for a supplier to grant to a customer a promotional allowance which is not available on proportionally equal terms to all other customers competing in the distribution of such products or commodities. The draftsmen of this provision could not have been interested in improving productivity in marketing. The FTC has answered queries from manufacturers as to how this clause might be implemented by suggesting that if a manufacturer provides ads or displays for large markets it should provide small merchants with "hand bills and the like".

The impracticability of such suggestions is apparent, but the confusion has been further compounded by the decision of the United States Supreme Court in the Fred Meyer case [8] in which the Court by a judicial tour de force decided for the first time thirty-two years after the Robinson-Patman Act had been passed that the word "customer" in this section of the Act does not mean what one would expect from common usage. Customers of an independent wholesaler are, in fact, customers of the suppliers to the wholesaler, according to the Court.

This interpretation saddles the manufacturer with responsibilities for policing of small retailers with which it has no dealings and whom it does not even know. If the economy has any concern for effective use of the time and resources of manufacturers in the food business, this misconstruction of legislative intent should be remedied.

Small Business and the Functional Discount

Although the Act was passed primarily to protect small businessmen, ironically most of the respondents in FTC Robinson-Patman Act proceedings have been small rather than large firms. In the food business the Act has hurt small independent operators by depriving them of the services of so-called rack jobbers who go from store to store and handle the purchase, stocking, and display of candy, health and

---

[8] FTC v. Fred Meyer et al,   390 U.S. 341 (1968).

beauty aids, housewares, and other items. The small indepen-

dent grocer cannot handle these departments efficiently him-

self because of the variety of slow-moving items involved.

The rack jobber buys in quantity and is able to provide the

small operator with valuable advice as to what items will

sell best.

But handling such small stores is obviously expensive.

The rack jobber contends that he is performing an important

function for the manufacturer in enabling the latter's mer-

chandise to reach outlets which would otherwise be beyond

his normal distribution network. Therefore, the jobber re-

quests a functional discount on the ground that he has to

perform services over and above those performed by the

wholesaler who buys in quantity and then simply reships to

his stores.

However, the Robinson-Patman Act does not recognize

functional discounts. Therefore, the manufacturer would be

in violation of the law if he granted a lower price (or an

additional discount) to a rack jobber than to a wholesaler

or retailer buying similar quantities. The result has been

that some rack jobbers are now dropping their smaller accounts

because they find they cannot service them on the discounts

presently granted by manufacturers.[9] Here again, the price

---

[9]
Small Business and The Robinson-Patman Act, Hearings before
   the Special Subcommittee on Small Business and The Robinson-
   Patman Act of the Select Committee on Small Business, House of
   Representatives, 91st Congress, 2nd Session, Vol.2,
   February 4, 1970, p. 613.

inflexibility resulting from the Act's arbitrary definition
of price discrimination has made impossible the adaptations
which would normally evolve in our competitive economy. The
rack jobber is an efficient mechanism for distribution of
slow-moving items to the thousands of small grocers in this
country. The Robinson-Patman Act ought not to be permitted
to interfere with that function.

The Impact of the Antitrust Laws

The decade of the seventies will be characterized by
increasing efforts on the part of business concerns to adapt
to the complexities of our economic system through cooperative action. Since most of such actions will be motivated by a desire to improve efficiency and to make it
possible for groups of smaller companies to compete more
effectively with industrial giants, public policy should in
general facilitate such efforts. However, the antitrust
laws may impose a barrier—both real and psychological—to
the implementation of such plans. If our nation is truly
interested in improving productivity in industry, then a re-
examination of the impact of the antitrust laws on business
efficiency is clearly in order.

Joint Ventures

Joint ventures provide a mechanism for major breakthroughs
in distribution efficiency. Although the antitrust laws do not
forbid such ventures, businessmen fear that normal operation of
such ventures may involve them in technical violations of the

law. Suppose, for example, that six grocery manufacturers
form a joint venture to build and operate a distribution
facility which would consolidate their various products into
shipments on a mixed carload basis to customers. The first
question which arises is whether or not they have to open
participation to all of their competitors—which they may
consider would make the whole plan unwieldy. Ever since the
Associated Press case,[10] it has been accepted doctrine that
when an association of competitors confers a competitive advantage upon them, they cannot exclude or discriminate against
competitors who join, or seek to join, the group.

A further problem is faced when rules are drawn up to
insure the efficient operation of the facility. Can the
competitors agree that they will only ship on pallets and
that they will only permit pick-ups for back haul on a truckload basis? These requirements, while quite reasonable in
terms of operational efficiency, come dangerously close to
the fringes of price since they affect the cost to purchasers.

Joint ventures might also be of interest to some of the
retail food chains, were it not for the risks imposed by the
antitrust laws. For example, many chains are installing delicatessen departments in their markets and then establishing central facilities to service the stores with product. These
facilities are expensive to construct and operate and require a
large volume of business to attain maximum efficiency. Several

_____

[10] *Associated Press v. United States*, 326 U. S. 1 (1945).

executives suggested to the writer that it would make good

economic sense for a number of retail food companies in an

area to operate such a facility jointly, thus avoiding

needless duplication of facilities and making possible a

higher volume operation. However, the overriding fear of the

antitrust laws has blocked any real investigation of the

feasibility of such a plan.

Since under present antitrust enforcement attitudes,

agreements among competitors are prima facie suspect, it is

understandable that businesmen, although cognizant of the

benefits which could accrue from joint ventures in terms of

increased productivity, are hesitant to run the risks in-

herent in such arrangements. This is particularly true of

the food industry where many large companies have already

been the subject of antitrust prosecutions and therefore tend

to be "gun-shy" with respect to cooperative ventures involving

competitors.

Cooperatives

Although the antitrust laws were supposedly enacted to

protect small business against the inroads of big business,

the fact is that much of the activity under these laws has

been directed against small businessmen who, through co-

operative action, are attempting to achieve some of the

advantages in productivity which large corporations already

enjoy. Thus, in one recent decision,[11] the Federal Trade

Commission held that a group of small jobbers, who set up a

---

[11]Southern California Jobbers, Inc., FTC Docket 6889 (1965).

distributing warehouse cooperative, could not lawfully receive
the manufacturer's discount of 20 per cent available to
regular warehouses. Commissioner Elman in his dissent warned
that this decision could have an adverse effect on many small
retailers in the food business who have formed cooperatives to
engage in wholesaling and distributive functions.

[The retail food industry is a highly competitive business with a narrow margin of profit remaining for retailers.]
If small grocers who band together in a cooperative warehousing
operation are going to be able to compete satisfactorily they
must be able to adopt the distribution techniques which enable
large chains to function so efficiently. One such technique
involves the billing out by the warehouse of orders on a computerized print-out basis which shows suggested retail prices.
This procedure, which is in common use by food chains and
independent wholesalers, enables the store to determine its
expected gross profit on that particular load and also provides the necessary data for maintenance of a retail inventory.
However, the Department of Justice has questioned the legality
of such a procedure where the warehouse is owned by cooperating
retailers since technically this amounts to an agreement among
competitors with respect to price.

The Franchise System

    The most significant development fostering small business
which has emerged since World War II is unquestionably the spread

of the franchise system. Under this procedure a small

businessman can put some capital into a business and have

the expertise of the franchisor assist him in purchasing,

site location, and other aspects of operation. In view of

the high mortality rate of small business, a system which

provides such assistance should be commended.

However, recent antitrust decisions are well on their

way to emasculating the franchise system. In the Schwinn

case, the United States Supreme Court declared illegal

per se an effort by a company operating in a competitive in-

dustry to restrict its outlets to the most efficient distri-

butors and thus to strengthen its distribution channels in

the competitive battle against large integrated sellers.[12]

We seem to be tending in a direction in which any

restrictions upon the freedom of the individual businessman

to buy or sell as he pleases will be deemed unlawful without

consideration of their reasonableness or their benefits to

the economy. This may satisfy some vague objective of pro-

hibiting "restrictions on alienation", but it makes little

sense in the complex business world. Reasonable restrictions

on a franchisee are a necessary part of the relationship in

order to protect the investment of the franchisor and to

compensate him for commitments made on behalf of the

franchisee.

---

[12] United States v. Arnold Schwinn & Co., 388 U.S. 365 (1967).

For example, in the food industry it is not uncommon
for wholesalers to select a site, put up a building, lease it
to an independent merchant and then require that he adhere to
certain aspects of a plan for affiliated merchants which involves maintaining certain standards of quality, participating
in advertising and promotional programs, and making a certain
amount of purchases from the wholesaler. Unquestionably
these provisions restrict the freedom of the store operator.
He undoubtedly would prefer that the wholesaler gratuitously
turn over the store to him and let him operate it the way he
wants to. But what would be the quid pro quo for the wholesaler doing so? The franchise system in the food industry
and in other industries involves restrictions, it is true;
but the entire system needs to be viewed in terms of its
effect upon productivity and efficiency in distribution.
Certainly it can make a major contribution to improvement of
the operation of the small businessman.

Productivity and Merger Policy

On May 30, 1968, the Department of Justice issued its so-
called "Merger Guides". Section I (10) provides that

....Unless there are exceptional circumstances the Department will not accept as a justification for an acqui-
sition normally subject to challenge under its horizontal
merger standards the claim that the merger will produce
economies (i.e. improvements in efficiency) because,
among other reasons,

    (i)   the Departments's adherence to the standards
            will usually result in no challenge being made
            to mergers of the kind most likely to involve
            companies operating significantly below the
            size necessary to achieve significant economies
            of scale;
    (ii)   Where substantial economies are potentially
            available to a firm, they can normally be
            realized through internal expansion; and
   (iii)   there usually are severe difficulties in
            accurately establishing the existence and
            magnitude of economies claimed in a merger.

The application of this rule to the food industry means,
in practical effect, that the Department will not consider
economies in distribution resulting from a merger. The Department's view, like that of the Federal Trade Commission, is
that in food manufacturing, the only relevant factor is the
size of plant and that generally because of the nature of the
business this will remain relatively small. In the case of
retail firms, the view apparently is that if the chain is
large enough to maintain one warehouse there are no economies
worth considering beyond that point. For both manufacturers
and retailers the Department of Justice is not interested in
examining the validity of claims that economies in distribution would follow from a merger.

This attitude does not conform with the facts of competitive life in the food business. It is time that our administrative agencies took proper account of the economies in
production and/or distribution that may flow from increased
size of operation. The effects of a merger upon productive
and distributive efficiency and the possible benefits to

consumers in the form of lower costs and prices should at
least be considered as an important criterion of lawful merger
activity.

Standards Setting by Industry Groups

Further application of the provisions of the Fair
Packaging and Labeling Act with respect to standardization
of package sizes as well as the possible decision by Congress
to "go metric" may lead to increased participation by industry groups in the coming decade in the process of setting
standards. As has already been indicated, such procedures
can contribute to improved efficiency and may also make comparisons in the market place more feasible for consumers. On
the other hand, there are cases in which standards setting
has been used by businessmen as a device to inhibit change
and indirectly to regulate price.

The Department of Justice has viewed with suspicion
any actions by businessmen to agree to standards where the
effect may prejudice smaller competitors. As a matter of
fact, the Department of Justice threatened to interfere with
agreements reached under the Fair Packaging and Labeling Act
and only a change in personnel and pressure from Congress
brought forth a more conciliatory viewpoint. Even in the
area of pollution abatement where other government agencies
have agreed that some degree of cooperation among competing
firms within an industry is desirable, Richard W. McLaren,
Assistant Attorney General in charge of the Justice Department's

Antitrust Division, has warned that such cooperation could "stray into anticompetitive arrangements."[13]

What is needed in this country is a basic change in attitude by officials entrusted with the administration of the antitrust laws toward the cooperative efforts of businessmen. If productivity improvement is to be given a high priority in our national objectives, businessmen should be encouraged to meet together and, subject to adequate safeguards to protect the public interest, to try to agree upon standards which will improve productivity in American industry.

Congressional decision that the United States should adopt the metric system may require further implementation of the standards-setting procedure, however. The procedures of the present leading standards organizations provide that no standard shall be approved if consensus is still lacking after efforts to resolve conflicts have been made. In a national metrication program the necessity for inter-industry coordination may require a mandated time schedule, however flexible, specifying certain final deadlines for adoption of standards in certain industries or product categories. Some procedure will have to be provided by government, either through an arbitration board or other means, to issue final rules on standards which cannot be resolved fully by mutual agreement. It is clear that private standards setting which seriously impairs the competitive position of individual companies

---

[13] Wall Street Journal, April 2, 1971, p. 3.

poses dangers which cannot be left to the action of private industry groups.

The Need for Reform

The foregoing brief analysis chronicles some of the ways in which the antitrust laws and the Robinson-Patman Act in particular inhibit the improvement of efficiency in our economy. Not only have the regulatory agencies and the courts given insufficient attention to the impact of these laws upon productivity, but also by an emphasis upon injury to individual competitors rather than to competition, they have sought to insulate from competition the least efficient firms in the economy.

Effective competition always hurts someone. Restraints by government on business policies aimed at achieving greater productivity only promote inefficiency. The goal of national policy should be effective competition, whether it results in competition among a few large companies or a large number of small companies. But this is not our policy today. What is needed is a complete re-examination of the antitrust laws with a view to determining how they can be revised so as to serve the needs of increased productivity while assuring the maintenance of a competitive society.

A nation, like a business, becomes great by using its assets to best advantage. The Japanese have taken a mono-polistic industrial structure, a paternalistic employer-

employee relationship, and aggressive management to build an
industrial complex which threatens our competitive position
in world trade. It is time that America took stock of its
assets.

The structure of most American industries is oligopolistic. For years this has been viewed as a taint, as if
atomistic competition were really the ideal. But a thousand
small companies cannot sit down together and agree upon a
standard pallet, nor upon the size of retail packs, nor can
they work out the intricate systems problems which are involved in the development and application of a Universal Product Code. Bigness in corporate size may, as some critics allege, inhibit intra-firm innovation and rapid change. However,
when the important consideration becomes inter-company cooperation in initiating complex system changes in the process
of physical distribution, there is little doubt that corporate
size and a small number of firms facilitate such developments.
In the struggle to improve our productivity, the oligopolistic nature of our major industries can be a boon—if we see
it as such and grasp the opportunity.

We are entering an era of voluntarism and cooperative
action, a decade when business should be encouraged to sit
down with government and work out cooperative arrangements in
the interests of improved productivity. If this is to be a
fulfilled promise rather than a lost opportunity, we must
change our attitudes toward bigness in industry and make government a partner rather than a prosecutor of business.

CHAPTER IX

LABOR AND PRODUCTIVITY

No review of the potential for increased productivity
would be complete in any industry without examination of the
labor input. The increased output per manhour generated by
patriotism during World War II and by Scanlan plans, profit-
sharing and other incentive arrangements attest to the
tremendous variation which is possible in human effort
applied to the daily job. If all employees in our economy
were induced to give 10 per cent more effort to their jobs,
it is doubtful if there would be any measurable increase in
fatigue or health problems, yet the increase in Gross National
Product would be enormous.

A major reason that employees do not step up the pace of
their work—whether they belong to unions or not—is the fear
that they will work themselves out of a job. The "lump of
labor" notion is deeply ingrained in the minds of American
labor. Therefore, when considering various restrictions imposed by organized labor on technological change and the
pace of work, it is important to recognize that the single
most important reason for labor's skeptical attitude toward
productivity is a deep-seated feeling of insecurity which
is continually nurtured by the fluctuating business cycle.

In theory, the area of employee motivation provides the
single greatest opportunity for increased productivity in this

nation's economy. Individual companies can attest to the increase in manhour output which has accompanied the successful
implementation of profit-sharing plans, job enrichment, and
other programs which seek to elicit greater involvement in his
job by the individual worker. In the economy as a whole, the
changes which are occurring in the nature of our labor force
make an understanding of employee motivation and needs more
important than ever before. Indeed, it is possible that without positive and constructive management programs to provide
job enrichment, greater employment security, and worker participation in operational decisions, the confluence in the years
ahead of a highly educated work force with a monotonous technology may produce an actual decline in manhour output, especially
in those manufacturing establishments where production line
specialization has reduced each job to highly repetitive dis-
crete functions.

Management emphasis, therefore, on employee motivation and
personnel relations generally is both necessary and desirable
as an essential ingredient in a national program to raise the
rate of productivity improvement. An analysis of management
efforts in this regard, however, lies outside the scope of this
text. This discussion will not dwell on such programs, not
because they are not important but simply because they raise a
host of problems and issues which cannot adequately be considered in the limited context of this volume. The emphasis

of this report is primarily focused upon the possibilities
for productivity improvement which can be achieved through
application of a systems approach in the area of physical
distribution.

In the following pages we shall direct out attention to
some of the union restrictions in the food industry which
directly affect the efficiency of the distribution system.
Although such restrictions represent an important aspect of
the productivity problem, they are only part of the problem
and must be viewed in proper perspective. Unions are not
responsible for proliferation of product or for the lack of
progress in developing the unit train or for the slow pace
of unitization of shipping loads or for many of the other
roadblocks to productivity which have been discussed thus
far in this report. Union officials have rationalizations
for restrictive union rules just as management officials
have justifications for product differentiation and proliferation. The fact is that productivity improvement is
not the primary goal of either group in guiding their
respective institutions.

The discussion of certain union rules and practices in
the following pages should not be interpreted as being "anti-
union" any more than the discussion of the inefficiencies in
unit-load handling is "anti-management". If we are interested
in improving productivity in the food industry we must be
ready to recognize impediments to efficiency wherever they

occur in the distribution system.

The precise impact of union rules upon efficiency is difficult to assess because very often organized companies will actually show higher productivity performance than nonunion firms. For example, in the retail food industry where union and nonunion markets may compete side by side, the organized stores are likely to show a higher level of labor productivity as measured by output per manhour, despite the incorporation in union contracts of various provisions restricting management's flexibility in use of the labor force. The higher cost of labor in organized markets compels management to control its use more rigorously. Thus, the level of physical productivity may be higher, but the level of customer service—which is not reflected in manhour statistics—may be less than in nonunion stores. However, unionized markets may be put at a substantial disadvantage relative to nonunion markets with respect to employee productivity if strict enforcement of the Clerks' Work Clause (discussed below) deprives the unionized stores of free vendor employee labor.

Some union contractual provisions may actually improve productivity. This may be true of union restrictions on the use of part-timers. Utilization of part-timers enables a store to meet peak demands without hiring full time personnel who may not be needed at less busy times. On the other hand, the excessive use of part-timers results in high labor turnover, indifferent work by young transient employees, and high training costs. Union and management spokesmen disagree on where the balance falls, but

it is possible that in the long run the creation of a mature
full-time labor force is more conducive to higher productivity.

Union Rules and the Supermarket Industry

Although many of the manufacturing concerns which supply
food stores are unionized, few reported to the writer any major
problems with unions with respect to practices inhibiting technological change or efficient utilization of the work force.
Practically all unionized manufacturing companies have senior-
ity rules, and these of course do restrict management's ability
to eliminate less efficient workers. But such provisions have
become part and parcel of the industrial jurisprudence of this
nation and progressive managers have come to agree with unions
that productivity must be viewed over a man's working life
as well as on an hourly basis.

The major problems with restrictive rules are encountered
in the retail sector and to some extent in warehousing and
delivery. It is therefore in these areas that this chapter will
focus attention. It is not surprising that in a supermarket
where two separate unions may represent different personnel
there is the greatest emphasis upon job classification and the
greatest restriction on interchange and flexibility in use of
the work force.

The supermarket industry is becoming a mature industry. As
such it is taking on certain of the characteristics of the railroad industry. The concept is well established—and the unions
continually seek to broaden and strengthen its application—

that certain employees in defined job classifications, in
effect, own specified work. A "bagger" cannot run a register
even if there are ten people in line and half the cashiers
are out sick! A supervisor cannot handle merchandise even
when an inventory is being taken and the store is closed.

Such rules have a decided impact upon productivity in
a supermarket operation because this still remains a labor
intensive industry. Over half of store level operating
costs consists of labor. Therefore, limits on effective
utilization of employees have a major impact upon profit
margins and service to customers. Furthermore, the peaks
and valleys in consumer demand make maximum flexibility in
use of personnel highly desirable to maintain service standards, but this is rendered extremely difficult by the excessive compartmentalization of employees created by union
contract provisions.

In the industry at the store level there are three major
unions involved: the Retail Clerks International Association,
the Amalgamated Meat Cutters and Butcher Workmen, and the
International Brotherhood of Teamsters, Chauffeurs, Warehousemen and Helpers. Generally the Meatcutters organize
meat personnel and the Retail Clerks the rest of the store.
However, in many cases any one of these unions may organize
the entire market on a so-called "wall-to-wall" agreement.
Teamster organization is concentrated in warehouses and among

deliverymen, whether employed by retailers, warehouses, or
vendors.

According to a recent study, about 60 per cent of companies
reporting to Super Market Institute are unionized to some degree
and these companies operate 88 per cent of all member supermarkets. The larger the company the more likely it is to be
organized. Among supermarket chains having sales of $100 million
or more per annum, virtually all are unionized in some of their
stores or divisions compared to only 39 per cent among the smallest
companies with annual sales under 2 million. Extent of union-
ization also varies regionally. In the Pacific region, nearly
all operators are organized. On the other hand, the Southeast
and New England have the fewest unionized companies.[1]

Types of Restrictive Practices

Restrictive practices in the supermarket industry include
rules which prevent management from utilizing the most efficient
methods, from introducing new technology and from utilizing the
workforce effectively. The provisions range from a local Teamster
requirement of a "helper" on a truck where one is not needed to
a local Meatcutters' ban on use of equipment not in use on
November 1, 1955. A determination as to whether or not such
provisions are reasonable requires a qualitative judgment which
necessarily reflects the bias of the viewer. Although the
writer, in the previous sentence, stated that the helper was
not "needed", the Teamster local in question would argue the

---

[1] The Super Market Industry Speaks, 1970, Twenty-Second Annual
Report of Super Market Institute, p. 30 .

point adamantly. Is such a provision an example of feather-

bedding or a legitimate exercise of the union's concern for

the health and safety of its members? As one writer has pointed

out, there is only a fine line between what is featherbedding,

what is restriction on output, and what is the protection to

the employee or a proper benefit for his labor.[2]

The impact of a restrictive work practice ought to be examined

not only from the point of view of a particular store or company,

but also from the point of view of the industry at large. This

is particularly true of the "Clerks' Work Clause" of the Retail

Clerks International Association. This clause states that all

work in the store relating to the categories of merchandise covered

by the union contract can be performed only by members of the union.

It has long been the practice for companies which sell

beverages, cookies, housewares, and other products to have their

drivers or salesmen stock the store shelves with the company's

products. The vendor believes that his own man will be more con-

scientious about seeing that shelves are fully stocked and that

perishable product is rotated than will store employees with

many other responsibilities. The usual form of the Clerks'

Work Clause bans such in-store work by vendor employees except

for a few departments such as cookies and crackers. However,

in recent negotiations, the Retail Clerks Union has been

attempting to eliminate all vendor in-store stocking of mer-

chandise.

---

[2] Herbert R. Northrup, Restrictive Labor Practices in the
Supermarket Industry (Philadelphia: University of
Pennsylvania Press ,1967),p. 71,

How does such a clause affect productivity? For the
unionized store operator, it means that he must now assign
this work to members of the bargaining unit who are on the
store payroll. The impact upon the store therefore is usually
a reduction in productivity measured by the usual manhour output indexes. From the point of view of the food industry,
however, all that has happened is a transfer of work from the
driver or salesman to the store clerk. The overall effect upon
productivity will depend upon a number of complex factors. For
example, the vendor may not be able to reduce his complement
of drivers or salesmen as a result of the shift in the stocking function. The driver must still deliver the merchandise
to the store. Often he will have to wait while stale merchandise is removed by the clerk from the shelf. From this point
of view a significant part of the driver's time can be wasted.
Furthermore, certain items such as housewares are small and
quite unlike grocery products in nature. The store clerk may
be less efficient in stocking such items than the vendor salesman who does it all day.

Thus, from the point of view of both the individual store
and the industry at large, strict application of the Clerks'
Work Clause may reduce productivity, at least as long as the
items continue to be direct store-door delivered. However,
if the entire distribution method were to be changed with the
product moving to the chain or wholesaler warehouse and then
to the store, considerable savings might be effected, although

it is possible that perishable items such as cookies and crackers
might not be rotated as well as they are today by salesmen.

There are other considerations in this already complex area.
From the point of view of the industry it is certainly inefficient
to require a salesman, who may be earning $15,000 a year, to per-
form a function such as stocking shelves which can be done by
a stock boy. However, this consideration relates to the cost
of the function rather than to physical productivity which has
been our major concern.

Likewise, many retail concerns dislike having vendor salesmen come into the store to stock shelves because of the risk of
higher pilferage created by this practice. The Clerks' restriction
may improve the store's gross margin by reducing pilferage loss,
but at the same time it can reduce productivity for the reasons
discussed.

The impact of various union contractual provisions upon
productivity is complex and may lead to different conclusions
depending upon whether we are looking at a particular company
or the industry at large. Furthermore, although certain provisions may reduce physical productivity, there may be offsetting
advantages which do not register in manhour output statistics.

In the following brief discussion, the writer has selected
a few of the more extreme provisions which are found in some
local contracts in the industry. Their inclusion in this analysis
does not indicate that they are necessarily unreasonable from the
point of view of the union, but rather that their impact upon
productivity is obvious and substantial.

1) As was indicated in Chapter VI, one of the most
promising developments in the supermarket industry in terms
of potential for increased productivity is the centralized
warehouse cutting and pre-packing of meat. In many cities
of the nation, companies have negotiated this issue with
locals of the Amalgamated Meatcutters and have been able to
work out some viable transitional arrangement. A common
basis for agreement is that no meatcutters shall lose their
jobs as a result of the change-over; meatcutters shall be
employed at the central warehouse without loss of pay; and
at least one meatcutter will be maintained in each store for
a specified period of time. Such a settlement, while depriving
management of the full labor-saving potential of the innovation, nevertheless makes sense in conserving the skill and
earning capacity of the members of this skilled trade.

Although officials of the International Union have not
opposed central meatcutting operations, some locals have taken
an adamant position against this development. This is said to
be the situation in Chicago and St. Louis. In Chicago, the
union will not permit centralized processing of retail packages
of fresh meat or even block-ready cuts. In St. Louis, the
Meatcutters' local for many years prevented organized markets
from purchasing prepackaged luncheon meats from independent
packers and still bars prepackaged poultry or red meat from
stores under its jurisdiction.

The union contract negotiated with a number of the retail
food chains in St. Louis provided in effect that all meat had

to be cut, weighed, sliced and wrapped on the premises, "except, however, the Employees covered by this Agreement will handle those items that were prepared and packed off the premises prior to October 2, 1950." As a consequence of the interpretation given this clause, supermarkets covered by this contract were unable to take advantage of the progress made by packers in pre-packaging many kinds of specialized meat products in the period since 1950. Finally in 1969, as a result of a settlement of a law suit brought by a number of retail food chains against Meat-cutters' Local No. 88, a stipulation was entered into which permits the purchase of prepackaged luncheon meats by the markets but still bars the prepackaging off the premises of red meat and poultry.

2) In Chicago, a customer going into a supermarket after 6:00 P.M. finds that the fresh meat case in the meat department is covered over with a board. Even though packaged fresh meat may be in the case, and even though the meatcutter has already been paid for the labor embodied in the package of meat in the case, the store is forbidden to sell it. This restriction affects output, in the form of meat sales, in an obvious and direct manner. The origin of this re-striction dates back to a time when there were many small meat markets in the city. The independent owners of these markets did not want to work evenings and joined with the union in incorporating such a prohibition in contracts which also became applicable to chain supermarkets. Today, despite a change in consumer shopping habits with more

and more shopping at night, consumers in Chicago are not
accorded the same privileges as customers in stores in other
cities of the United States. Jewel Tea Company, a Chicago-
based supermarket chain, sought to have this clause declared
unlawful, but after lengthy litigation the prohibition was
upheld by the Supreme Court as a lawful exercise of union
bargaining rights.[3]

3) As was indicated in Chapter V, many large retailers
and wholesalers are attempting to eliminate inefficient direct
deliveries to stores and to handle these products instead
through the warehouse where the items in question can be consolidated with other products and shipped in a full load to
the store. A major barrier to such a change-over is presented
by union contracts with vendors which provide that driver-
salesmen for such items as milk and other beverages and bakery
products shall be paid a commission on all products delivered
to particular stores in their respective territories, whether
or not the driver himself makes the delivery. As a consequence,
if a vendor agrees to deliver in one large load to a chain's
warehouse, he will still be liable to pay commissions to his
drivers whether they service the stores or not. As a result
of this kind of provision, bakery drivers in Washington, D.C.
earn over $20,000 per year. Similarly processors of smoked and
packaged processed meats have been loath to enter into consolidated

---

[3]Local 189, Amalgamated Meat Cutters v. Jewel Tea Co.
381 U.S. 676 (1965).

delivery arrangements which would eliminate the present
inefficient direct store door delivery pattern, because although delivery would be made to one central distribution
facility the processor would still be liable for payment of
commission to the drivers to whose stores the meat was ultimately delivered.

The union driver commission provision has had three
adverse repercussions:

a) It has inhibited the development of more efficient
distribution arrangements.

b) It has stimulated the duplication of facilities.
Since chains have been barred from handling the branded products
of vendors through their warehouses, they have been encouraged
to build their own facilities to produce private label.

c) These arrangements have added significantly to the
cost of food for items such as bread for which the already
high distribution margin has been the subject of continuing
criticism and investigation by Congress, the FTC, and the
National Commission on Food Marketing.

Recommendations for Action

The foregoing represents only a few of the union rules
and restrictions which supermarket executives, in interviews
with the writer, listed as having an inhibiting effect upon
productivity in distribution. In many cases they represent
the result of local practices and local demands which may be

quite inconsistent with national patterns and may, in fact,

be frowned upon by International Union officials. Nevertheless,

they do exist and once they have become part of the fabric of

collective bargaining contracts they are difficult to remove,

even though the reason for their existence may have long since

passed from the economic scene.

Can anything be done to eliminate such restrictions or to

lessen their inhibiting effect upon productivity? Management's

first reaction is to urge government to "pass a law". However,

it seems clear that this is not the way to deal with such

problems. Indeed our experience with legislation in this field

is an object lesson of the failure of this approach.

Section 8 (b) (6) of the Taft-Hartley Law makes it an un-

fair labor practice for a union to "cause or attempt to cause

an employer to pay or deliver or agree to pay or deliver any

money or thing of value, in the nature of an exaction, for

services which are not performed or not to be performed."

Despite the Congressional intent in enacting this provision,

the United States Supreme Court has held that this language

does not prohibit the International Typographical Union from

insisting on "bogus" work—that is the reproduction of adver-

tisements which have already been set and have already appeared

in print.[4]   Nor does it apparently prohibit the American

---

[4]American Newspaper Publishers Association v. NLRB,
    73 Sup. Ct. 552 (1953).

Federation of Musicians from forcing a local theater to pay local musicians to stand by while a name band plays for the audience.[5]

The Lea Act of 1946 was passed to outlaw a number of the restrictive practices and featherbedding measures adopted by James Caesar Petrillo, then President of the American Federation of Musicians. The Act may have had some effect on the practices of this Union, but Mr. Petrillo managed to escape liability for violation of the Act.[6]

The factors entering into the development of the myriad of make-work rules and restrictions which honeycomb American industry are too complex to be encompassed by a single law. Nor is any Board or tribunal gifted with such wisdom that it can substitute its judgment for that of labor and management in dealing with such restrictions.

What affirmative action can then be taken in this critical area? To attempt to cope with such restrictions directly by legislative fiat is politically infeasible and administratively impractical. It is therefore suggested that the problem be dealt with by indirection on the basis of (a) restoration of a balance of bargaining power; (b) exposure to public opinion; and (c) education of workers.

---

[5]NLRB v. Gamble Enterprises Inc., 73 Sup. Ct. 560 (1953).

[6]See Northrup, op. cit., p. 145.

Restoration of the Balance of Power

Restrictive labor provisions, like excessive wage increases, are incorporated in union contracts because employers
are too weak to resist them. As has been pointed out earlier,
this is a very real problem in the supermarket industry where
many companies simply cannot risk a lengthy strike because
of the tremendous losses which could be incurred. The nature
of the business, the over-capacity which exists in the industry, the fact that nonunion competition exists in many areas
and would benefit by a strike of organized companies—all
of these factors put the organized supermarket operator at
a disadvantage in his bargaining relations with unions.

The retail food business is unlike the coal industry or
the steel industry. The latter can stock pile output and
make up lost sales after a strike has ended. By contrast,
the business that a supermarket loses is lost forever. More
serious is the fact that the loss of market position suffered
by a company whose stores are closed for months may take
years to recoup. [The losses which a retail food chain incurs
by a strike have to be measured not only by the decline in
sales revenue during the strike period but also by the
additional costs which must be incurred once the strike
has ended to woo customers back to their former shopping
habits.

Strikes can now be so prolonged that even if management wins in principle it may lose economically. A number
of factors have strengthened the staying power of unions
in industrial conflicts: the power of the picket line,
state laws prohibiting use of "strike-breakers", availability of welfare payments and food stamps to strikers,
union strike benefits, and so forth. As a consequence,
the damage that a prolonged strike can do to the business
of a food chain can in some circumstances far exceed the
economic injury sustained by the individual union members.
Management must weigh these risks in determining whether
or not to accede to union demands. All too often the line
of reasoning taken runs as follows: "If I fight for
principle, I will lose my business; if I yield, the chances
are that my competitors will eventually have to give the
same benefit, so we all will be in the same boat together."
Such logic, reflecting the realities of union bargaining
power in a competitive market place, inevitably leads to a
multiplication of bad settlements—bad in the sense that
they permit onerous work restrictions to be incorporated in
union contracts or provide for wage adjustments far in excess
of the rate of productivity improvement.

Direct governmental restrictions seeking to regulate

rules or wage adjustments are unworkable and inimical to
the long run health of collective bargaining. In the retail
food industry—and perhaps in other industries selling
perishable products—an indirect way of slowing the rate
of introduction of union rules which impair productivity
would be to strengthen management's bargaining power. Some
stiffening of the employer's position without substantial
detriment to the union position could be achieved through
the following measures:

1) The right of employers to bargain through employer
   associations should be affirmed and strengthened.
   If employers have elected to bargain jointly through
   an association, the union should be compelled to
   honor such agreement and to deal with the association,
   whether or not there has been a past practice in
   this regard. The rule laid down by the NLRB which
   permits a union to serve a sixty-day notice on an
   employer group and require bargaining on an individual company basis despite a long history of multi-
   employer bargaining should be rescinded.[7]

2) Strike and picketing action should be limited to the
   area actually covered by the bargaining unit involved
   in the dispute. If a retail food chain has stores

---

[7]Evening News Assoc. 154 NLRB No. 121 (1965).

in Florida and California, as well as in New York,
and a dispute develops between the company and a
union with respect to wages, hours and working conditions of employees covered by the New York local,
the union ought not to be able to picket stores in
other areas in a manner which interferes with shipments to those stores or ingress to or egress from the
stores. Such action unduly enlarges the area of
industrial conflict and in effect permits a small
group of union members to exact extreme concessions
by imposing heavy losses on a chain-wide basis. Of
course, no restriction should be placed on simple in-
formational picketing by the union which does not
interfere with store operation in other areas.

3) If a strike is called, a food company should be given
at least 72 hours to dispose of perishable product
before the strike action becomes final. Loss of
perishable product in warehouses or stores can be
huge in the event of a walkout. The nature of the
food business requires special protection in this
regard to avoid losses of perishable food which
cannot be carried over in inventory.

4) The good faith bargaining section of the Taft-Hartley
Law—Section 8 (d)—should be enforced by the NLRB
with the same vigor against unions as it has been

against employers. Unions should be obligated to
bargain about prohibitions against technological
change—such as the St. Louis restriction on
processed meats—which affect managerial rights,
just as employers are now compelled to bargain
about decisions such as sub-contracting, which
affect employee rights.

Exposure to Public Opinion

Publication of reports by fact-finding boards is a common
and generally ineffectual device for dealing with problems in
the labor field. For example, in the railroad industry, numerous and repeated Congressional hearings and reports of arbitration boards have not been notably successful in eroding
union make-work tactics even though considerable publicity
has been given to union practices and demands. Perhaps public
apathy stems from the fact that the railroad is relatively
remote to the lives of most Americans.

The food industry, however, is a matter of vital concern
to every housewife. It is possible therefore that exposure
of certain practices to the light of public opinion might
arouse sufficient wrath on the part of housewives that pressure
would be felt by union members and officials to change restrictive practices which ultimately have an adverse effect upon
food prices and the service provided by supermarkets.

In the food industry, therefore,—and perhaps in certain

other industries as well—there would be some value in
establishing a Board of Productivity, staffed on a tripartite
basis with labor, industry, and public members, which could
hear management grievances on major labor restrictions.
The function of the Board would have to be limited to hear
only major issues since otherwise the Board would be inun-
dated with a plethora of petty complaints which should be
resolved by the parties without recourse to such an administrative procedure. Such a Board should not have any power to
enter any order respecting a provision in a union contract;
it could merely make public its findings of fact.

However, the power and influence of the Board could be
broadened by giving it the authority, in exceptional cases,
to recommend that the employer involved in the dispute have
access to a government established buy-out fund. This would
be a fund established by an appropriate agency in government
to assist various companies or industries to eliminate
practices that impose major obstacles to significant potential improvements in productivity. Such funds could be made
available to employers on a long term loan basis at low
interest rates. Unlike a continuing subsidy, allocation would
be on a one-time basis. For years our government has paid
individual farmers to restrict production. Perhaps now in
this era of inflation it would make good sense to assist
business to increase production.

A condition of access to such a fund might be an agreement

by management that part or all of the net reduction in costs
effected would be reflected in lower prices to buyers.   In
England, the so-called 1965 White Paper dealing with productivity bargaining under an incomes policy required that "some
of the benefits from proposed productivity agreements should
accrue to the community as a whole in the form of lower prices."[8]

Of course there are obvious problems in such a procedure.
If organized labor knows that there is a governmental fund
ready to buy out wasteful practices, it may be tempted to
devise new and more costly work practices which then can be
"sold" for a price. Likewise, employers who have already
bought their way out of a bad contract provision may feel it
inequitable that competitors should have access to a low
interest fund to accomplish the same objective. Such a fund
should be sparingly used. However, it could add a valuable
resource in the arsenal of weapons available to modify and
eliminate restrictive work rules in industry.

Education of Workers

Many union officials are concerned about the increasing
belligerence of union members and the extreme demands which
are emanating from union membership meetings. There is little
that union officials can do to convince members that such
demands are unsound, because too conciliatory an attitude
towards the employer's problems may result in a more vocal

---

[8] Lloyd Ulman, "Collective Bargaining and Industrial Efficiency",
in R. E. Caves, ed. Britain's Economic Prospects
(Washington, D.C.: The Brookings Institution, 1968), p. 367.

member replacing the official in his post at the next union

election. This is particularly a problem in the retail food

industry where 50-60 per cent of employees in bargaining

units are part-timers, many of them youths, who have very

little long-term interest in the company for which they are

working and know little about the basic economics of the

industry.

In this situation, union officials privately have told

the writer that they would appreciate "the facts of economic

life" being communicated to employees by some governmental

source. One of the basic problems which employers face in

bargaining with respect to wages, for example, is that em-

ployees have no conception of the percentage of profit which

the business makes after taxes. It has been the writer's

experience that most employees will estimate profits after

taxes to represent about 10 to 20 per cent of the sales

dollar whereas in the food industry they constitute only

one per cent.

Even though our workforce is better educated than ever

before in our history, the fact remains that most Americans

have little understanding of economics and the interrelation-

ship of productivity, output, costs and prices. In the long run,

the most useful function that a permanent National Commission

on Productivity can perform is to educate the American
worker to the meaning and significance of productivity in
American economic life. The employer cannot do this; whatever figures he may issue are immediately suspect. Interest-
ingly, employee misunderstanding of the level of profits seems
to be as prevalent in public companies as in private, even
though in the former every employee may receive a copy of
the company's annual statement showing neatly the small percentage of the dollar which the company has retained as after-
tax profit.

Any educational campaign attempted by the National Commission
must be well-conceived if it is to be even moderately successful.
The starting point must be a recognition that productivity is
a dirty word in labor circles. It has been associated too much
in the worker's mind with the stretch-out, and time studies, and
displacement of labor. In the last few years, productivity has
been used as a reason why employees should not get wage adjustments to which they believe they are entitled. Perhaps a new
approach is needed using a concept which is less emotionally charged

Such an approach might be based on the concept of real wages
and real income. In a period of inflation, workers—and in particular unionized workers—have become acutely conscious that they
are on a treadmill seeking to maintain the purchasing power of
their money incomes. Perhaps this lesson can be used to drama-
tize the need for action which will make possible higher real
wages and a bigger pie to divide among all Americans.

If union officials and union members could interest themselves in improving productivity, they could serve as a medium
for publicizing new methods, new equipment, and new procedures
throughout an industry. A substantial improvement could be
achieved in the overall rate of productivity advance in an
industry if we could find a way to bring less efficient firms
in line with the most efficient in terms of operating practices
or at the very least to reduce the lag which presently exists
between the time of introduction of improved practices by the
most advanced companies in an industry and the final adoption
of such new methods by all firms within the industry.

A union such as the Meatcutters or the Retail Clerks has a
communications network which could be used to spread information
about new methods and new equipment throughout the retail food
industry. Although most major breakthroughs—such as the automatic checkout—are well publicized in the trade press, there
are many lesser developments which are not generally known but
which nevertheless make for more efficient operation. While
employers may wish to keep new improvements of this type confidential so as not to benefit competition, unions should have an
interest in making all organized employers as efficient as
possible; for it is only if the organized sector of the industry
is kept healthy and profitable that the union can in the long
run continue to win gains for its members.

CHAPTER X

SUMMARY AND RECOMMENDATIONS

The food industry contains the potential for a substantial acceleration in the rate of productivity advance in the decade of the seventies. However, the various institutional, legal, and systems barriers are such that it is unlikely that the actual rate of change in manhour output will vary materially from that in past years unless government promotes a more rapid rate of progress by adopting appropriate affirmative policies. It is sobering to consider that in the entire period from 1929 to 1958 which was marked by one of the most revolutionary changes in the long history of food distribution—the transition from service to self-service stores—the rate of improvement in manhour output in food wholesaling and retailing averaged only 2.8 per cent per annum.[1] The coming decade will require truly significant breakthroughs in organization and technology if there is to be any marked acceleration in the rate of increase of manhour output, for the continuous proliferation of product variety will exercise a downward drag on productivity at all levels of the industry.

The food industry is the largest industry in the nation. Furthermore, the products purchased in supermarkets form a major component of the cost of living for most Americans and

---

[1] Output per Man-Hour in Distributing Foods of Farm Origin. U.S.Department of Agriculture, Economic Research Service, Technical Bulletin No. 1335, April, 1965, p. v.

therefore a rise in their cost has a widely felt impact on the
rate of inflation. Since there is evidence that the size of
wage adjustments currently being negotiated in the food industry
is probably in excess of that occurring in the economy at large,
and in view of other inflationary factors affecting the price
of food, it would seem to be in the public interest for government to consider what positive steps might be taken to stimulate
productivity improvement in this industry.

We cannot pass a law to give us greater productivity. Rates
of productivity change are deeply imbedded in existing technological and organizational systems and do not respond easily to outside action. To accelerate the rate of improvement in productivity
in the food industry will take time, and patience, and planning.
Programs must be adopted which will extend over long periods of
years and will not be disrupted by the change in political admin-
istrations.

The role of government should be to lead, not to manage; to
develop a climate in which business can look to government for cooperation in solving complex problems; and to foster better lines
of communications with business on productivity matters. In no
other highly industrialized country is there such a barrier of
mistrust and misunderstanding as exists today between business
and government in the United States. The first step toward higher
productivity is to break down this barrier.

In the last analysis, a more rapid rate of productivity advance can only be produced through business initiative. Business
must supply the ideas, but government can assist by supplying the

organizational structure which will foster the setting of new
goals and the generation of a creative systems approach to the
solution of productivity problems.

A procedural device which would be helpful as a beginning
would be to follow the consultative system developed under the
Fair Packaging and Labeling Act and to appoint industry productivity task forces. Such task forces could meet in conjunc-
tion with labor and consumer representatives and draw up goals
for productivity improvement based upon their knowledge of the
developments within the particular industry. Out of the com-
bination of various voluntary industry goals could come a
national objective of achieving, say, a five per cent annual
improvement factor. The first such industry task force ought
to be established in the food industry.

However, in order for such groups to function effectively,
government would first have to commit itself to a wide-ranging
program in support of increased productivity which should include the following specific measures:

Research

There is an urgent need for increased research effort with
respect to the possibilities of improving productivity through
implementation of system economies in distribution. Relatively
little research has been undertaken in the past in this industry
and therefore there is no information bank of basic data on which
to rely in attempting to make decisions as to whether or not
certain policies will produce quantifiable improvement in manhour
output. Some of the necessary research should be undertaken by

trade associations, individual companies, and other private groups. Other projects, however, are so complex and have so many inter-relationships with other industries that they are beyond the scope of privately financed research effort. For example, the question of what benefits, if any, would flow from standardization of carton sizes could only be undertaken by a quasi-governmental agency with authority to relate such research to ongoing projects in other agencies and industries dealing with the metric system, size of railroad cars, size of containers, etc.

A number of research projects suggest themselves which would provide useful data as part of an overall program to improve productivity in the food industry. Such projects include the following:

1) An investigation of the soundness of current measurement techniques for productivity in the food industry which would attempt to answer some of the conceptual questions raised in this report. Total factor productivity indexes should be developed and compared with conventional labor productivity indexes to ascertain the degree of discrepancy which will be likely to develop between the two measures during the coming decade as a result of more intensive capital utilization. Consideration should also be given to the concept of social productivity and the extent to which indexes should reflect the impact of industry actions upon the general public.

2) A study building upon research already underway at the American National Standards Institute which would set up a long run goal of a modular distribution system in which carton sizes, pallet dimensions, container sizes and dimensions of trucks and

railroad cars would be compatible. Such a study should seek to quantify projected savings in distribution costs as well as resulting diseconomies. In addition, consideration should be given to incentives or cost penalties which may be necessary in order to move the industry in the direction of standardization if cost-benefit analysis indicates this is desirable.

3) If Congress decides that the United States should adopt the metric system, an inquiry as to the advisability of using the change-over period as a means of achieving greater standardization in retail package sizes, and, if so, in what respects.

4) An experimental study in some metropolitan area applying simulation and other operations research techniques to determine whether a central clearing house to which shippers would direct their trucking needs could achieve better utilization of trucking capacity and reduce empty ton-miles.

Such research projects ought not to be conducted on a haphazard basis. There is a need for coordination of effort and for interchange of information. Such a function could be performed by the National Commission on Productivity or a permanent food industry committee on research in productivity.

Tax Policy

Technological change in the food industry during the decade of the seventies will involve developments which are so capital intensive that without some tax relief it is questionable whether an industry operating on such a low margin of profit and with a declining rate of return on investment will be able to shoulder the burden of investment required to adopt the innovations which

are now in view. Reinstatement of the investment credit is, of
course, helpful. However, additional tax relief may be required
if the present downward trend in profit margins continues.

Labor

Because of the vulnerability of the retail and wholesale
food industry to strike action, specific legislative changes
should be considered which would strengthen the bargaining
power of employers. In particular, bargaining through employer
associations should be facilitated, special provisions should
be enacted to protect firms against loss of perishable products,
and picketing action which interferes with operations should be
limited to the locus of the principal dispute. A special Productivity Board should be set up to hear disputes with respect
to major contractual impediments to productivity improvement.
As an ancillary to such a Board, a special fund should be provided which in exceptional cases could be used to make low
interest loans to employers to buy out labor practices which
retard productivity improvement.

Unions should be encouraged to use their communications
network to spread information about new methods and new techniques throughout the industry. Whereas it may be in the
interest of an individual company to keep a new labor-saving
method confidential so as not to benefit competition, unions
have an interest in making all employers as efficient as
possible. If we could bring up the level of productivity of
the least efficient firms in the industry to the standard of
performance of the most efficient, there would be a tremendous

improvement in the rate of productivity advance for the industry as a whole.

Antitrust

A new rule of reason is called for by government in relation to big business. It should be recognized that an oligopolistic industry structure can facilitate the implementation of systems improvements in physical distribution. The role of franchising as a legitimate arrangement with mutually advantageous restrictions should be affirmed through appropriate legislation. Joint ventures and cooperative arrangements designed to share facilities and otherwise improve efficiency should be encouraged, whether the participants are large or small companies. Merger guidelines for large companies should be revised so as to include the effect upon efficiency as one of the relevant considerations in the determination of the lawfulness of the merger.

The opinion rendered by the FTC in the General Foods case with respect to back hauls under a delivered price system should be rescinded as a direct barrier to greater efficiency in transportation. The Commission should be encouraged to relax its requirements for the showing of a cost-saving defense. A policy statement should be issued by the Commission indicating that where improvement in efficiency can be demonstrated, arrangements between suppliers and large buyers with unique facilities will not be considered discriminatory.

Transportation

The Interstate Commerce Commission should encourage development of an experimental unit train which could serve the food

industry as well as manufacturers of other commodities. If
such a service were inaugurated, private interests have indicated
their willingness to proceed with construction of the necessary
intermodal terminals.

The unit train is a viable concept which has demonstrated
its effectiveness in other industries. General Motors Corporation
dispatched its first unit train from Chicago to Los Angeles on
March 20, 1970. Today General Motors has four daily unit trains
in service between various points. According to Edward N. Cole,
President of General Motors Corporation, the unit train has
halted a ten-year rise in transit damage and substantially reduced in-transit time across the country.[2] The same benefits
can accrue to the food industry from the development of unit
trains to serve its needs. The current extreme rise in East
Coast cities of the cost of produce gives additional emphasis
to the need for reducing transportation costs which constitute
such a large proportion of the total cost of perishable agricultural products originating on the West Coast.

The Interstate Commerce Commission should also investigate
the problem of truck detention, not with a view to imposing
stricter standards, but rather with the objective of determining
how the present wasteful loss of time can be reduced. The possibility of extending the appointment system to less than truckload lots should be considered.

---

[2] General Motors Corporation, Press Release, January 27, 1972.

Miscellaneous Governmental Regulations

If government is interested in improving productivity in industry, it must realize that the proliferation of laws and regulations which take time for compliance and enforcement erodes productivity just as does the proliferation of product discussed in this report. Before new laws and regulations are passed, their cost impact in terms of efficiency ought to be weighed carefully against the benefits expected.

A case in point is the Department of Transportation order effective December 31, 1967 which provides that a vehicle carrying explosives, dangerous articles or other hazardous material must carry shipping papers giving a detailed description of every item which is explosive or flammable and naming the chemicals involved. Technically this regulation covers items shipped to supermarkets such as aerosol cans, bleaches, charcoal, and other items. The National Association of Food Chains has developed data which shows that in 3,300,000 dispatches of food chain trucks there were only 25 fires and not one originated from the merchandise being carried.

The regulation provides an exemption which would cover most loads in the food business, but requires that shipping papers must nevertheless be prepared listing the items "by administratively prescribed names" and providing other information. The preparation of such shipping papers for millions of shipments where statistical data indicate no real risk exists imposes unnecessary clerical tasks upon firms in the food industry and reduces productivity.

A major contribution could be made by government to the improvement of productivity in industry if each government department would review its regulations and question (a) whether or not they are really necessary; and (b) whether their coverage can be narrowed without detriment to the public interest.

Education

In the long run, the most important function of a permanent National Commission on Productivity would be to promote a broad understanding of the importance of productivity to the welfare of our nation. The goal, which could be monitored by public opinion testing on a year-to-year basis, would be to develop a constantly increasing proportion of the population which understood the relation of profits to business income, the inter-relationship of wages, productivity and unit labor cost, and other basic economic principles. We are today reaping the harvest of a long history of economic illiteracy in our nation. Perhaps the Commission can serve as a source of reliable information which might be used throughout our educational system and in particular in the labor force. Ultimately we must develop an understanding among our workers as to the essential function of profits in fueling the productivity machine.

The Road Ahead

As has been reiterated many times in this report, productivity ought not to be set up as a national goal without a full understanding of its limitations and of the problems it may produce. Certainly a productivity program should have as an essential

component a companion program of adequate subsidies, payments
and retraining for employees who may be dislocated as a result
of an acceleration in technological change. Although particular
groups may have some fear of the consequences of such a commitment to productivity, the end result should have broad support,
for, if successful, it can provide the increase in Gross National
Product which is needed to improve the lot of the disadvantaged
in our society. The Council of Economic Advisers has estimated
that if we could increase the rate of productivity growth by one-
tenth of one per cent per year, we could produce 15 billion dollars
of additional output per year by the end of this decade.[3]

The United States is rapidly becoming a have-not nation.
The abundant natural resources which made us a great industrial
power are slowly but surely being exhausted. In such a situation,
we cannot afford to be an inefficient nation.

We can meet the challenge of low cost output from other
nations by erecting tariff walls or paying industry subsidies;
if we take this path we shall reward inefficiency and pave the
way to our becoming a second-class industrial power. Or we can
meet these challenges by utilizing our management and labor skills
to the fullest and assume a major national commitment to accelerate the rate of improvement in our productivity. Such a program
will not cure inflation; it will require time and patience and
cooperation among all the elements in our economic structure.
But in the long run it is the only program that can guarantee
a rising standard of living for the American people.

---

[3] *Economic Report of the President*, February, 1971, p. 91.

The Need for a Systems Approach

The slowdown in rate of productivity advance which has characterized American industry during the past five years has led to some speculation that we may as a nation be running out of technological steam and that it will be difficult to achieve an accelerated rate of productivity growth in the years ahead. This diagnosis may well be true if we cling to our past practice of seeking productivity improvement primarily in the intra-company orbit. However, in the inter-firm locus—in the vast wasteland of uncoordinated activity which lies outside the corporate door—there are abundant opportunities for improving labor productivity if we will only adapt our vision and our capabilities to exploit them.

The main thrust of this book has been that the greatest improvements in productivity in the food industry can be brought about only through a cooperative systems approach among various sectors of the industry. The same admonition applies to other major industries in our economy. The systems approach has demonstrated its efficacy in improving productivity within in-dividual departments of companies, within entire plants, and is now being extended by many companies to the control of physical distribution in and among the varied plants and facilities of a multi-unit firm. The next logical stage in the extension of the systems approach would seem to be the inter-firm relationship within an industry. The problems of making and implementing systems-oriented decisions among separate corporate entities within the confines of our legal structure are fraught with

difficulty. But the opportunities for productivity improvement
are enormous. While managers have been concentrating on applying the most advanced techniques to improve output per manhour
within facilities subject to their control, they have ignored
the effect of their action upon other units within the industry
system. The result has been an appalling degree of waste within
the system as a whole.

The basic idea which has motivated the gradual extension of
the systems approach has been that integrated system performance
will produce an end result greater than that from non-coordinated
performance. Management has come to recognize that even though
individual components of a total system are each working at top
efficiency they will not necessarily generate maximum efficiency
for the company as a whole. In its handling of pallet sizes and
container sizes, the food industry presents some graphic examples
of how fragmented actions in a competitive industry can generate
high productivity within individual facilities yet create inefficiency on a broad scale when the industry is viewed as a
total system.

The Changing Nature of Technology

The locus of opportunities for major breakthroughs in productivity improvement is changing in this country. We as a
nation must be flexible enough in our concept of business and
government relationships to exploit this changed situation. Not
only are the major inefficiencies in the inter-corporate orbit,
but the nature of technological progress itself may be changing
so as to require uniform industry action as a condition of

utilization of major innovations. A number of significant technological developments—some already applied and others on the
horizon—can only be feasible if introduced on an overall industry
basis. Examples are the computer-readable check in the banking
industry, the elimination of stock certificates in the securities
business, and the universal code and automatic checkout in the
food industry.

Experience so far with the development process for the
universal code has demonstrated the benefit of planning and the
need for standardization. In Europe, where there was no centralized planning with respect to merchandise codes as among nations,
two separate and distinct codes have developed in the food
industry—one in Germany and one in France. They are not compatible and the Common Market now has one more complex problem
to unravel. The lesson is that technology which runs off in all
directions at once may have been satisfactory for a less complex
economy, but it will not necessarily meet the needs of the future.
This is not to suggest that all technological improvements require
standardization or that limits should be placed on the initiative
of individual inventors to design new and better systems which
may conflict with old established ones. What is needed is some
mechanism whereby an industry can discuss, appraise, and implement
various improvements on a uniform basis without fear of government
antitrust action.

In the next few years there will be much discussion about
the need to increase governmental and industry research and
development expenditures in order to stimulate productivity.

Perhaps at the same time there should be consideration of how given research and development expenditures can be used more productively. Joint research by the automobile companies with respect to anti-pollution and safety devices has been frowned upon by the Federal Trade Commission and the Department of Justice. Admittedly there are dangers in such procedures. But there are great benefits which can flow from a slightly different approach which does not necessitate cooperative research by competing companies. This alternative involves industry meetings to develop a consensus as to the kinds of new technology required and an industry commitment to implement devices meeting certain agreed upon specifications.

In the food industry the concept of the automatic checkout has been talked about for 15 years but very little was done about it in terms of research expenditures by equipment manufacturers. However, once the food industry agreed upon the specifications of a code and a consensus was adopted among all sectors of the industry concerning the utilization of some kind of scanning device, equipment manufacturers spent millions of dollars on research in the hope of exploiting the market. New technology always involves high marketing risks. The development of industry goals, priorities, and specifications can help to channel research funds into areas which are most productive and most likely to result in implementation.

Trade associations have in the past sought to perform some of these functions of achieving systems economies, and in some cases have met with considerable success. However, member companies

are becoming increasingly hesitant to participate in such informal industry agreements because of the fear of governmental
prosecution. If our nation is to be in a position to exploit
the advantages which can flow from the application of a systems
approach to problems of productivity, it must have a format for
inducing and implementing industry action.

There are today two legislative sources from which such
action might flow. In the first place, as has already been
observed, if Congress acts favorably on the recommendation of
the Secretary of Commerce that the United States adopt the
metric system, there will be a need for the establishment of
industry committees to agree upon new standards. In the
second place, the 1971 amendments to the Economic Stabilization
Act of 1970[4] added to the duties and powers of the National
Commission on Productivity by providing in Sec. 4 (c) (1):

> It shall be the duty and function of the Commission
> ...to encourage and assist in the organization and
> the work of labor-management-public committees and
> similar groups on a plant, community, regional,
> and industry basis.

Perhaps what will evolve will be regularly functioning industry
committees with representation by labor and public members,
meeting under the watchful eye of the Department of Justice,
which will be able to discuss high priority needs for technological advancement and to formulate ideas and programs
which can promote an accelerated rate of introduction of
desired improvements.

---

[4] Public Law 92-210, 92nd Cong. S.2891, Dec. 22, 1971.

The movement toward standardization and joint industry
action is not without its dangers. But both inflation and
wage and price regulation also pose dangers to the future of
private enterprise. If we are really committed to improve
productivity in this country, the possibility of a broadened
systems approach to industry-wide problems deserves the
attention and support of business, labor and government.

INDEX